Genre: The Musi

British Film Institute Readers in Film Studies

Genre: The Musical

A Reader/Edited by Rick Altman

Routledge & Kegan Paul
London and New York

in association with the British Film Institute
127 Charing Cross Road, London WC2H 0EA

First published in 1981
by Routledge & Kegan Paul plc
11 New Fetter Lane, London EC4P 4EE
Published in the USA by
Routledge and Kegan Paul Inc.
in association with Methuen Inc.
29 West 35th Street, New York, NY 10001
Set in Sabon and Helvetica by
Input Typesetting Ltd, London
and printed in Great Britain by
St Edmundsbury Press Ltd
Bury St Edmunds, Suffolk
Reprinted 1986

Library of Congress Cataloging in Publication Data

Genre, the musical.
(British Film Institute readers in film studies)
Bibliography: p.
Includes index.
Contents: Vincente Minnelli / Thomas Elsaesser –
George Sidney / Alain Masson – Some Warners musicals and
the spirit of the New Deal / Mark Roth – [etc.]
1. Moving-pictures, musical – History and criticism –
Addresses, essays, lectures. I. Altman, Rick. II. Series.
PN1995.9.M86G4   791.43'09'09357   81–11966

ISBN 0–7100–0816–3   *AACR2*
ISBN 0–7100–0817–1 (pbk.)

Contents

Acknowledgments

The editor and publishers gratefully acknowledge permission to reprint the following material:

Thomas Elsaesser, 'Vincente Minnelli', *Brighton Film Review*, no. 15 (Dec. 1969), pp. 11–13; no. 18 (March 1970), pp. 20–2; Alain Masson, 'George Sidney: Artificial Brilliance/The Brilliance of Artifice', *Positif*, 180 (April 1976), pp. 48–54, translated by Liz Heron © British Film Institute 1981; Mark Roth, 'Some Warners Musicals and the Spirit of the New Deal', *The Velvet Light Trap*, no. 17 (Winter 1977), pp. 1–7; Robin Wood, 'Art and Ideology: Notes on *Silk Stockings*', *Film Comment*, vol. 11, no. 3 (May–June 1975), pp. 28–31; Lucy Fischer, 'The Image of Woman as Image: the Optical Politics of *Dames*', *Film Quarterly*, no. 30 (Fall 1976), pp. 2–11; Dennis Giles, 'Show-making', *Movie*, no. 24 (Spring 1977), pp. 14–25; Raymond Bellour, 'Segmenting/Analysing', *Quarterly Review of Film Studies*, vol. 1, no. 3 (August 1976), pp. 331–53. Reproduced here in a different translation, by Diana Matias © British Film Institute 1981; Jane Feuer, 'The Self-reflective Musical and the Myth of Entertainment', *Quarterly Review of Film Studies*, vol. 2, no. 3 (August 1977), pp. 313–26; Richard Dyer, 'Entertainment and Utopia', *Movie*, no. 24 (Spring 1977), pp. 2–13; Rick (Charles F.) Altman, 'The American Film Musical: Paradigmatic Structure and Mediatory Function', *Wide Angle*, vol. 2, no. 2 (January 1978), pp. 10–17. (Note that the articles by Collins, Williams and Sutton are specially written for this volume. A French translation of the Collins article is forthcoming in *Ça/Cinéma*.)

Stills from *Bye Bye Birdie* by courtesy of Columbia Pictures Industries, Inc. Stills from *Dames*, copyright © 1934. Warner Brothers Pictures, Inc. Renewed 1961. United Artists Associated, Inc. All rights reserved. Stills from *Twenty Million Sweethearts*, copyright © 1934. First National Pictures, Inc. Renewed 1961. United Artists, Inc. All rights reserved. Stills from *Top Hat* by courtesy of RKO General Pictures. Stills from *Singin' in the Rain, Silk Stockings, The Band Wagon, New Moon* and *Gigi* by courtesy of Metro-Goldwyn-Mayer Pictures Ltd.

Introduction

If Hollywood measured its success by the quality of criticism inspired by its films, then the musical would certainly be its worst investment. For three decades more money was poured into the musical than into any other genre (the *average* musical made by MGM's Freed Unit coming in at well over two million dollars). For its musicals Hollywood recruited the country's most talented performers – comics from the vaudeville circuit, composers from Tin Pan Alley, choreographers and designers from Broadway, orchestra leaders from the world of jazz or the concert hall, directors from Europe, singers and dancers from every corner of the performing world. Technically, the musical has also been in the vanguard, from the 1929 colour sequences to Gene Kelly's animations, from Berkeley's top shots to the split-screen trick photography of the 1950s, from the early use of the playback to sophisticated recording techniques in later years. Money, talent, technique – the musical had it all. What the musical has never had, however, is the sustained attention of careful but friendly critics.

In the early years, nearly every critic was either a detractor or a mindless scribbler of fan magazine hype. More concerned with a film's novelties than its meaning, even the best of the fan magazines devoted their pages to articles like the following notice from the September 1929 issue of *Photoplay*:

> Here's the ultimate. There can't be anything more to add to pictures. MGM has now introduced the smell-a-tone. At the opening of *The Hollywood Revue of 1929* at Grauman's Chinese Theater the audience thought the orange blossom finale was so realistic that they could actually smell orange blossoms. Well, they could. A gallon or so of perfume was put in the ventilators when the finale flashed on the screen.

When a serious critic like Otis Ferguson took on the musical, the results were hardly more satisfactory. For all his wit and careful observation, Ferguson's comments are so influenced by his profound dislike for the genre that their considerable insight disappears beneath a layer of all too clever criticism. Just what, he asks in *The New Republic* for 2 October 1935, can you expect from the musical?

> And that is the main trouble: you can't expect anything. A musical rarely attempts to be more than a ragbag of various show tricks; and even when it does, there is no relation between its comedy,

> which is mostly wisecracks, and its songs, which are mostly sugar. As for possible plots, there are two in use: the Hymie-the-Hoofer type, where the boy makes the grade with his act; the My-Gal-Daisy-She-Durrives-Me-Crazy type, where the boy makes the girl. These are naturally followed with no conviction, the chief problem in any given picture being how to bring in the first number. Somehow, before the film has gone many feet, somebody has got to take off from perfectly normal conversation into full voice, something about he won't take the train he'll walk in the rain (there is suddenly a twenty-piece band in the room), leaving everybody else in the piece to look attentive and as though they like it, and as though such a business were the most normal of procedures.

From time to time – as in the criticism of the Russian-American Alexander Bakshy – an imaginative writer would turn a sympathetic ear to the musical, but by and large early criticism of the musical is more concerned to judge than to analyse.

Not until the 1950s does this judgmental tendency give way to a new impulse. Faced with an extraordinary number of musical films (well over a thousand by then), critics began to formalize the categorizations which had slowly developed over the previous decade – and by so doing established the chapter headings of the numerous histories of the musical written over the past two decades. Many of these classifications are simply borrowed from the vocabulary of Broadway. The book musical is opposed to the revue; the dancer's musical is distinguished from the singer's musical (with the latter category broken down into an operatic strain and a crooning counterpart); the operetta is set apart from all musicals which take place in a contemporary setting. Other distinctions dwell on similarly superficial characteristics, such as the source of the film's plot material (e.g. Broadway adaptation or original Hollywood) or the location of the film's story (e.g. backstage, college, Navy, western, Ruritania, etc.).

By far the most important classificatory device, however, derives from Hollywood's common practice of signing a star or successful director to a long-term contract at a single studio. The history and theory of the musical have long been tied to a series of separate categories, each teaming one or more names with the studio where they flourished. More than perhaps any other genre, the musical is remembered not film-by-film, but in groups of films sharing a recognizable style: the series of spectaculars which Busby Berkeley choreographed and then directed for Warners in the mid-1930s, the Astaire-Rogers pictures at RKO, the extraordinary sequence of films which Arthur Freed produced for MGM in the post-war years. Few would doubt that these films reveal a distinctive style properly expressed by a specific personal or studio catch-phrase such as 'a Berkeley film' or 'a Metro musical'. On this model, the production of other studios and individuals is often treated as having a similar coherence: Paramount had the genius of Ernst Lubitsch treating the traditional operetta with his lightly ironic touch; MGM in the later 1930s had the successful pair of Jeanette MacDonald and Nelson Eddy; Fox was characterized from the 1930s through the 1950s by its policy of one blonde at a time (Shirley Temple, Alice Faye, Betty Grable, June Haver, Marilyn Monroe); the later Paramount musicals had the inimitable Bing Crosby.

This convenient method of classification supported an even more convenient method of writing the history of the film musical, a method which remains prevalent today. A section on beginnings (stressing the contributions of Paramount's European directors) is followed by a chapter on Berkeley's work for Warner, another on the Astaire-Rogers films at RKO, and perhaps a shorter treatment of MGM's MacDonald/Eddy films, at which point a catch-all section on Fox/the blondes, Paramount/Crosby, Universal/Deanna Durbin, and Columbia/Rita Hayworth intervenes, preparing the way for the major chapter on MGM, its star producers (Freed, Pasternak), performers (Garland, Kelly, Astaire), and directors (Minnelli, Donen, Walters). This leaves only the period of the late 1950s and 1960s – with their emphasis on Broadway adaptations – and the contemporary musical, which emphasizes rock, disco, and other new musical styles. Every general history of the musical accepts this account, either explicitly or implicitly. The emphasis is on groups of films, not on individual masterpieces. Only when a film lies outside the area covered by this overview does it regularly receive individual attention, as if by compensation for the fact that it fits no established category (e.g. *A Star is Born*).

The advantages of this studio/personality approach for the general film historian are plain. Without dwelling on a particular film, which might not be known to the reader, the historian can still make his general points about the 'evolution' of the musical from the artificiality of the stagy European operetta to the 'Platonic Ideal' of the integrated musical, as Jerome Delamater has termed it, where music and dance are never allowed to arise artificially from a realistic environment. The disadvantages of this approach are not quite so obvious, yet they are legion. As long as our comments on the dancing of Astaire and Rogers need depend on no extended analysis of a specific dance, then we hardly need to occupy ourselves with the fundamentals of dance. As long as each director is linked to a particular studio, then we are not likely to isolate that director's particular contribution. As long as production personnel and performers receive all the attention, then technology must remain ignored. In short, the studio/personality approach has long bred sloppiness and artificial limitations into the study of the Hollywood musical. The history of the genre has seemed so clear, and its modalities so fixed, that few scholars, critics, or fans have revealed a desire – and a capacity – for going any farther.

Nevertheless, over the past decade (and especially in the last couple of years) a number of studies have appeared which reach beyond the more traditional approach outlined above. In general, changes in film theory have been slow to penetrate the rather conservative circles of genre film criticism. This is especially true in the case of the musical, which is often denigrated as hollow, silly, and escapist even by the very critics who value European popular film or the American western. The few outstanding essays on the musical have thus often appeared in out of the way places, limited distribution journals like the *Brighton Film Review* or *The Velvet Light Trap*, specialized foreign-language magazines like *Positif* and *Ça/Cinéma*, or academic journals like the *Quarterly Review of Film Studies.* Anyone who wants to go beyond the traditional studio/personality approach to the musical must do so blindly, groping through journal after journal with little return.

The present collection should put an end to that situation. Thirteen articles and an annotated bibliography provide an introduction to the present state-of-the-art in analysis of the Hollywood musical. All of the articles have been published since 1975 in English, French, or American journals or specially commissioned for the collection (including one earlier article newly revised and accompanied by a new preface). Nearly all the articles undertake analysis of specific films, but on the whole they have been chosen not for the excellence of those analyses but because they shed new light on the musical genre as a whole – on its history, its theory, its meaning. Not surprisingly, they represent most of the important currents of film criticism prevalent during this decade: the *auteur* 'theory', ideological concerns, structuralist analysis, the ritual function of entertainment, the contribution of technology. All, however, take the musical seriously, and thus provide new clues to the genre's structure, function, and meaning.

In grappling with the complexities of the musical, the contributors to this collection have consistently returned to half a dozen problems which constitute the nodal points not only of this volume but of contemporary genre criticism as a whole. The embattled *auteur* 'theory' no doubt constitutes the most obvious of these nodes. In the face of increased research into the standard practices of the studio system (see, for example, the books by Knox and Fordin listed in the bibliography), *auteur* criticism has largely turned to new interpretations of acknowledged masterpieces or the recovery of little-known directors of unrecognized genius. The problems of the *auteur* approach are brought much more clearly into focus by the articles which Thomas Elsaesser and Alain Masson have contributed to this collection. Elsaesser makes the possibility of remaining an *auteur* in a genre/studio world the very thematic base of Minnelli's oeuvre, thus foregrounding the individual/community problem which is fundamental to the musical's very existence. Masson makes a virtue of the bad taste of which George Sidney is commonly accused; if you work in MGM's Freed Unit, Masson implies, where good taste and high production values are a given, then the only road to a personal style is through 'bad' taste. This rather eccentric position has the virtue of foregrounding the self-preserving strategy of all auteurist analysis: in order to function, the *auteur* approach must recognize and ultimately criticize the industry's standard practices, because only divergence from those practices can give rise to a personal style and thus to an *auteur*.

The *auteur* approach and its studio counterpart thus appear throughout this volume not as diametrical and mutually exclusive opposites but as the two elements in a symbiotic, if dialectical, relationship. Neither the notion of single authorship nor emphasis on the Hollywood system can long survive alone in the context provided by the musical. Indeed, many familiar notions of authorship and artistic integrity are contested in the essays which follow. For Elsaesser and Masson, the particular film originates in a director's individual attempt to escape, creatively, the restrictions of an industrial system; for Roth the choreographer is the source of a given film's personal style; Wood derives the text's 'life' from the excesses in a specific performance. Fischer is joined by Feuer in revealing the means by which film-makers become the scribes of cultural ideology, while Dyer, Sutton, and Altman offer a sense that the musical is somehow authored by the very audiences which consume it. More than any other genre, the musical seems to invite such a confrontation. Whereas most genres privilege one category of production over others (especially direction and acting), musical fans regularly lionize individuals representing an extraordinarily wide range of responsibilities, from directors, dancers, actors, singers, and comedians to writers, composers, choreographers, producers, and even lyricists, designers, and cinematographers. When the other commonly proclaimed authors of the musical – the studio, the audience, technology – are added to this list, interminable questions of authorship, unity, and responsibility are bound to result.

Closely tied to the problem of authorship is that of textual ideology. Robin Wood confronts the question head on, Lucy Fischer and Richard Dyer grapple with it openly, others touch on it in passing. Yet not even the most basic questions elicit agreement. Where, for example, is ideology to be discovered? In a particular political position (Roth)? As a sort of *tertium quid* beyond recognized political stances (Wood)? In the apparatus's overt (Fischer) or covert (Giles) positioning of the spectator? In the use of the culture's rituals to dissemble the flaws in the culture's logical discourse (Sutton, Altman)? Or is it to be located in the masking of the work necessary to produce a musical show (Feuer)? In many ways the musical is Hollywood's rhetorical masterwork: we pay our money for the right to have our desires predetermined, but instead of being upset at this unequal exchange we come away convinced that life is rosy, that we belong to the worldwide community of music lovers, and that love set to music will always result when people of good will 'get together to put on a show'. Clearly foregrounding the ideology underlying this rhetoric, the articles in the collection nevertheless reach no common position. Far from closing off debate, location of the genre's ideology only creates a new space for further discussion.

It is not surprising, therefore, that the musical's self-reflecting nature should be repeatedly alluded to. Often characterized as conservative and classical in its technique, the musical has nevertheless repeatedly sent proponents of reflexivity back to the drawing board. Propounding the politically radical function of reflexive technique in, say, Dziga Vertov's *Man with a Movie Camera*, these critics have been brought up short by the recognition that the reflexive techniques characteristic of 'radical' practice are just as common in the supposedly conservative musical. We thus find several of the articles which make up this volume treating the musical as a more or less transparent example of Hollywood practice (Wood, Bellour, Giles), while others challenge the traditional identification of the musical with classical narrative (Collins, Altman); indeed, one article specifically confronts the special function which conservative forms of entertainment ascribe to the same self-reflective techniques which other texts turn to radical purposes (Feuer). Here arguments might well move in two different directions. The most obvious question to be asked would seem to be: 'Is the musical genre a subset of the classical narrative category?' More is to be gained, however, if we ask the other – more difficult – question: 'Is classical narrative by nature reflexive?' The latter question wreaks havoc with traditional descriptions of classical narrative, yet it brings back to the surface many of the questions repressed by insistence on Hollywood's transparency (at the expense of intertextuality, reflexivity, and self-parody).

What is at stake here is the very constitution of the spectator as viewing/hearing subject. Nearly every separate article in this collection proposes a different model of the constitution of that spectator. Some see a specifically sexual positioning whereby the spectator necessarily takes on a male point of view (Fischer, Giles). Another approach stresses the intensive use of internal audiences designed to facilitate positioning of the external spectator (Collins). Those who advance a ritual hypothesis see the spectator not so much constituted anew as firmly held within the position reserved for him/her within society at large (Dyer, Sutton, Altman). According to this approach, the spectator is positioned (by the structures of society, by the status of entertainment, by the commercial nature of cinema) long before he/she even begins to watch a specific film. In fact, this opposition between pre-positioning of the spectator (dependent on cultural codes, intertextuality, or the ideology of the apparatus) and textual positioning (based on the text's form, rhetoric, and technology) constitutes a basic leitmotif of this collection.

Another constant concern involves the nature, status, and function of entertainment as a category fundamental to American life in general and to the Hollywood experience in particular. Just what kind of a concept is entertainment? Is it a category of consumable experiences, like travel, or is it the focal point of an American myth? How can it be simultaneously related, as it seems to be, to a communitarian, spontaneous, folk ethic and to the crass commercialism of Hollywood at its worst? In short, how can entertainment lead down the road to Utopia when it so clearly seems to pave the way to second-rate art, anti-intellectualism, and total disrespect for the values of culture? The problem of American entertainment – and especially the Hollywood variety – is everywhere implicit in this volume, but it appears with special force in the essays by Jane Feuer and Richard Dyer, two articles which bring to the surface categories and practices long taken for granted by critics of the American scene.

These are but a few of the critical problems foregrounded by the articles in this collection. Taken singly, these essays present important contributions to the study of a too long neglected genre. Taken together, they do still more: they focus our attention in new ways on problems basic to film criticism and theory today. Constantly complementing and contesting each other, these articles bear eloquent testimony to the contemporaneity of a genre once thought *passé*. The musical will stay with us, because it forces upon us the questions which probe at the heart of the film-viewing experience. The musical is always about Hollywood; more than any other genre it foregrounds those problems which are particular to and characteristic of Hollywood. Constantly reminding the viewer that he/she is watching a film, the musical regularly transforms itself into an experimental discourse on the status of film viewing – and hearing. It is ironic that the most escapist of the entertainment arts should also be the most reflexive, the most aware of its status, and thus the most complex of all the Hollywood genres. Not only is the musical a *Gesamtkunstwerk*, an art form more total than even Wagner could imagine, but it regularly invites us to consider why we spend our time watching films, what we find in them, how they form our values and psychology. As the articles in this collection clearly reveal, to study the musical is to study Hollywood, the cinema, and the things which make them go.

1 · Thomas Elsaesser: 'Vincente Minnelli'

Brighton Film Review no. 15, December 1969, pp. 11–13 and no. 18, March 1970, pp. 20–2.

The late 1950s and 1960s in France were a time of intense excitement for devotees of cinema. The young directors of the New Wave, it seemed, had finally solved the traditional problem of film authorship. In the previous decade a film was not the work of, say, Claude Autant-Lara, but a collaboration between Autant-Lara the director, the well-known script-writing partners Bost and Aurenche, and a studio team of technicians who worked in more or less the same tradition for various directors. With the generation of Malle, Truffaut, Godard and company, it suddenly seemed possible to speak of the director as *auteur* because he took on the role of screenwriter and technical director as well as that of artistic director. Developed under the influence of New Wave practices, the *auteur* 'theory' was soon applied to a more problematic realm, that of the Hollywood studio system. Producing perhaps the best, but most conservative, criticism of the 1960s, the *auteur* approach lionized any director who – supposedly in spite of the studio system – managed to turn out a series of films with a sense of personal style and philosophy. Among the directors so honoured none was so appreciated in Europe while being neglected in America as Vincente Minnelli. French *auteur*-oriented criticism pointed up a unity of inspiration in Minnelli's work which American critics had not yet sensed.

Nevertheless, as Thomas Elsaesser reminds us in his preface to the article which follows, *auteur* criticism was soon branded as sentimental, aestheticist, and conservative, and thus fell into disrepute. Had all *auteur*-oriented criticism shared the qualities of Elsaesser's article, however, I doubt that such a lot would have befallen it. Whereas other articles of the same period continue to isolate repeated themes, point out habitual techniques, or dwell on a director's preferred plot patterns, rarely sensing the interrelationship among the three, Elsaesser reveals an extraordinary sensitivity to the wide range of problems implicit in 'straight' *auteur* criticism. How, for example, does an author's individual genius relate to the conventions of his preferred genres? To what extent are a director's films self-conscious of their status as products of the Hollywood dream-machine? From what source do the structures typically identified with a given *auteur* derive the energy which drives them? To these and other important questions, Elsaesser provides answers which seem prophetic in the light of the direction which critical debate has taken during the 1970s.

Not reading Minnelli's films in terms of a stable structure such as 1960s structuralists might have found, Elsaesser speaks instead of the drives which have become such an important part of post-structuralist vocabulary: 'energy in search of a material form'. Viewed from this vantage point, Minnelli's protagonists take on the identity of the Hollywood director himself, for both seek to impose their inner dynamic on the world's outward static reality. The musical thus becomes an ideal image of the medium itself, while Elsaesser's analysis prefigures the interest in self-reflexivity which has characterized film criticism throughout the 1970s. Indeed, the preface to this reprinting foreshadows an attitude which, I believe, is sure to be that of the 1980s – a certain nostalgia for the human qualities of *auteur* criticism, for thematics, for meaning, for the attention to living concerns which, I might add, so characterizes Elsaesser's criticism itself.

Preface (1979)

When this article was published early in 1970, auteur studies were already becoming highly unpopular. And although I was addressing myself to a student audience that probably understood little and cared less about the debates then gathering momentum in Britain around questions of auteur vs genre, structural vs thematic criticism, ideological vs textual analysis, I felt sufficiently involved in these issues to hope that an expository manner of arguing might still carry a polemical edge: under cover of convenient provincialism the contributors to the *Brighton Film Review* had, for the previous two years, been trying to divert the mainstream auteurist emphasis on themes in the direction of 'style'. The Minnelli piece wanted to push a little further towards genre (all of his films are musicals, and the melodramas are musicals turned inside out) in order to relate the concept of the musical itself to some more general notion of a 'drive-oriented' structure that was assumed to underpin all Hollywood film-making of the time. The individual genres and their historical mutations could then be understood as partial aspects of a totality whose constellation was centred elsewhere. Perhaps the argument is somewhat circular: Minnelli is seen as an auteur because his practice of the musical/melodrama allows us to observe principles and structures to which much of Hollywood film-making conforms, and this aesthetic his work incarnates in a strikingly pure state. I am quite sure that at the time I failed to see just how close such a set of equations gets to pulling the rug from under my own attachment to the auteur theory.

After positing a 'drive-oriented' structure, the article doesn't pursue the point, except to explain its presence (at that time I had neither read nor heard of Lacan) in terms of the exigencies of audience identification, and to express the truism that Hollywood's global strategy was aimed at binding its audiences on a psychic level. These psychic continuities (today one would say 'fantasms') define both the narrative and the visual rhetoric (the *mise en scène*) of a given film, and they also create the illusion of unity that constitutes the form of alienation specific to a director's work. What seemed to make Minnelli exemplary, along with others such as Renoir and Fritz Lang, was that in his films the act of seeing, the constraints and power-relations it gave rise to, appeared so uncannily foregrounded that the action always tended to become an adumbration or metaphor of the more fundamental relation between spectator and *mise en scène*, audience and (invisible, because reified) director. Fortuitously, but perhaps fittingly, my article ends with a brief analysis of *Two Weeks in Another Town*, which Paul Mayersberg had already called a 'testament film'. There the director (visible, but split between two protagonists) definitely loses control, evidently a direct comment on the changes that were taking place in Hollywood film-making during the sixties: the very same changes that made auteur/*mise en scène* criticism (whose unspoken third term had always been the studio-system) historically obsolete and by that token, available as a theoretical construct.

What remains is to ask the paradoxical question, why critics should have invested, and still invest, so much energy in the auteur theory, given that it had always been perverse, deliberately flying in the face of what we know about social psychology or cultural history. Its victories had to be snatched from the jaws of common-sense.

In Eisenstein's *October* there is a scene where a Bolshevik soldier, after penetrating to the Czar and Czarina's bedrooms, turns everything upside down and finally slits the eiderdown with his fixed bayonet: in vain is he looking for the source of misery that forced him to revolt. None of the banal objects before his eyes can satisfy his desire for a glimpse at origins, in a scene as 'primal' as any critic could wish. A similarly frustrated voyeurism is documented from those who stormed the Bastille, and it was undoubtedly what moved the Sansculottes to tearing up Marie-Antoinette's bed-linen during the occupation of the Tuileries. Such may be the auteurist's thirst, except that he is after the source of his pleasures as much as after a scapegoat for events and feelings that elude his grasp. In the history of the American cinema, apparently so completely dedicated to the impersonality of *histoire*, a dimension of *discours** had always been intermittently visible, which it was the privilege of the auteur critic to attribute to the director. And this for good reason: the criticism we have today seems to have settled the vexing question of why films give pleasure, by deciding that in the cinema the spectator enters into a dialogue merely with his own alienated self, be it Marxian or Lacanian. Insofar as auteur criticism has not sufficiently acknowledged the narcissism of the film-viewer, it stands exposed by its fanatical obsession with the narcissism of the film-maker. But for those who can speak to themselves only through the discovery of an 'other', there will remain the need, however rhetorically displaced or nostalgically recalled, to reinvent the author, if only, as Barthes has remarked, because his disappearance implies that of the critic and reader. The auteur is the fiction, the necessary fiction one might add, become flesh and historical in the director, for the name of a pleasure that seems to have no substitute in the sobered-up deconstructions of the authorless voice of ideology.

'Vincente Minnelli' (1970)

Minnelli's critical reputation has known a certain amount of fluctuation. Admired (or dismissed) in America as a 'pure stylist' who, in Andrew Sarris' phrase 'believes more in beauty than in art', his work reached a zenith of critical devotion during the late 50s and early 60s in France, with extensive studies in *Cahiers du Cinéma*, especially in the articles by Douchet and Domarchi, who saw in him a cinematic visionary obsessed with beauty and harmony, and an artist who could give substance to the world of dreams.

In England *Movie* took up his defence, from their first number onwards. But strangely enough, they concentrated almost exclusively on Minnelli's dramatic films of the early 60s (a memorable article by Paul Mayersberg on *Two Weeks in Another Town* comes to mind), and gave rather cursory treatment to the musicals, while the later films, such as *Goodbye Charlie* (1964) and *The Sandpiper* (1965) were passed over with visible embarrassment. With this, Minnelli joined the vast legion of American directors whose work

* For an exposition of this distinction between *histoire* and *discours* see the article below (p. 134) by Jim Collins.

was supposed to have suffered decline, if not total eclipse in the Hollywood of the middle and late 60s.

The following remarks are merely a preliminary attempt to disentangle a few essential characteristics from a singularly rich and varied body of work, and to trace some of the dominating lines of force in his style. Above all, I am concerned with the fundamental *unity* of Minnelli's vision.

At the risk of displeasing the genre-critics and antagonizing those who share the view that thematic analysis generally exhausts itself in what has (rather summarily) been referred to as 'schoolboy profundities', I would like to look at some of Minnelli's constant themes and furthermore, conduct some kind of special pleading for Minnelli as a *moralist*, even though this will mean flying in the face of the 'stylist' school – both of the Sarris variety and *Movie*, who claim for Minnelli as for Cukor that he never writes his own scripts, and therefore never uses other people's material for the propagation of his own views, that he confines himself to the interpretation, the *mise en scène* of the ideas of others, and that, consequently, his work is best regarded as lacking in consistent themes, and rather excels on a supreme level of visual competence.

I think this is a fundamental misunderstanding. True, there are superficially two 'Minnellis' – one the virtual father of the modern musical, and the other the director of dramatic comedies and domestic dramas. Other critics – even sympathetic ones – would probably claim a different Minnelli for almost every film – the loving 'pointillist' of American period pieces or of 'Gay Paree' (*Meet Me in St. Louis*, *Gigi*, *An American in Paris*), the catalyst for Gene Kelly and Fred Astaire musicals (*Ziegfeld Follies*, *Yolanda and the Thief*, *The Pirate*, *The Band Wagon*, *Brigadoon*), the ingenious vulgarizer of painters' lives (*Lust for Life*) and best-selling novels (*The Four Horsemen of the Apocalypse*), the handiman who puts together a star vehicle for an ambitious producer (*The Reluctant Debutante*), and lastly perhaps the 'difficult' director of such problem pieces as *Some Came Running*, *Home from the Hill*, and of Hollywood self-portraits – *The Bad and the Beautiful* and *Two Weeks in Another Town*.

Altogether, Minnelli has directed some thirty-two films, not counting the episodes and sketches contributed to other people's films. It might seem difficult to find a personal vision in as vast an oeuvre as his, not to mention the fact that all films (except one) have been made in the M-G-M studios, under the supervision of a few, themselves very gifted and articulate, producers like John Houseman (4 films) and Arthur Freed (12). But surely anyone who is reasonably familiar with his films will see in Minnelli more than the glorification of the *metteur en scène*, the stylish craftsman of the cinema, the dandy of sophistication. I for one am convinced that Minnelli is one of the purest 'hedgehogs' working in the cinema – an artist who knows one big thing, and never tires to explore its implications.

In Walter Pater's famous phrase all romantic art aspires to the status of music. My contention is that all Minnelli's films aspire to the condition of the musical. In this resides their fundamental unity. However, in order to substantiate this point, I shall insert a few remarks to explain what I mean by 'musical'.

The classic Hollywood cinema is, as everybody knows, *the* commercial cinema par excellence – out merely to entertain. Usually this is taken to be a fundamental drawback, at worst utterly precluding its products from the realms of serious art, at best, presenting the film-maker with formidable odds against which he has to test his worth, as artist *and* entrepreneur. (I shall try to show how deeply Minnelli's conception of his art, indeed his 'philosophy' of life, are formed by the conflict between the necessity of circumstance and the vital need to assert – not so much one's self, but rather one's conception of meaning, one's vision of things. It furnishes his great theme: the artist's struggle to appropriate external reality as the elements of his own world, in a bid for absolute creative freedom. When I say artist, I hasten to add that this includes almost all of Minnelli's protagonists. (Insofar as they all feel within them a world, an idea, a dream that seeks articulation and material embodiment.)

Yet there is another side to the 'commercial cinema' syndrome, which is rarely ever given its full due. (At least in England: in France, the *Positif* and *Midi-Minuit* équipes have always paid tribute to the commercial cinema *qua* commercial cinema.) I am referring to the fact that perhaps the enormous appeal of the best Hollywood cinema, the fundamental reason why audience-identification and immediate emotional participation are at all possible, lies in Hollywood's rigorous application of the *pleasure principle* – understood almost in its Freudian sense, as the structure that governs the articulation of psychic and emotional energy. It seems to me that a vast number of films 'work' *because* they are built around a psychic law and not an intellectual one, and thus achieve a measure of coherence which is very difficult to analyse (as it must be extremely difficult for a film-maker to control and adhere to), and yet constitutes nevertheless an absolutely essential part of the way the cinema functions – being indeed close to music in this respect.

For a superficial confirmation of this fact, namely that there is a central energy at the heart of the Hollywood film which seeks to live itself out as completely as possible, one could point to the way in which – superimposed on an infinite variety of subject matters – the prevalent plot-mechanisms of two major genres of the American cinema (the Western and the Gangster film) invariably conform to the same basic pattern. There is always a central dynamic drive – the pursuit, the quest, the trek, the boundless desire to arrive, to get to the top, to get rich, to make it – always the same graph of maximum energetic investment.

For the spectator, this means maximum emotional involvement, which depends upon, and is enhanced by, his maximum aesthetic satisfaction – or rather, by the skilful manipulation of his desire for as total a sense of satisfaction as possible. Intellectual insight and emotional awareness are transmitted in the best American cinema exclusively as a drive for *gratification* which the audience shares with the characters. The more a film director is aware of this interrelation of morality and aesthetics in the cinema, the more his *mise en scène* will be concerned with the purposeful ordering of *visual* elements, to achieve a kind of plenitude and density, which inevitably, and rightly, goes at the expense of ideas. In other words, there seems to exist, particularly in the American cinema, an intimate relationship between the *psychological* drives of the characters (i.e. the motives *beneath* the motives that make them act), the *moral* progression which they accomplish, and the *aesthetic* gratification afforded to the audience by the spectacle; and these are held together by some profound mechanism, identical in both audience and characters – be they criminals, detectives, gunfighters, shop-assistants, song-writers or millionaires.

Perhaps one of the most interesting consequences of this fact is that this, if true, would entail a thoroughly different concept of cinematic realism, which would have nothing to do with either literary realism or the realism of pictorial art. In a very definite sense, the Eisenstein–Rossellini–Bazin–Metz–Wollen controversy has seriously underrated the question of a psychic dynamism as part of our aesthetic experience. Even the most rudimentary awareness of its existence would dispose of such arrant nonsense as Metz's claim that 'in the last analysis, it is only by the richness of its connotations that a film by Visconti differs from a documentary on the methods of surgery' (*Communications*, no. 4, pp. 81–2). If semiology is not to degenerate, I think it must find, above all, a more positive validation of a film's sense of physical *continuity*, and that, it would seem, necessitates a novel idea of cinematic realism – not just as continuity of space and time, but both dimensions seen as elements of a perhaps predominantly *psychic* continuity. (To forestall certain obvious objections, this evidently applies to the American cinema more than it does to the modern European cinema. There is no such 'psychic continuity' to be found in the later films of either Godard, Bergman, or Pasolini – and whatever continuity there is, situates itself on a more complex level which is often an uneasy mixture of intellectual, symbolic and 'old-fashioned' emotional appeal – with varying degrees of success.

After this rather devious excursion, I am back to Minnelli and the assertion about the 'musical' nature of his films. For what seems to me essential to all of Minnelli's films is the fact that his characters are only superficially concerned with a quest, a desire to get somewhere in life, i.e. with any of the forms by which this dynamism rationalizes or sublimates itself. What we have instead, just beneath the surface of the plots, is the working of energy itself, as the ever-changing, fascinating movement of a basic impulse in its encounter with, or victory over, a given reality. The characters' existence is justified by the incessant struggle in which they engage for total fulfilment, for total gratification of their aesthetic needs, their desire for beauty and harmony, their demand for an identity of their lives with the reality of their dreams. Minnelli's films are structured so as to give the greatest possible scope to the expansive nature of a certain vitality (call it 'will', or libido) – in short, to the confrontation of an inner, dynamic, reality and an outward, static one. Minnelli's typical protagonists are all, in a manner of speaking, highly sophisticated and cunning day-dreamers, and the *mise en scène* follows them, as they go through life, confusing – for good or ill – what is part of their imagination and what is real, and trying to obliterate the difference between what is freedom and what is necessity. (This is not the place to analyse whether there is, philosophically or ethically, something suspect about such a conception of the self and the world – suffice it to say that these ideas have a long, intellectual tradition, which is relevant, even if Minnelli has neither heard nor even read about it.)

What, in this context, characterizes the Minnelli musical is the total and magic victory of the impulse, the vision, over any reality whatsoever. The characters in his musicals transform the world into a reflection of their selves, into a pure expression of their joys and sorrows, of their inner harmony or conflicting states of mind. When Gene Kelly begins to dance, or plays with the first words of a song, say in *Brigadoon*, the world melts away and reality becomes a stage, on which he and Cyd Charisse live out their very dream. Or when Louis Jourdan, in utter confusion about his feelings, rushes to the Jardin du Luxembourg to sing the title number of *Gigi*, Minnelli leads him into a wholly mysterious, wholly subjective landscape of the imagination, pregnant with the symbols of his newly discovered love for the one-time schoolgirl. Such a confrontation with their innermost worlds always gives the characters a kind of spontaneous certainty from which, ultimately, they derive their energy.

The Minnelli musical thus transforms the movements of what one is tempted to call, for lack of a better word, the 'soul' of the characters into shape, colour, gesture and rhythm. It is precisely when joy or sorrow, bewilderment or enthusiasm, that is, when emotional intensity, becomes too strong to bear that a Gene Kelly or a Judy Garland has to dance and sing in order to give free play to the emotions that possess them. And it is hardly exaggerated to compare what Minnelli did for the musical with Mozart's transformation of the comic opera. One only needs to hold a Busby Berkeley musical – with its formally brilliant but dramatically empty song-and-dance routines and elaborate visual compositions – against even an early and comparatively minor Minnelli effort, say, the 'Limehouse Blues' sequence from *Ziegfeld Follies*, to see how the musical with Minnelli has been given an authentic spiritual dimension, created by a combination of movement, lighting, colour, décor, gesture and music which is unique to the cinema.

Thus defined, the world of the musical becomes a kind of ideal image of the medium itself, the infinitely variable material substance on which the very structure of desire and the imagination can imprint itself, freed from all physical necessity. The quickly changing décor, the transitions in the lighting and the colours of a scene, the freedom of composition, the shift from psychological realism to pure fantasy, from drama to surreal farce, the culmination of an action in a song, the change of movement into rhythmic dance – all this constitutes the very essence of the musical. In other words, it is the exaltation of the artifice as the vehicle of an authentic psychic and emotional reality. Minnelli's musicals introduce us into a liberated universe, where the total freedom of expression (of the character's creative impulse) serves to give body and meaning to the artistic vitality in the director, both being united by their roles as *metteurs en scène* of the self.

The paradox of the musical, namely that a highly artificial, technically and artistically controlled décor and machinery can be the manifestation of wholly spontaneous, intimate movements, or the visualization of submerged, hardly conscious aspirations, becomes not only Minnelli's metaphor for the cinema as a whole, but more specifically, it makes up his central moral concern: how does the individual come to realize himself, reach his identity, create his personal universe, fulfil his life in a world of chaos and confusion, riddled with social conventions, bogus with self-importance, claustrophobic and constricting, trivial and above all artificial, full of treacherous appearance, and yet impenetrable in its false solidity, its obstacles, its sheer physical inertia and weight? – epitomized in the sticky, rubbery substance Spencer Tracy has to wade through, as he is trying to reach the altar, in the nightmare sequence of *Father of the Bride*. Minnelli's answer, surprisingly enough for this supposedly obedient servant of other people's ideas, is a plea for chaos, where his characters embrace flux and movement, because it is closest to the imagination itself. Minnelli's motto might well be that 'rather no order at all than a false order'.

And here we have the crux of the matter: for the Minnelli musical celebrates the fulfilment of desire and identity, whose tragic absence so many of his dramatic films portray. Looked at like this, the dramas and dramatic comedies are *musicals turned inside out*, for the latter affirm all those values and urges which the former visualize as being in conflict with a radically different order of reality. In his non-musical films – from *The Clock* to *Home from the Hill*, from *Meet Me in St. Louis* to *Two Weeks in Another Town* – tragedy is present as a particular kind of unfreedom, as the constraint of an emotional or artistic temperament in a world that becomes claustrophobic, where reality suddenly reveals itself as mere décor, unbearably false and oppressive. That is when the dream changes into nightmare, when desire becomes obsession, and the creative will turns into mad frenzy.

It is in this absence of that freedom which the musical realizes and expresses through dance and song, through rhythm and movement, by indicating that peculiar fluidity of reality and dream which alone seems to offer the possibility of human relationships and of a harmonious existence – it is in the absence of this that Kirk Douglas or Judy Garland, Robert Mitchum or Glenn Ford and Ronnie Howard (*The Courtship of Eddie's Father*) suffer anguish and despair, neurosis and isolation, spiritual and physical enclosure, if not death. And it is precisely the possibility, the promise of a return to chaos, to movement, which saves Spencer Tracy or Judy Holliday (*Bells are Ringing*), Gregory Peck and Lauren Bacall (*Designing Woman*), Rex Harrison and Kay Kendall (*The*

Reluctant Debutante) in the dramatic comedies from becoming hopelessly trapped in their own worlds.

Minnelli's films invariably focus on the discrepancy between an inner vision, often confused and uncertain of itself, and an outer world that appears as hostile because it is presented as a physical space littered with obstacles. Life forces upon the characters a barely tolerable sense of rupture, and the Minnelli universe has its psychological raison d'être in a very definite and pervasive alienation. But instead of lamenting this modern condition, almost all his films concentrate on portraying the energies of the imagination released in the individual during this process of (social?) decomposition. Too often this has been seen merely as a total abandon to the faculty of make-believe, of the beautiful appearance through which Minnelli is supposed to celebrate Hollywood escapism.

This view, even if applied only to the musicals, is an untenable simplification. Minnelli's concern is always with the possibilities of a human creativeness asserting itself in and through a world which is so obviously imperfect. True, imperfections are taken for granted, they are global, because Minnelli is dealing not with a given reality, but with the psychological and emotional predicament it produces. Two types of heroes come to symbolize this situation: the artist and the neurotic, two ways of dealing with the actual which are obviously not unrelated. That he sees them as intimately connected states of being constitutes the coherence of his moral vision and the unity of his themes.

Whereas the 'neurotic' dilemma is either treated comically (*The Long Long Trailer*, the dream becoming a nightmare, or *Goodbye Charlie*, in which the hero is so traumatized by American society that he involuntarily undergoes a sex-change) or tragically (*Home from the Hill, The Four Horsemen of the Apocalypse*), art and neurosis form the explicit subject of *The Bad and the Beautiful, Lust for Life, Two Weeks in Another Town*. Even in the musicals, where the triumph of the creative temperament seems assured, it is not by a 'naive' assertion of will-power or happy-go-lucky bonhomie, but through a complex process of metamorphosis which transforms both the individual and his world. For the inner vision is essentially flawed, and so long as the protagonist cuts himself off from life, his dream is static, a passive nostalgia or worse, a self-limiting delusion. As a consequence, the external world seems to him nothing but oppressive, false and alien – an attitude which none of Minnelli's films vindicate as an adequate response, though they often make it their starting point.

Three of Minnelli's greatest musicals, *The Pirate*, *Brigadoon* and *The Band Wagon*, open with such typical situations of the 'self-in-exile'. In *The Pirate* Judy Garland, about to be married to a fat, wealthy businessman, sighs over her fate and looks romantically into the distance while dreaming of Macoco, the legendary Caribbean pirate, coming to take her away. In *Brigadoon*, a disenchanted Gene Kelly, playing an American tourist, stalks about in Scotland, having lost his way in the wilderness of the Highlands. And in *The Band Wagon*, Fred Astaire in the role of a once-famous star, gets off the train in New York to discover that the big party at the station is cheering some other celebrity.

Though these may seem archetypal situations of the genre, they recur in all of Minnelli's films, whether musical or not. *The Courtship of Eddie's Father* is a particularly striking example, with father and son feeling completely lost in their own home (a family situation common to at least a dozen Minnelli films). And the implications are finally made explicit in *Two Weeks in Another Town*, where the hero is first seen in a mental hospital. In other words, Minnelli starts from a characteristic disorientation about the relation of self and world, from which originates the impulse towards action. Whatever his protagonists do becomes therefore automatically identified with a desire to realize themselves by transcending an indifferent or restrictive environment.

This makes the Minnelli character live in the tension of a necessary isolation and an inevitable drive towards domination. It is as such a central theme of the American cinema. But whereas one easily assumes this to be in Minnelli's earlier films an exclusively aesthetic concern – a need for beauty, for living out a romantic fantasy – the moral dimension is never obscured. And if the very early films do emphasize the final articulation of a harmony, the later ones turn to the ambiguous conditions of the creative will itself, whether in the form of a self-destructive obsession (*Lust for Life*), a manic manipulation of others (*The Bad and the Beautiful*) or a tenacious determination (*Home from the Hill*).

In some of the earlier films, for example, Minnelli's attitude can be seen to alternate between an optimism about the individual's potential to make the world conform to his dreams, and an equally acute sense of the tyranny over others implicit in its realization. But this is never blown up to the dimensions of ponderous moralizing; on the contrary, it is always contained in the insignificant story, the unprepossessing event. In *Meet Me in St. Louis*, for example, near-tragedy ensues when the father of the heroine decides to move his family to New York, and thus to uproot them from their small self-contained world. It is the typical Minnelli dilemma of the will of the individual opposed to the always fragile fabric of human harmony. The father's announcement of his intention falls on the family like a spell, and their world is visibly coming to a halt. Finally, the father relents, they stay, and, in a very complicated camera-movement, Minnelli conveys the precise feeling of a rhythm recommencing, and the characters 'circulate' once more through the house as if their blood had begun to flow again, with gestures and movements that approximate a graceful dance. By contrast, in *Father of the Bride*, the same situation is inverted, and Spencer Tracy, as the father, is progressively more exiled from his own home because of the banal and conventional ideas and preconceptions which his wife and daughter are trying to foster upon him.

The clearest expression of a corresponding optimism is in *The Clock*. It is the story of a GI on a 24-hour leave and a girl from the country who happen to meet in a railway station. In this film, full of the most unpromising stereotype material, Minnelli magnificently communicates the elements of his vision. For example, the obligatory stroll through Central Park becomes the pivot where the real New York in all its oppressive strangeness transforms itself into an integral part of the couple's experience of themselves. As they listen to the bewildering noise of the city, the sounds merge into a kind of music, and through its rhythm, the couple find each other – the city literally brings them together. This is important, because the film is built on the tension between the fatality of the Clock, the diffuse chaos of the city, and the will of the lovers. Against a world circumscribed by time and ruled by chance (their initial encounter, the various accidental separations, the careless indifference that surrounds them), Minnelli sets the determination of the couple to realize a common happiness. Insignificant though they are in the human sea, their naive trust in love-at-first-sight appears as heroic because it is supported by a belief in the human will and its power to transcend the given. Judy Garland and Robert Walker here exemplify the Minnelli 'philosophy' par excellence: the freedom of the individual, his creative potential, consists in perceiving order and design in chaos, whose meaning is revealed when it becomes dance. The film opens with a crane shot into the crowd at Pennsylvania station, showing the aimless movement. It ends with the camera tracking out from the station, and as Judy Garland is seen walking away, even the crowd has a regular flow and a definite rhythm.

Although the polarity between two worlds, or world-views, is

Minnelli's central structural device, the meaning of the themes is defined by the nature of the energy which the characters bring to bear on the world as they find it. The spectrum is wide, with innumerable shades and variations. Whether it is the genteel 'joie de vivre' of *Meet Me in St. Louis*, the instinctive stubbornness of Eddie in *The Courtship of Eddie's Father*, the dream of a luxury caravan (*The Long Long Trailer*), or the fantasy life of a switch-board girl (*Bells are Ringing*) – common to all of them is the sense that without this energy the world would always disintegrate into mere chaos.

As with many Hollywood directors, the basic purpose of Minnelli's handling of visual elements is to encourage audience identification. But no other director has such a keen and differentiated eye for the mesmerizing qualities of a setting, a particular décor. Not inappropriately, the French critic Domarchi once compared Minnelli to Hitchcock, saying their conception of the cinema is 'alchemistic'; the elements of Minnelli's *mise en scène* are indeed geared towards producing an overall impression of unreality, wholly engrossing the spectator by a sense of timing and a fluidity of movement which exaggerates the natural relativity of time and space in the cinema to a point where the visual spectacle becomes a kind of hallucination.

This means that the mechanism of identification (or projection) normally understood rather crudely as referring only to the audience's empathy with the protagonist, is amplified to include the setting, which no longer functions as an objective point of correlation, but becomes wholly absorbed into the action as the natural extension of the protagonist's being. The characterization of the Minnelli hero therefore reduces itself to the barest outlines of a specific individuality. His role is to indicate a sequence of psychological *situations* of general significance, and not to illustrate the ramifications of a unique case. What matters is not his character (i.e. his moral principles, his credibility as a rational and sentient human being) but his personality (i.e. the set of attitudes and physical responses he displays in given situations).

Where it is a question of substantiating or explaining a human relationship in terms of psychological motivation, Minnelli therefore invariably presents the conflict as a clash of settings, an imbalance of stylistic elements, such as a contrast of movements or a disharmony of colours or objects. The bright yellow caravan in the landscape of *The Long Long Trailer*, for example, jars so painfully that in itself it suffices to undermine the couple's pretensions to a free and natural life. At other times the violence of a gesture is set off against an otherwise smooth or harmonious visual surface, and when Barry Sullivan in one of the opening scenes of *The Bad and the Beautiful* slams down the telephone, an incongruous but highly dramatic contrast is created in opposition to the dream-like setting in which Lana Turner is being filmed by the camera-crew. Minnelli constantly reduces his stories to their moments of visual intensity, where he can project the dramatic conflicts into the décor. Where other directors use the cinematic space to clarify the intellectual complexities of their plots (Preminger, Lang), Minnelli relates distance (or lack of distance) to varying degrees of subjective intensity. Thus, an important function of the *mise en scène* is to interiorize the rapport that exists between spectator and action, by reproducing a similar tension of identification and projection within the film itself – achieved very often by a typically Minnellian camera movement which consists of an unobtrusive, but very fluid, travelling forward, interrupted by an almost imperceptible craning away usually held as a general shot until the fade-out. This makes the Minnelli hero emerge in many ways as the creator *and* spectator of his own life, realizing himself most fully in a world which he can transcend by using it as the décor of his own *mise en scène*.

Conversely, the moment of rupture – doubt, despair, nightmare – is equally dramatized in the interrelation of hero and environment, and the world of objects becomes either solid, immobile or bristling with a recalcitrant life of its own.

In these cases, it is the gesture, sometimes aggressive, more often hesitant, which is extended into the alien territory that defines the protagonist's sense of personal identity, and the most subtle changes in his state of mind are relayed through his position and behaviour vis à vis the setting. Barry Boys in an article on *The Courtship of Eddie's Father* has given a fine analysis of the opening of the film, with Eddie precariously poised in the once familiar kitchen, which through the death of his mother has become a hostile world.

This means that there is an obvious analogy between the approach of his characters to their predicament and the cinematic medium. Thus the mechanism of projection and identification are reflected in Minnelli's films as the two phases of a character's development: projection of his vision upon an environment, identification (or breakdown of an identification) with a décor, a created world.

In the musicals, where the characteristics of Minnelli's cinema are most transparent, one can see a kind of recurrent pattern of situations, which forms the archetypal Minnelli structure (what differentiates his non-musical films is mainly that though these situations are present, they are not necessarily in this order): 1 The moment of isolations (the individual vision as imprisonment). 2 The tentative communication (the vision materializes as décor). 3 The rupture (the décor appears as mere appearance and delusion). 4 The world as chaos. 5 The world as spectacle/the spectacle as world.

In a sense, this pattern represents a kind of catharsis of vision, to which corresponds the clarification of emotions through the purging of their opposites: what emerges from the contradictory impulses of solitude and euphoria, frustration, despair and delirious monomania is a measure of self-fulfilment, often merely implicit – where all emotional extremes feed into the creation of the 'show', and where the energy is finally disciplined in the movement of the dance. The classical example of this is *The Pirate*: Judy Garland (Mañuela), dreaming of the pirate, sees Macoco materialize in Gene Kelly, only to discover that he is an imposter – a discovery that creates emotional chaos for her (she loves him all the same) and actual chaos on the island (there is a price on his head). Mañuela, finally renouncing her romantic fantasies, joins Kelly's humble theatrical troupe, and the film ends with an ironic number, significantly entitled 'Be A Clown'.

Likewise, in *Brigadoon*, Gene Kelly's desire for another world materializes in the legendary village of Brigadoon where he meets the girl of his life, only to discover that the whole village and its inhabitants will have to disappear again for another hundred years. He returns to New York, but the mad chaos in the fashionable bar makes him long so much for the enchanted world of Brigadoon that he returns to Scotland, and miraculously, Brigadoon appears once more, conjured up by his faith. But now Brigadoon is threatened by one of the inhabitants who wants to escape from the magic spell and live a 'real' life. The villagers hunt him down and he is finally killed. Gene Kelly on the other hand, marrying Fiona, his dream girl, accepts the 'unreality' of Brigadoon and is prepared to live for only a day every hundred years – metaphor for the artist living only through his art.

In *The Band Wagon*, too, the pattern is in evidence. Here it is particularly the different stages of Astaire's reimmersion into the world of showbusiness, the different and often disastrous shows, that liberate the character from his wholly egocentric projection, and by a series of debunking manoeuvres and parodies (e.g. the staging of *Oedipus Rex*), Minnelli establishes the idea of the spectacle as the measure of things. This is summed up in the theme song 'That's Entertainment': 'everything that happens in life/can happen in a show . . . anything, anything can go/ – The world is a stage/the stage is a world/of entertainment'.

The notion of the artist as actor, however, not only relates the hero in a complex way to his environment, it also allows Minnelli to pursue the theme of artistic creativity into its most banal guises, where a common human denominator – the role-playing of all social life – serves to illuminate what is after all normally considered a privileged state of being. An essentially artistic temperament is revealed in all those who – from switchboard girl to Hollywood tycoon – want to act upon a given reality, change it, transform the material of their lives through the energy of an idea, an obsession, or merely the tentative groping to live up to the boldness of their imagination. But this theme of an energy in search of a material form hardly ever communicates itself in Minnelli as achievement. On the contrary, it is radically relativized as process – a permanent becoming – and rhythm, gesture and colour are the properly cinematic signs of a spontaneous and contagious vitality, embodied in the musical as in no other genre.

Thus, despite the obvious difference between Judy Holliday's blunt vivaciousness in *Bells are Ringing* and Lesley Caron's spiritual and graceful sensibility in *Gigi*, both films share the common drive for a liberation which inevitably leads to the spectacle, and both films are, in this sense, concerned with the ethics of the *mise en scène* – in one film understood as the (benevolent) influence on other people's lives, in the other as the assumption of a role in a formalized and stylized society. In *Bells are Ringing*, Judy Holliday wants to play the good fairy to the clients of a telephone answering service, but at first she creates merely confusion, chaos and mischief. But although her role-playing makes her seem unreal to herself, her clients eventually bind together – to produce a theatre-play. In an important aspect, however, her predicament highlights one of the inspirations of Minnelli's art. Through Judy Holliday's escapades we see a dichotomy between the richness of the American imagination and the restrictive force of a conventional morality. Significantly, the police handcuff her for her flight of fancy, ironic symbol of society's attitude to the creative artist.

If *Bells are Ringing* concerns the responsibility of the *metteur en scène*, *Gigi* is an example of the apprenticeship of the *mise en scène*. Gigi has to learn how not to be natural, how to calculate her movement and judge the meaning of each gesture. She has to learn the conscious use of appearance, as a way of retaining a personal spontaneity and freedom through the language of social grace. In *Gigi* it is difficult to know how to take this aesthetic education – the colour symbolism tells the story of a degradation, with Gigi's red and green becoming gradually a merely fashionable mauve and pink. On the other hand, the process seems inevitable, and Minnelli obviously prefers a conscious grace to a false innocence. In this sense, *Gigi* more than any other film is about the commercial cinema. And by subjecting his inspiration to the rigours of the system, Minnelli himself seems to praise the chains that tie the Hollywood artist so often to the banal story, the vulgar sentiment, the platitudinous cliché. However, unlike other aesthetic moralists such as Ophuls or Renoir with whom he has much in common, Minnelli has a wholly American reliance on an unbroken stream of vitality and energy. But as with them, what defines value for him is the *conception* of the world, not its material basis. In this sense, even the most 'unreal' of his melodramas or musical comedies acknowledges a level of existence, a dimension of the actual that many a European director studiously ignores, and which Hollywood itself seems to have lost under the impact of TV-style instant realism. Who is then to say whether Minnelli's aestheticism is pernicious mystification or not rather the realism of the truly cinematic artist?

But Minnelli himself has dramatized the dilemma of film-making explicitly in his two films *The Bad and the Beautiful* and *Two Weeks in Another Town*. In both films seemingly fundamental moral distinctions between art and life are seen to become more and more ambiguous, as the laws and conditions of film-making impose themselves on an already inauthentic model of life. The film-to-be, the artefact, assumes the dimensions of an inexorable necessity, exposing the moral flaws and human weaknesses of those involved in its creation – a banal point perhaps, had not Minnelli balanced this indictment of Hollywood in *The Bad and the Beautiful* by the dramatization of a grandiose, all-devouring obsession of an artist who spares neither himself nor others in order to remain true to his inspiration. Through the character of producer Jonathan Shields – cynical, cunning and demonic, who sacrifices everything in order to make films – Minnelli explores the nature of his own commitment to the cinema. Shields, by destroying their private lives, liberates the creative potential of his director, scriptwriter and leading lady, who had all been imprisoned by their petty worries and emotional fixations. *The Bad and the Beautiful* shows the visionary as the most ruthless realist, dominating a world with an energy so radical that it can only come from the intimate knowledge of its degradation.

Art as the destruction of 'ordinary' life – this is the central ambiguity which is at the heart of Minnelli's vision. And in *Lust for Life*, the film about Vincent Van Gogh, he pays homage to a greater artist, yet at the same time sharpens his own theme to its paroxysm. The Nietzschean intensity of Van Gogh's vision produces paintings of life as no human eye has ever seen it, but it is also a demonic urge that dissolves and severs all human bonds and finally destroys Van Gogh himself. In the film, the two sides are linked symbolically. As his isolation grows, the yellow colours of a superhuman light invade the canvas. But here Minnelli confronts a dilemma that transcends the framework of Hollywood, namely that of the morality of art itself. What are the values it creates, whom does it serve and to what ends?

If these questions receive an ambivalent answer in Minnelli's films, where the artist finally redeems and justifies his trespass on 'life', it is partly because for Minnelli the artist is not privileged in either status or sensibility. All those who are capable of experiencing existence by its intensity ('why must life be always measured by its duration?' – this complaint of Deborah Kerr in *Tea and Sympathy* is symptomatic) and have the courage of their inspiration are artists in Minnelli's films, whether creative in an accepted sense or not.

It is when dealing with the 'real' artist, as in *Lust for Life*, that the question of the value of ordinary life becomes problematic, and in *Two Weeks in Another Town* the demonic element in the Shields-Van Gogh personality is portrayed as unambiguously neurotic and incapable of dealing with his life. Through Jack Andrus (all three characters, significantly, are played by the same actor – Kirk Douglas) Minnelli insists above all on the human price to be paid for the artist's venture. For in this film, the 'art' is shown to be inept, and the society is simply decadent. The assertive energy which in the early films mediated the rupture is explicitly and nostalgically evoked by Minnelli quoting his own *The Bad and the Beautiful*. A feeling of guilt and failure, by contrast, always makes reality seem apocalyptic. In *Two Weeks* it is the spectacle in its corrupt form (one director taking over from another, everyone working behind one another's back) that comes to dominate, and the actor, instead of being the force that precariously balances two mutually complementary orders of reality, is a schizophrenic, just released from a mental hospital. Although the film in the end appears to suggest the possibility of a new start, this is both a return and an escape, and the issue is finally left open. What weighs, however, more heavily is the 'death' of the director in the film – Minnelli's alter ego – whose once creative vision has turned into a morbid and self-destructive introspection, to which he finally succumbs.

2 · Alain Masson: 'George Sidney: Artificial Brilliance/The Brilliance of Artifice'

Positif, no. 180, April 1976, pp. 48–54, translated by Liz Heron

In the musical more than in any other genre, the critic has been called upon to recover given films, directors, or even studios from the accusations of 'bad taste' which have been levelled against them. As Alain Masson demonstrates in his article on George Sidney, the standards responsible for a particular notion of bad taste are nearly always artificial ones, often evolved within the film world to justify a particular cinematic practice. The excessive numbers of Busby Berkeley or the garish colours of Minnelli's décor are felt to be in poor taste only when they are compared to contemporary standards; later decades have come to appreciate such excess precisely because it tends to point up the very artificiality of the codes which it contests. In like manner, George Sidney has been labelled as a minor MGM director whose success is due to the studio's équipe rather than to the director himself. In an era when the musical's ideal form was the so-called 'integrated' style (where the numbers seem to arise so naturally out of the narrative that a clear distinction between the two seems beside the point), Sidney time after time weighted down his films with production numbers reminiscent of the 1930s extravaganzas. The logic of taste necessarily takes over at this point: Sidney is an anomaly, *ergo* Sidney has bad taste.

In response to this all-too-familiar progression, Masson proposes a clever and extremely persuasive alternative: from beginning to end of his not inconsiderable *oeuvre* Sidney pursues an aesthetics of anomaly. By mixing diverse generic conventions, by consistently casting against type, by heightening the narrative/number tonal contrast, Sidney succeeds in stressing the supplemental nature of music, its orchestration, and the numbers which introduce it. Where the logic of the 'integrated' musical calls for a constant attempt to reduce the distance between narrative and number, Sidney voluntarily heightens the contrast between the two, thus creating for some a consummate example of bad taste, but for Masson a conscious attempt to contest the conventionality of narrative, to show up its givens and its gaps. Masson thus places himself with Elsaesser on the side of those who see in the musical a reflection on the conditions of existence of Hollywood narrative, rather than a transparent example of classical narrative itself. I take it as a sign of the good health of the field of genre criticism that a genre director as little heralded – indeed as poorly known – as Sidney should attract an article of such high quality.

Critical appreciations of George Sidney differ little; the references in Andrew Sarris and Jean-Pierre Coursodon-Bertrand Tavernier all concur in their emphasis on the disparity between the bulk of his work, where they acknowledge certain films as important, interesting and enjoyable, and the looseness of his *mise en scène*, or at least the incoherence of his vision of the world, and even the ugliness of his world. The historians of Hollywood, Charles Higham and Joel Greenberg (*Hollywood in the Forties*) or Gordon Gow (*Hollywood in the Fifties*) mention him quite a lot, and books on musical comedy devote a substantial amount of space to him, but everywhere you can sense a certain reticence: skill and unfailing hard work are all he is ever credited with. What is more, his colleagues have divergent opinions of him: Charles Walters comments (*Positif*, nos. 144–45) that at MGM 'L. K. Sidney was vice-president, George Sidney was his son, and Lillian Burns was the "drama coach"* and George's wife.' On the other hand, according to Stanley Donen (*Cahiers du Cinéma*, no. 143), Sidney 'has a great interest in everything to do with musical comedy. Moreover he studied music and plays the piano extraordinarily well. He's also a man who has an amazing amount of experience in films. He knows a thing or two about musical comedy.' That Sidney had a taste for the limelight is amply testified by his position on the Directors Guild; that he profited from nepotism to a degree is highly likely; but his career can't be reduced to that. His survival outside MGM testifies in his favour in that respect. His last film, *Half a Sixpence*, was made in London in 1967, which suggests that at that time Sidney, like many other Hollywood directors, was collaborating in one of numerous attempts at the financial rationalization of production in the face of the crisis. Furthermore, at MGM between 1932 and 1955 his upward trajectory was by no means the overnight affair that Walters's ideas would have us believe: he crossed one hurdle at a time, moving on from shorts to small-scale productions, and from Joe Pasternak to Arthur Freed. When all is said and done his success is in the same mould as that of other directors of his generation, an Aldrich or a Fleischer, for instance.

Such success can be explained primarily by the success his films

* Translator's note: in English in original.

have had with audiences. They're still one of the staples of American television. It's also strange to note how French critics over the last few years have shifted slightly in the same direction: already in no. 81 of *Cahiers du Cinéma* the anonymous Zoilus* acknowledged the charm of *Pal Joey*, while bemoaning the 'too-slick picturesqueness' of the *mise en scène*. In no. 153 of the same journal Jean-Louis Comolli praises *Bye Bye Birdie*, but he too finds fault with the 'limp and unassuming' production. (I'd like to know: does Sidney overdo it or does he underplay it?) Olivier Clouzot's eulogy of *Jupiter's Darling* (*Cinéma 60*, no. 40) doesn't prevent him from making the point that 'Of course, George Sidney is not a director capable of great rigour in his plot construction.' René Gilson in the same journal (no. 84) acclaims *Birdie*, recognizing in Sidney a 'craftsmanship' (transposition of the previous 'lack of rigour'), which he assesses as 'discreet' (embodiment of the 'limp and unassuming') and 'occasionally inventive' (transmutation of the 'too-slick picturesqueness'). What is more, these niggardly praises make no pressing demands on their authors to revise their assessment of Sidney. The overall impression is that Sidney made some good films, but had very little to do with it himself. This is the world upside down in terms of the *auteur* theory. It is therefore not surprising that the journal which least troubles itself over this would-be theory should be the only one to reinstate *Bye Bye Birdie* within the perspective of Sidney's work, through an article by Gérard Legrand (*Positif*, no. 60). In fact in the '*auteur* theory' it isn't just the obviously over-ambitious 'theory' that's so ill-chosen, but also the word '*auteur*' which is much too close to the humanist tradition in literature. The case of Sidney, whose work owes its coherence and its singularity far less to themes or some moral position than to artistic experiments, could serve as a potent example of this.

Artifice

One starting point for characterizing these endeavours would consist in using the notion of mixed genres, but extending its scope beyond the mere conjunction of the serious and the comic. Since the genre central to Sidney's career happens to be musical comedy, then it comes down to a broadening of that genre. In Arthur Freed's

---

* Translator's note: Zoilus was a severe critic of Homeric poems in the fourth century BC, hence, any ill-natured critic. The review in *Cahiers* referred to is unsigned.

studios in the same period the primary aim was pure musical comedy, of which *Singin' in the Rain* remains the supremely classic example. Its first constituent is the location of the plot in a world that lends itself to a degree of fantasy, but without giving the sense of being no more than a pretext for it, like the old backstage musicals; so a space is created where song and dance seem natural. As a result the conventions of this kind of musical comedy are constituted principally through exclusions: care is taken not to make particular scenes or characters too realistic; conversely, anything too highly stylized is kept at a distance. This is how the big numbers in *Singin' in the Rain* or *The Band Wagon*, whose extravagance is none the less declared by their context, come to be really much less unrealistic than the numbers in the 1930s films they parody. If one can define musical comedy as the improbable meeting of prosaic comedy and the poetry of song and dance, and thus of two extremes, then the project of MGM around 1950 essentially consisted in an obscuring of the gap that separated these two heterogeneous elements. It is a project, then, that is both indispensable to the coherence of the genre and paradoxical in relation to its constituents. However important it may be, this exceptional success could not, therefore, constitute a universal model on the basis of which criteria of judgment could be arrived at that would be applicable to the whole history of the genre. Now this fundamentally restrictive enterprise, by its application of imperatives such as taste or decency – in the sense that the theoreticians of classical drama might give to these terms – amounts to a formal exclusion of any attempt at extension, since it is based on a kind of aesthetic censorship. Despite appearances, the work of George Sidney in this way comes to be positioned against the mainstream, which would partly explain the distrust on the part of critics who still make elegance a decisive factor in their appreciation of musical films. But ten years on from the re-evaluation of Busby Berkeley's work, this kind of dandyism really ought to be a thing of the past.

For Sidney, the mixing of genres probably begins with what the Americans call 'miscasting'. In *Pilot No. 5*, Gene Kelly, already well known as a dancer on the stage and in films after the success of *For Me and My Gal* (B. Berkeley, 1942), plays an airman of Italian extraction, a part that's anything but musical, no doubt awarded out of admiration for the intensity of his performance in Berkeley's film. Kelly's tendency to use signification rather than expressivity as a means of conveying emotions, as befits a dancer, was in itself obviously not unattractive to Sidney, for whom the human face and body are not the register of an infinity of nuances, but rather display totally characterized emotions in a deliberate and disconnected manner. Kim Novak's acting in *The Eddy Duchin Story* or in *Jeanne Eagels* is in this respect a perfect illustration of the paradox of the actor, which really seems to involve the reduction of emotions to a system of coded unities. A personage as grotesque and gross as Red Skelton is thus not entirely out of place in such a world. His exaggerated grimaces simply mask the lowest boundary of such stylization. Xavier Cugat and indeed the Barbara Nichols of *Pal Joey* or *Who Was That Lady?* can easily be included; or better still, the Judy Garland of *The Harvey Girls*, which reveals the demise of someone who was still regarded as the frail adolescent. The same gap opens up between the petulant Ann-Margret and the shy, rather mannish young girl that she plays in *Bye Bye Birdie*.

The advantage of this artifice of imposing conventions on the expression of emotions which could never achieve a natural level is that it can contrive essential intervals when emotional expression can be given free rein. When predictable psychology is transgressed by the violence of an emotion to which it is foreign, then there is really no question of translating inner disturbance into significative mimicry. Since they are supposed to be the windows of the soul, but are in themselves utterly expressionless organs, the eyes may become the symbolic locus of this process: just remember the close-up on Sinatra's look while he is watching Kim Novak's strip-tease, in *Pal Joey*! Because it constitutes the *mise en scène* of the viewer's concupiscence it is filled with shame, and that is what determines, out of a necessity that goes deeper than the internal logic of the narrative, that the act of undressing should stop there, and that Sinatra should call out – to our great relief. It is a complex piece of play which entails the viewer's complicity in censorship, but with great care re-inscribes the forbidden and the intimate in the spectacle. At any rate, the emotional excess and the expressive dimension of this passage derive much less from what the actor expresses than from the absence of expression: it is the incapacity to translate an emotion which manifests ambiguity, or even ambivalence of feeling. The expressive value of a face that cannot be read exists in two other forms in Sidney's work: the impassivity of Tyrone Power after the death of his wife and before his own, in *The Eddy Duchin Story*, and Ann-Margret overwhelmed by her own desire in *Viva Las Vegas*, or Kim Novak on the stage in *Jeanne Eagels*. Moreover, in this last instance the close-up is not enough for Sidney. He multiplies the inserts and the camera movements in a genuine frenzy of *mise en scène*. However questionable such business may be in aesthetic terms, it at least has the virtue of a complete integration of the filmed reality with the film and the viewing of the film, by emptying this would-be reality of any internal coherence. Such violence is not unexpected in a melodrama, in moments of climax, but it is quite out of place in musical comedy, where it formally ushers in a mixing of genres.

The injection of the serious (*The Harvey Girls*) or the burlesque (*Bathing Beauty*), the uncertainty created by the hazardous conjunction of classical music and the rumba (*Holiday in Mexico*) or the melodies of the high-class night-club (*The Eddy Duchin Story*), the meeting of Shakespeare with the operetta (*Kiss Me Kate*), musical comedy with car racing (*Viva Las Vegas*) or the Russian ballet and rock 'n' roll (*Bye Bye Birdie*) or Roman mythology (*Jupiter's Darling*), the use of animation (*Anchors Aweigh*) or the sequence of abstract images (*Pal Joey*) – so many gambles that must seem foolish *a priori*. What is more it isn't hard to tell that in most cases it wasn't Sidney himself who was responsible for these surprising decisions. It was Kelly who had the idea for the dance with the Hanna-Barbera mouse; the problems with the trick photography also seem to have restricted both the choreography and the *mise en scène*. The extravagances of *Bathing Beauty* and *Holiday in Mexico* derive from the riotous ambitions of producers lacking in rigour and anxious to show off every card up their sleeves: Jack Cummings and Joe Pasternak. But you then have to see how Sidney applies himself to delivering the goods! In what seem to be the more personal films he operates the same procedures, handling the duels in *The Three Musketeers* and *Scaramouche* like choreography; entrusting the part of the colourful spy in *Who Was That Lady?* to an extraordinarily stiff actor (J. Whitmore); etc. . .

Brilliance

The truth is that Sidney is an activist of *mise en scène*; the shoddier the project the more scope he will have for the exercise of his mastery. It is in unceasing movement, not in its continuity, that his art has its fulfilment. It is not enough for him that *Bye Bye Birdie* lampoons television, rock, ballet, youth, middle-aged women, parents, composers, and whatever else I could mention. He also has to slip in a photograph of Sinatra looking discountenanced by the irresistible rise of Conrad Birdie, and stresses the heights of absurdity reached by the Bolshoi when its conductor suffers the effects of a pill that can speed up movement. Sidney's solution is precisely to film the whole sequence speeded up, giving it a scientific justification and making it possible to go beyond the mere build-up of comic effects, and towards a generalized uneasiness. He adds a Hitchcock pastiche by giving us a floor-level tracking-shot that follows the squeaking shoes of the already caricatured possessive mother character. It is in this way that the *mise en scène* utterly dominates the theatrical material that it has taken as its object. The sudden brilliance of the first shot, with its high chromatic tensions and its striking camera movements, has as its function this domination, more than that of showing us Ann-Margret; in fact this is an introduction, intended to make the viewer familiar with a definite formal purpose, and underlining a specific aesthetic value: the display of artifice. Confirmation of this intention could be found in the numerous tricks of the film: it is on the very surface of the screen that Dick Van Dyke finger-traces happy faces to cheer up Janet Leigh – it is only her shadow that he manages to bewitch at first – we'd be apt to say her film image. Similarly, the famous telephone ballet doesn't take place in any one possible space, but in the simultaneity of several places which only the editing can unite: Sidney takes care to emphasize this by using what is unmistakably a painted backdrop whenever a background is needed.

This taste for display is made manifest to a privileged degree in the way Sidney films the big bands, and he does this intentionally: Kay Kyser, Bob Crosby and Benny Carter in *Thousands Cheer*; Xavier Cugat in *Bathing Beauty* and *Holiday in Mexico*, and of course the reconstruction of Eddy Duchin's band. And this predilection is by no means exclusive: a mere pianist can provide enough for the director's verve to get its teeth into whether it is José Iturbi or Duchin. The musical sequence is never dealt with independently; the shots never break from the musical structure: the music is regarded as a series of happenings, a plot in other words. In Sidney's aesthetic these happenings must necessarily be translated with force, and that is why he likes to hold them within the orchestration, which governs the cutting of the band scenes. But isn't *mise en scène* itself for him a kind of orchestration? A score starts to bc interesting when it goes beyond the mere function of background music, when the arpeggios, the trills or the quavers seem to acquire a certain independence in relation to the theme and in fact become something more. It is precisely the role of camera movements, visual effects (a soloist rises or comes forward and the whole band seems to move away into the distance behind him), and the unexpected (a pair of dancers filmed back-lit in a Cugat number) which Sidney makes use of over and over again in his *mise en scène* of bands. Note, too, that he proceeds in identical fashion when he is filming a pianist.

An orchestral figure

So the reiterated presence of a dominant figure can be recognized in his oeuvre, but this orchestral figure is employed not just with the band numbers; its structure also exists in numbers like 'Atchison, Topeka and the Santa Fe' (*The Harvey Girls*), the departure or arrival of the boat in *Show Boat*, etc. First there is a series of waiting shots: the band, the townspeople waiting for the train, the boat on the river. Then closer and closer shots pick out one section of the musicians, knots of growing activity; the captain and a child who is the first to catch sight of the show boat. The second phase is constituted by the setting up of spatial relationships between the different groups: a soloist is detached from the band with a camera movement: a lateral tracking-shot leads the townspeople as far as the station, where the train, also tracked laterally by the camera, has just come in; a shot-reverse-shot cut with lead-in sets up a clear relation between the boat and the crowd waiting on the quay. The third phase is the most difficult to describe for it is the most free. It consists in a simultaneous extension and increase of activity: in the band there is a rapid succession of crescendi, with a multiplication of strange camera angles: the camera moves back to hold the Harvey Girls as they get off the train, then focuses on the joyous excitement of the townspeople (one of them throwing his lasso in time to the music); overhead shots show the crowd dancing on the quay and follow the passengers as they disembark. Final phase: the band comes together again as a triumphant ensemble; the train moves off again and as it picks up speed the townspeople run alongside, and the camera tracks in on the Harvey Girls grouped in the form of a pyramid; the same pyramids figure in the boat scene with a long shot to establish the whole scene, and a close-up of Howard Keel kissing the lovely Kathryn Grayson against the background of the sky, as if to emphasize the idea of reunion. Waiting, setting up of relationships, rhythmic centre, reunion: this is really the schema of this orchestral figure, whose chief moment, it must be emphasized, is entirely constructed in the mode of its expansion. Aside from this the function of each phase is noted in different ways: thus the pyramid easily becomes a mark of closure, by virtue of the function of conclusion it has so long assumed on the stage of every music-hall in the world, but it also has the advantage of suggesting convergence; the sense of anticipation is often associated with a psychological motivation, as we have seen; the moment of the composition of spatial relationships is ultimately defined by the appearance of arbitrariness in the shots which instead of considering the different elements all together or separately is applied to pushing them towards the point of their conjunction or their rupture, while at the same time conveying the impression that henceforth it is the camera movements that constitute the driving force of the action.

Irrespective of the meanings that it contains, this figure can develop and be understood in strictly formal terms. The sense of anticipation is then to be considered only as the subject that engages the viewer's attention in the introduction of the whole. The second moment illustrates the formal possibilities of *mise en scène*, those which in fact are about to be freely developed in what follows. The last phase contains all the characteristics of a conclusion: in answer to the initial anticipation there is a closing of all the relationships, a suggestion of the circularity of the figure. However, it is seldom that Sidney's art functions as pure and empty form, despite his predilection for music. What is added is also often an addition in meaning.

In the first place it happens that this setting-up of meaning is not immediate. In *The Eddy Duchin Story* the complexity and the virtuosity of the *mise en scène* of the band or piano numbers would be quite gratuitous if it did not carry with it an emotional excess: it is across a piano that Tyrone Power first catches sight of Kim Novak, which adds up to no more than an amusing little scene, but it is effected in the same visual terms as the pathetic reunion between the dying Eddy Duchin and his long-lost son at the end of the film. The vigour of the Central Park Casino number hardly conveys anything more than the image of a band working smoothly, but when the pattern of this *mise en scène* is repeated in a rehearsal to which the father invites the son and some friends of his, then it suggests the beginnings of a reconciliation between the two characters.

Moreover, there can be no doubt that the very revelation of what is added engenders a certain anxiety. Thus in the aquatic number which functions as the finale in *Bathing Beauty* the swimming pool appears to be deeper than its outer proportions would lead us to believe – a second, secret depth into which Esther Williams will dive all the more voluptuously, and so its erotic significance is consequently undeniable. So for Sidney the very existence of what is added is linked with a world of trouble which is expressed in the big panic numbers – 'Plenty of Living to Do' in *Bye Bye Birdie*, Ann-Margret's rock 'n' roll number in *Viva Las Vegas* or the banjo sequence in *Half a Sixpence*. There is another no less insidious obsession in his work: with the mirrors that fragment Lena Horne's reflection in *Thousands Cheer* or multiply the sensual contortions of Ann Miller in *Kiss Me Kate*.

The comedy

These are not isolated elements. What is really at stake is a whole conception of musical comedy, and perhaps the narrative film. Unlike a Minnelli or a Donen, Sidney has hardly attempted a total integration of the heterogeneous elements that constitute the raw material of a musical film, or quite simply a film. So music and dance are not exclusively a function of revelation or commentary in relation to the narrative; they are not content just to illustrate the story told by the narrative. Their role is rather that of a challenge to the plot in its more conventional moments. Spleen, jealousy, day-dreaming, the encounter, the discovery of femininity, are all the basis for plenty of scenes that are devoid of any originality because they are, so to speak, mandatory in the concoction of any love story. Faced with this constraint one can conceive of a number of strategies: ellipsis or litotes, hyperbole or the sublime. Sidney doesn't care one way or the other: he gets comedy pure and simple, without it entering his head for a moment to pretend that it is anything else. He even pares it down to its barest working essentials: the triangular plot of *Pal Joey*, the parallel couples in *Bye Bye Birdie*, the oppositions in *Half a Sixpence*, to say nothing of the obstacles to the happiness of the lovers constituted by the fear of water in *Bathing Beauty* and racing car madness in *Viva Las Vegas*. It all comes down to a geometry that leaves little room for surprises. You will search Sidney's films in vain for any trace of complexity in the piecing together of the story-lines, and that is why he seems so much at home with big spectaculars like *Thousands Cheer* or *Pepe*. His intention is to compensate for the simplicity of the story-line, or its absence, by the richness of the *mise en scène*, and notably in the musical numbers.

For the music seems to enrich each of the characters with a double superfluity. The existence of this tendency has been well commented on by Gérard Legrand (*Positif*, no. 114) with reference to *Scaramouche*, but it can, without doubt, be extended to the whole of Sidney's work, and connected to the director's preoccupation with the score. In *Bye Bye Birdie*, for instance, young Kim McAphee is a wholesome, smiling virgin, who is quite properly in love with her fine boyfriend. The only trouble is that rock 'n' roll sends her into a frenzy, particularly the idol Conrad Birdie, an exaggerated yet flabby character who is a wonderful incarnation of the paradox of phallic motherhood, which moreover links him with Dick Van Dyke's mother. So the narrative outline which sets up a parallel between the two couples and the obstacles to their happiness is confirmed on another level. And there is more: as she changes after school Kim sings her joy at reaching womanhood, but simultaneously she swaps her dress for a wretched pair of jeans and a shapeless sweater, thereby adopting the desexing uniform of the American teenager. Over and above the possible disturbances generated by this transvestism, there is here a valuable pointer to the character: doesn't Kim thus confirm her own conception of femininity? It is also clear that in both cases it is the forms of musical comedy – the intrusion of the music and the singing – that seem to be responsible for the splitting of the character. It would be easy to call on psychoanalysis here, and make the musical the theatrical unconscious of comedy. Perhaps we can do without it. It will be enough to bear in mind that in the music the function of the orchestration is to add depth to the melody which it thus puts in perspective.

A supplementary world

So music introduces a supplementary world, and on occasion a world of excess. It is music that turns Red Skelton into an undignified puppet prepared to make a fool of himself in a tutu, and Esther Williams into an insatiable siren. It is music that governs Rita Hayworth's mock strip-tease and Kim Novak's real one, where costumed as an eighteenth-century aristocrat, in accordance with an established convention, she takes off an article of clothing each time the music is jazzed-up. It is music that prevents Eddy Duchin from simply accepting his lot. So it makes us see that the simplified geometry of the plot is indeed fragile. There is another world, made of uncertainties, masked desires, duplicity, and probably bad taste. A certain amount of artistic hypocrisy has to be got rid of in order to accept this Dionysian world.

For their part Sidney's heroes seem hardly prepared for such resignation. On the contrary, they consciously practise a kind of headlong flight. This explains the fascination with speed in his films. In *Bye Bye Birdie* Dick Van Dyke invents a pill that speeds up animal motion; Elvis Presley is a racing driver in *Viva Las Vegas*; we witness a rowing contest in *Half a Sixpence*; in the same film the hero flees from problems by travelling; Gene Kelly is transformed into an intrepid sea-dog in *Anchors Aweigh*. All these movements are really part of a search for some kind of blindness. That could also be regarded as the key that Sidney himself gives to his art. What in fact is the difference between blindness and the dazzle that his *mise en scène* is so purposefully bent on producing, instead of aiming at the precise delineation of his characters within the complexity which he seems to accord them with reluctance?

Moreover, the crowning moment of the film often remains the one where, in the belief that they are escaping, the characters plunge into their supplementary world. This simultaneously seductive and disturbing world appears in the final number of *Bathing Beauty*: in what could have been just another display of Esther Williams's talent we are actually obliged to recognize a truly strange festival. The neutralizing of the oppositions between the pool and dry land, between swimming and dancing; the union of water with fire; the movement of the colours, pinks and greens, yellows and whites; the connections between the loud flourishes of the Harry James Band and the swimmer's teeth or make-up, and her gestures, emphasized by the chorus; the magic passage, with the aid of underwater devices, from the darkness of the depths to the deep-blue of the surface or the whiteness of the water fountains sparkling in the firelight; nothing seems to obey the laws of nature. Sidney's passion for decoration doesn't impel him to embellish the world, but to create another one. In the same way dance extracts another truth from the body: Esther Williams's fluidity, Janet Leigh's sharpness, Kim Novak's charm, Ann-Margret's great sensuality of movement. This is a world where the theme is a repeated calling into question of identity, a world of metamorphosis and communication.

But none of that is seriously dealt with in a plot. Instead, it turns out that the narrative is contradicted by the appearance of these erotic nuances, these fragile truths of artifice, these superficial glimpses, these spangles.

The orchestration, Sidney's *mise en scène*, challenges the unfolding of the narrative by unmasking all that it hides, by releasing the confused images of the dream which is the foundation on which it is constructed. So we go beyond conventional codes to approach reality, which is unreadable. Making abundant use of the standard forms of musical comedy or melodrama, he forces them to open onto that which transgresses them instead of making them appear realistic, so that the form itself becomes transgression. You can accuse Sidney of bad taste or complacency, but you can't deny him the merit of having gone to the very limit, to the point where it becomes clear that in 'musical comedy', as in 'dialectical materialism', the meaning lies in the epithet.

3 · Mark Roth: 'Some Warners Musicals and the Spirit of the New Deal'

The Velvet Light Trap, no. 17, Winter 1977, pp. 1–7

No attack on the musical has been so persistent and forceful as that which brands the genre as escapist. The musical is an opiate, its critics contend, a drug which puts the spectator to sleep, thus inducing him to ignore the problems of the real world. Instead of ignoring the escapist critique, as most advocates of auteur criticism and art-for-art's-sake have done, Mark Roth confronts it directly. The apparently escapist film, he claims, may in fact permit the spectator to rehearse, perform, and resolve real-life problems. Overt political concerns and specific economic terminology may be absent from the Warners musical in the Busby Berkeley years, but political and economic considerations are nevertheless implicit within the film because of its ability to mime the familiar configurations of contemporary public life. In particular, the strong leadership of Franklin D. Roosevelt, both inducing and supported by a strong sense of community, is recalled by the strong director figures in Berkeley's 1933 films and their devoted troupes. Berkeley's famous pattern-dances thus become more than a convenient example of self-focusing surrealist art; their careful co-ordination of movement, where each individual is valorized only as part of a coherent whole, becomes symbolic of the spirit of co-operation characteristic of the early days of Roosevelt's presidency.

The advantages of this type of approach are obvious. Instead of refusing to admit the musical's escapist qualities – as most attempts to treat the musical as high art must do – Roth is free to affirm both the genre's escapist nature and its symbolic function. Indeed, the musical is better able to play the ritualistic role which Roth assigns to it precisely because the musical's air of frivolity disarms the spectator, lowers his resistance, and permits the film's symbolic properties to operate at a sub-conscious level. Furthermore, Roth's approach has the virtue of explaining certain problems which heretofore remained unsolved. Why in heaven's name did Ruby Keeler and Dick Powell become the darlings of the decade? By what logic did these relatively untalented and lifeless performers attain a level of success never known by such comparative geniuses as Eleanor Powell and Jack Buchanan? Seen from within the structure elaborated by Roth, the repeated success of Keeler and Powell provides the perfect model of the man-in-the-street biting the bullet in an effort to follow Roosevelt's directives and help restore the country to economic stability. They thus locate the spectator, giving him a clear sense of purpose not only within the film, but by extension within the country as a whole.

In sum, Roth's approach establishes a homology between the spectator/context relationship and a corresponding relationship in the film. Such a strategy is of course not without its drawbacks. Just what is the status of the homology established? Is it in the film or in the interpretation? Was it recognized when the films appeared or does it exist only retrospectively? Does a homology between Hollywood and Washington imply that the entertainment capital reflects the opinions of the political capital or vice-versa? These are questions which Roth chooses not to tackle, yet which require resolution before his sensitive and intriguing reading of specific films could ever serve as the basis for a fuller understanding of the relationship between Hollywood and its political/ideological context.

The New York Stock Market crashed in October, 1929. The next month President Hoover said, 'Any lack of confidence in the economic future or the basic strength of business in the United States is foolish.'[1] In February 1931 he said, 'Nobody is actually starving. The hoboes, for example, are better fed than they ever have been.'[2] Finally, as the depression continued, he was forced to recognize its existence; but he was ready with an excuse, not a plan for action. 'The depression has been deepened by events from abroad which are beyond the control of either our citizens or our government.'[3] By March of 1933 and the inauguration of Franklin Roosevelt there were between 14 and 16 million unemployed. Into the void of political leadership came Roosevelt with his promise of a 'New Deal' for the 'forgotten man at the bottom of the economic pyramid.' His first session of Congress lasted from March 9 to June 16, 1933. In its first issue since resuming publication (July 1, 1933) the *Literary Digest* gave a partial summary of the results of that session of Congress: Emergency Banking Relief, Economy Act, legalization of 3.2 beer, farm relief, inflation of currency, creation of the Tennessee Valley Authority and Civilian Conservation Corps, power for government control of hours, wages and production in all industries, relief to homeowners, railroad reorganization, banking reform, and a $3.3 billion public works program.[4] With these actions and inspiring rhetoric Roosevelt created, for a time at least, a spirit of unity, optimism and pride which found expression in the best of the Warners musicals of the period.

The archetypal Warners musical was born during the Presidential campaign of 1932, and began to decline by the end of 1933. It was a precursor and product of the optimism-in-the-midst-of-depression created by FDR. The high points of the Warners musical were *42nd Street* (1933) and *Footlight Parade* (1933). They have the dynamism and power, lively dialogue and inspired direction by Lloyd Bacon and Busby Berkeley to raise them far above other efforts in the genre. These films focus on the production of the show-within-the-film. The directors of these shows-within-the-film, Warner Baxter and James Cagney, are seldom off the screen. They dominate their respective films. As the musical form weakens, the production of the show-within-the-film becomes progressively less important and the director of the show becomes a weaker figure or is lost in the crowd. In *42nd Street* Warner Baxter is central and Ruby Keeler and Dick Powell are (thankfully) subordinated. This is also the situation in *Footlight Parade* where Cagney dominates and Keeler and Powell have minor parts. In *Gold Diggers of 1933*, however, the stage director is a weak and somewhat foolish figure and the Keeler-Powell team is much more important. The decline of the figure then accelerates: he is essentially absent from *Dames* (1934), minor in *Fashions of 1934* and *Gold Diggers of 1935*, absent from *Gold Diggers of 1937*, and played by the stiff Rudy Vallee in *Gold Diggers in Paris* (1938). *Gold Diggers of 1933* is a good film, but it is weakened by the lack of a strong male lead (such as Baxter or Cagney). After 1933 the musical form at Warners declines noticeably. *Dames* has some of Berkeley's most elaborate spectacles, but the film drags badly until the last reel when Berkeley is allowed to do his stuff. *Fashions of 1934* is weaker still. *Gold Diggers of 1935* belongs in a class of its own and can't fairly be compared with the other Warners musicals. After 1935 we see the form stiff with age in *Gold Diggers of 1937* and stiff with death and the wooden movements of Rudy Vallee in *Gold Diggers in Paris*.

As we all know, the Depression not only raised questions about the viability of American capitalism, but also called into question the ethos and mythology which was both the product and support of that system. Musicals and crime films were the two major film genres to explore this crisis. Each in its own way tried to come to terms with the effects of the worst economic crisis ever experienced by Americans. Both the gangster film and the musical were basically urban. For the gangster, 'making it' meant 'making it' in Chicago or New York. There was no such thing as being a 'big shot' in a small town or rural area. Similarly, success in the theatre meant success in New York. As Douglas Newton wrote in *Sight and Sound*, '[the musical] is an urban product designed to please the townsman. . .'[5] The relationship of each genre to the ideal embodied in the term American Dream is interesting and ambiguous. Discussion at length is beyond the scope of this essay, but one point is essential: the gangster is basically a loner, and ultimately he fails; the musical hero and heroine (most often Powell and Keeler) are parts of larger groups, and they succeed. The gangster has his gang, but he can fully trust no one and must therefore be self-reliant. To the extent that the gangster represents the American ideal of 'rugged individualism' his career illustrates that that formula no longer works. In the Warners musicals, on the other hand, each person is shown to be part of an interdependent group: the overall impression emphasizes the importance of social cohesion and harmony – symbolized most clearly in the dances. To what extent does this represent a change in the traditional American ethos of success?

The secularized version of what Weber called the Protestant Ethic was realized as a conscious (if not quite serious) doctrine by Ben Franklin. Ben may not have taken his preachments as seriously as is usually assumed, but his ideals met little opposition and flourished. This doctrine was formulated in its most popular form by Horatio Alger, Jr, in the years immediately after the Civil War. His books, over a hundred of them, reached their greatest popularity between 1890 and the beginning of World War I. Alger's stories are mostly urban. His hero is generally a boy of obscure birth (usually from the country) who is trying to survive in the big city (usually New York). He has no material advantages, but he has most of the virtues recommended by Franklin: thrift, honesty, diligence, etc. The plots generally involve some incident through which the boy's virtues are called to the attention of a benefactor who suitably rewards the hero. Generally the boy is not given an outright gift of money, but is offered a job and allowed to support himself decently.

Two other elements which allow the typical Alger hero to rise in the world are often overlooked. First, the hero must have diligently prepared himself to take advantage of the situation when it presents itself. Usually this means that he has taught himself to read and do arithmetic. In *Ragged Dick*, for example, Dick's quickness doing sums is his major asset. Also Dick has somehow, somewhere, taught himself to swim. But despite diligent preparation, success ultimately depends on luck. In Dick's case, while on a ferry to Brooklyn he jumps overboard to save a girl who is drowning and is rewarded by her father with a job. Of course, if Dick could not have swum he would not have gotten his chance; but at the same time all the swimming ability in the world would have done him no good had he not had the luck to be in the right place at the right time.

How does this Alger version of the American Dream relate to the Warner musicals? On the surface there is some similarity. Their typical plot does seem to echo an Alger novel. In *42nd Street*, for example, Ruby Keeler works hard, learns to dance, has her opportunity when the star of the show (Bebe Daniels) breaks her ankle, and 'makes it.' The myth of individual initiative, hard work, luck and ultimate success does seem to be supported by the typical musical plot. But while the myth is supported by the plot, it is contradicted, or at least significantly modified, by the dance numbers in which we see the individual subordinated to the will of a single person – the director. In short, it seems there is a subtle shift in the content and realization of the Dream. The message is that cooperation, planning and the guidance of a single leader are now necessary for success. The political implications of this change are of major significance.

Much confusion among critics is created by the general misunderstanding of what exactly the Warners musical form was and what it was trying (not necessarily consciously) to do. Douglas Newton states the aim of the musical precisely. He writes: ' . . . the musical film performs the important function of creating a modern myth.'[6] The importance of this cannot be over-stated. The musical form is essentially ritualistic. It is meant to reaffirm faith – not to illuminate conditions or states of being. The Warners musical of the early 1930s tried to come to terms with the questioning of the American Dream and to reaffirm faith in that ideal. (Though, as has been noted, it was unconsciously creating a new myth.)

From this point of view Cy Caldwell's criticism of *Footlight Parade* written in November 1933 is interesting. He writes:

> The indefatigable Warner Brothers have rolled up their sleeves and ground out another of those lavish cinema musical-comedies all of which look and sound almost exactly alike to me. In fact after *42nd Street* and *Gold Diggers of 1933* I was able to predict with a reasonable degree of accuracy every move that Ruby Keeler and Dick Powell were going to make in the current standard work. There must be something sacred about the plots of these Warners musicals that the high priests of the studio guard the ritual so religiously and beat off any

> suggestion for a major change. Apparently they abhor all suspense, all humor, all excitement, and pin their faith on the dance routines, which in this picture are almost fantastically lavish: slightly clad ladies wade and swim about a pool, bask on rocks with water cascading over them, form into ensembles shaped like stars, like a sea serpent and other interesting and beautiful groups that are refreshing to watch. . .[7]

Though of course he uses the religious terminology ('sacred; ' 'high priests,' 'ritual,' 'religiously') sarcastically, Caldwell has hit on the essence of the musical. It is in fact like a religious service or ritual. Once we understand this, the repetitious nature of the plots and much else becomes self-evident. The musical form, to succeed, must create a 'poetic' atmosphere in order to separate the action from everyday reality. To quote Newton once again: 'The fact is that the musical has deep roots in myth and sentiment, in all that the average man feels as poetic. . .'[8]

What about the repetitiousness of the plots? The plots do repeat and of course we know how they will end. But does one not know the end of the Christ story before he hears it repeated each Easter? He gathers with his fellows not to hear a new story (or plot), but to rededicate himself to the meaning of a story he already knows. Repetition is the essence of a ritual-religious experience. Innovation and ritual are diametrically opposed. Thus, as we know, it was essential to the ritualistic aspect of Greek drama that the plots be already known to the audience. Similarly with the Warners musicals: through repetition (among other things) these musicals achieved a ritualistic aspect – in this case specifically a ritualistic rededication to the ideal of the American Dream. This ritualistic distancing was more than ever necessary in the early 1930s in order to separate the ideal from the dismal economic reality.

What about the dances? Almost everyone (those who wait bored through the plot for Berkeley to be turned loose, and those who feel the dances slow up otherwise good comedy) agrees that the dances are removable, isolated units having little integral relation to the rest of the film. John Baxter's objection to the dances in *Gold Diggers of 1933* is not atypical. 'In the end Berkeley's dance numbers seem an imposition on (Mervyn) LeRoy's skilful comic pattern; without them *Gold Diggers* might well be an even more entertaining film than it is now.'[9] Nonetheless, once one is aware of the ritualistic nature of the musicals he can quickly dispose of the idea that the dances are expendable. They are no more expendable than chanting in religious services or Greek tragedy. They function as part of the fabric to raise the work to a poetic or mythic level and separate it from commonplace reality. Obviously a story can be told more quickly by talking than by chanting or singing; but it would no longer be the same story. Similarly with *Gold Diggers of 1933* or any of the other musicals: perhaps they could be played as straight comedy, but if they were they would become something other than what they are.

It might be noted at this point that in terms of the ethic they embody, the Fred Astaire musicals, rather than being akin to the Warners products, are their opposite. Astaire is too skilled as an individual performer to be a suitable vehicle for an ethic of collective effort and cooperation. We are awed by his individual achievement rather than by sheer mass as in a typical Berkeley number. The implication of the Berkeley-directed numbers is that individual skill matters much less than coordination, cooperation and leadership. The individual movements are usually very simple. So too it is worth noting the functional importance of having the Warners films often star the notably untalented Ruby Keeler and the not much better Dick Powell. The effect is opposite to that induced by Astaire. With Astaire we sit back and marvel at his grace and sophistication; with Keeler and Powell we say to ourselves, 'If they can make it, anyone can.'

In the light of what has been said about the social-political-ritualistic nature of the Warners musicals, we can see that the patriotic climax of *Footlight Parade* is not an odd aberration, but the logical culmination of the essence of the musical form. Shot from above, we see hundreds of chorus boys and girls dressed as American sailors form an American flag, superimpose a picture of Roosevelt over it, and then form an NRA eagle and fire their guns in salute. This patriotic display is the quintessence of the musical spirit. The musical is patriotic in the sense that it is affirmative and optimistic and tries to create those emotions in its audience. The end of *Footlight Parade* tries to function as the Parthenon did for Athenians and the Crystal Palace did for Victorian Englishmen, saying in effect, 'Must we not be a great nation, who could produce such a monument to our greatness?'

Both *42nd Street* and *Footlight Parade* are dominated by strong male characters (Warner Baxter and Cagney) who play directors. The so-called 'little people' who 'make it' are not central characters in these films. (Though they later become major characters as the musical form loses its vitality.) The parallel between the strong director of the show-within-the-film and the new strong political leadership in the country is apparent. In these films the 'little people' who succeed do so only by following the orders of the director. This change represents a major modification of the American Dream. The ideal of individual success has been transformed into an ideal of success through collective effort under the guidance of a strong director. This change echoes the new ethic espoused by Roosevelt in his first inaugural address. Two paragraphs toward the end of that address summarize the new ethic:

> If I have read the temper of our people correctly, we now realize as we have never realized before our interdependence on each other; that we cannot merely take but we must give as well; that if we are to go forward, we must move as a trained and loyal army willing to sacrifice for the good of a common discipline, because without such discipline no progress is made, no leadership becomes effective. We are, I know, ready and willing to submit our lives and property to such discipline, because it makes possible a leadership which aims at a larger good. This I propose to offer, pledging that the larger purposes will bind upon us all as a sacred obligation with a unity of duty evoked only in times of armed strife. . . .
>
> We do not distrust the future of essential democracy. The people of the United States have not failed. In their need they have registered a mandate that they want direct, vigorous action. They have asked for discipline and direction under leadership. They have made me the present instrument of their wishes. In the spirit of the gift I take it. . .

In *Footlight Parade* (released November 1933) we see the clearest embodiment of this New Deal Spirit. In it James Cagney plays Kent, a director of musicals momentarily put out of work by the movies. He then contrives the idea of mass-producing 'Prologues,' short, live musical entertainments to accompany movies (a form briefly popular in the early 1930s). We see him trying to come up with ideas and beginning to rehearse them only to have a competing producer consistently steal his ideas before he can stage them. We also know, though he does not, that his two partners, Frazer and Gould, are stealing the profits and preparing a false statement for him showing that the company is barely breaking even. As the crisis approaches, Kent has only three days to prepare as many Prologues for Apollinaris, an owner of 40 theaters who will decide after seeing the Prologues whether Kent or his competitor will get the contract. Before the big effort begins Kent assembles his cast and tells them, 'Nobody leaves this place till Saturday night. . .You'll eat here. . .sleep here. . .for three days you'll live right in the studio. . .It's war. . .a blockade. . .You're gonna work your heads off. . .day and night. . .we're gonna drive you. . .and curse you. . .and break your heart. . .but by Saturday night we'll have what I want! . . .' Kent's military terminology echoes FDR's inaugural address. The military-political aspect of Cagney's leadership is pointed out in the film by a montage of headlines, one of which is, 'Military Tactics Used in Prologue Factory, Studio in State of Siege.' Cagney, like Roosevelt, is asking for sacrifices from the people, but promising to provide the leadership to make the sacrifices worthwhile. His dance director, played by Frank McHugh, mutters constantly, 'It can't be done.' Kent, however, is confident and urges him on, one time shouting, 'Well, what are you waiting for. . . an okay from Roosevelt?' The military atmosphere is developed as we see the cast sleeping in barracks-like conditions on cots in large rooms and being summoned to meals by the army chow call played on a bugle. During this 'siege' Kent learns that his partners have been cheating him. They approach him trying to mollify him and we have another verbal allusion to the New Deal. Gould says: 'er-r. . .about that accounting mistake. . .' Kent: 'Mistake my Aunt Fanny!' Frazer: 'We're giving you a new deal. . .' Kent: 'And I'm the dealer!'

Footlight Parade ends with the great 'Shanghai Lil' dance number directed by Busby Berkeley. The young man who is supposed to play the lead in the number opposite Ruby Keeler gets drunk trying to overcome his stage-fright, so at the last minute Cagney, reluctantly at first, takes over. (Suggestive of the political lead who did not seek power, but had power thrust upon him.) In the number Cagney plays the part of an American sailor out of uniform searching for his love, the prostitute 'Shanghai Lil' (Ruby Keeler). He searches for her through a huge, smokey bar-opium parlor among various nationalities and races. When someone insults Lil in front of Cagney by implying that she is a prostitute, Cagney hits him and a huge multinational fight breaks out. The fight is striking because of its size and because such chaos is rare in Berkeley's work. When order is restored, miraculously, everyone in sight is wearing an American sailor's uniform, including Cagney and Shanghai Lil. They march in military formations, do drills with their rifles, and finally form an American flag, portrait of Roosevelt and NRA eagle. The political message couldn't be more clear: through discipline order triumphs over chaos, and the father of that order (not an ungodlike figure) is Roosevelt.

In the earlier *42nd Street* (March 1933) we discover the beginning of the spirit which reached its climax in the Shanghai Lil number of *Footlight Parade*. The script for *42nd Street* was prepared during the Presidential campaign of 1932. If *Footlight Parade* is the best expression of the early spirit of the New Deal, *42nd Street* was its most perceptive precursor. An interesting sidelight on the connection between these Warners musicals and the New Deal concerns the train chartered by Warner Brothers to publicize *42nd Street*. On March 18, 1933 *Newsweek* reported the following item: 'Warner Brothers chartered a special train, painted it gold and silver, loaded it with 14 stars and a galaxy of chorus girl satellites, had it driven across the continent, stopping off to drop in on Mr. Roosevelt during the inauguration ceremonies. . .and had it arrive in New York to ballyhoo a picture called *42nd Street*.'[10]

The tone of the dialogue in *42nd Street* is harsh and strident. Ginger Rogers plays 'Anytime Annie' of whom another character says, 'She only said No once, and then she didn't hear the question.' Ruby Keeler plays the virginal but (supposedly) talented young theater hopeful Peggy Sawyer. When Peggy first wanders bewildered backstage a chorus girl asks, 'Looking for somebody? – or just shopping around?' Later a girl remarks to her, 'You can't be only eighteen: a girl couldn't get that dumb in only eighteen years.'

Warner Baxter plays Marsh, a director of musicals who has lost his money in the Stock Market, is weakened by ill health, and stakes his life on the success of one more musical which, if successful, will allow him to pay his debts and finally listen to his doctors and take a rest. Baxter has the force and drive of Cagney, but lacks his overall confidence. He is the product of the pre-New Deal image of man. In some ways he looks back to 1929 more than forward to the first hundred days of the New Deal. One of the differences between their situations is that financing is a problem for Marsh, but it is really no problem for Kent. Kent's problem is not a general scarcity of funds, but merely the dishonesty of his partners who are stealing his share of the profits. Marsh, on the other hand, must depend on Abner Dillon (Guy Kibbee) to supply the backing. And since Dillon is more interested in chorus girls than in the show, first Bebe Daniels and then Ginger Rogers have to play prostitute parts in order to keep the play afloat. Obviously the pre-New Deal financial world is represented as being far more sordid than what was to replace it.

At times Marsh sounds like Kent (and Roosevelt). When rehearsals are about to begin Marsh gathers his cast and tells them: '. . . you're going to dance your feet off. . . It's going to be the toughest six weeks you ever lived through. . . '. During the week before the show is to open he tells them, 'Now it's up to you. Not one of you leaves this stage tonight until I get what I want.' Yet though Baxter at times sounds exactly like Cagney, we could never imagine him jumping on stage and taking over a part in his musical: he is too reserved and self-contained. And this is the crucial difference between them, and between Roosevelt and his predecessors. Despite his being clearly the boss, Cagney can give the impression that he is one of the common people. Baxter is always apart. He is an isolated individual, in a way the last of the Franklin-Alger line. He tells others what to do; Cagney shows them. Cagney is constantly demonstrating dance steps; Baxter never is. Thus the end of *Footlight Parade* is completely in keeping with its spirit. Cagney belongs on stage with everyone else, each contributing what he can to the collective effort. Significantly, and again properly, *42nd Street* ends not with the success on stage, but with a short scene with Marsh exhausted and alone sitting on an iron fire-escape in an alley outside the theater listening to passers-by dismiss his contribution while praising his play. His last words, and the last words in the film, are Marsh's weary and cynical, 'Just another show.' In effect, nothing has changed. There will be the alternation of success and failure, boom and bust for eternity. This attitude was changed, for a time at least, by the New Deal, and we have seen the effect of that change in *Footlight Parade*.

As was mentioned earlier, the later Warners musicals such as *Gold Diggers of 1937* and *Gold Diggers in Paris* are tired reworkings of a worn-out formula. From the hopeful, if frenzied, drama of the early 1930s the films degenerate until we reach the wooden pseudo-sophistication of Rudy Vallee in 1938. But even in 1933, though more often in 1934, Warners produced weaker musicals. Generally, as has been noted, the weaker films lacked a strong male lead. Another difference between the best musicals (*42nd Street* and *Footlight Parade*) and the lesser ones (*Gold Diggers of 1933* and *Dames*) is that in the latter the success of the show-within-the-film is not really a necessity. In both of the latter films Dick Powell *wants* to get into 'show business'. He is an amateur seeking amusement. Cagney and Baxter, on the other hand, play professionals whose lives depend on success. They are like Indians hunting for food compared to rich sportsmen shooting pheasant for pleasure. Another factor, perhaps the causal one, is that by mid-1934 the ideals which inspired the earlier films seem to have hardened into ideology. In *Dames*, for example, Horace Hemingway (Guy Kibbee) is a comfortably wealthy man who wants to be a millionaire. On a train returning to New York from Buffalo he finds a woman (Joan Blondell) in his compartment and asks the conductor to change him to another one, to which the conductor replies, 'Sorry, sir – we're all filled up. NRA's good for business.' How pallid is this obeisance to the New Deal compared to the triumphant end of *Footlight Parade*!

An exception to the generalization that the Warners musical declined after 1933 is the Busby Berkeley-directed *Gold Diggers of 1935*. But in many ways this film is different from the others in the genre to which it ostensibly belongs. The whole film takes place in a fantasy world quite different from the fevered urban settings of *42nd Street* and *Footlight Parade*. *Gold Diggers of 1935* is set in a resort hotel. Also there is an ease about the production of the show-within-the-film which contrasts sharply with the frantic preparations of the earlier films. Here the production is the charity whim of an eccentric, rich widow. Nothing in particular is dependent on the success of the show, and little is made of its preparation aside from some Jack Benny-like jokes about the thriftiness of the old dowager. In this film either everyone has enough money, or lives as if he did. Some people, such as Nicolif (Adolphe Menjou), the show's director, complain, but we see no evidence of their shortage of funds.

Success in this film is based on marrying someone who has money, not struggling and learning to dance, or whatever, and hoping for the lucky break which will lead to success. This fantasy of waking up one day to suddenly find wealth is the opposite extreme from the Calvinist-collective ethos of *42nd Street* and *Footlight Parade*. It has more in common with fairy tales (such as Cinderella or Sleeping Beauty) than Ben Franklin or Horatio Alger. This myth of success finds no reflection in the Ruby Keeler heroine (Keeler is absent from this film). Ruby Keeler succeeds (with luck as when the star breaks her ankle and she takes over), but she rehearses and works like hell to do it. While it's true that many people work like hell and don't succeed, it's another order of fantasy to have success be the result of no effort at all, as it is in *Gold Diggers of 1935*.

Berkeley prepares the audience for this kind of fantasy at the very beginning of the film. After the titles we fade-in to a close-up of a glossy magazine in the style of *Vanity Fair* being held open by jeweled, manicured hands to an advertisement for the Wentworth-Plaza Hotel. From the magazine picture of the hotel doorway we wipe to the real doorway. Thus the whole film is enclosed in a briefly established, but significant, story-book framework. The frame advises the audience that what it is about to see is fantasy; there's no reason to get upset or to take anything too seriously. This atmosphere contrasts sharply with the tension propelling many of the earlier musicals – *42nd Street*, *Footlight Parade* and to a lesser extent even *Gold Diggers of 1933*. In these films, though we know the hero will succeed, there is established a realistic alternative to success. There is no such alternative in *Gold Diggers of 1935*.

Perhaps paradoxically, while *Gold Diggers of 1935* is more of a fantasy than the earlier musicals, it also assumes a greater cynicism. This cynical tone is established in the first dialogue scene in the movie. After a meeting of the hotel's personnel they break up into groups and we cut to each group in turn. The head bellhop is telling the other bellhops, 'Remember this, guys: whatever the guest tips you, *I* get fifty per cent . . . '. The Maître d'Hôtel is telling the waiters, 'But remember, I get my percentage – otherwise –'. The head barman is warning the bartenders, '. . . the tips are split even except in special cases when I take two-thirds.' Actually the relationship between this awareness of the cynicism of the real world and the fantasy is more causal than paradoxical. In such a world fantasy is the only imagined means of success. Obviously this again contrasts with the earlier films where hard work, collective effort and skilled direction were shown to be the means to success.

The shift from an idealistic-collective ethos to a cynical or at best amoral attitude can be seen also in the attitude toward money displayed in the films. The economic problem common to most musicals is distribution of money. Always there is someone who has money, and the problem is to get him to do something socially useful with his money. In the context of the films this something 'socially useful' is of course to back the show the hero wants to put on. The change from the idealism of 1933 to the cynicism of 1934 can be seen in the contrasting roles played by Joan Blondell in *Footlight Parade* and *Dames*. In *Footlight Parade* Blondell is the devoted secretary of Cagney. She gets a check for $25,000 from his two partners by threatening to reveal their dishonest bookkeeping. She then turns the check over to Cagney who needs the money to get his shrewish wife to grant him a divorce. When Blondell wants money in *Dames* (this time for Dick Powell to put on a show) she sneaks into the house of the wealthy Horace Hemingway (Guy Kibbee), lies down in his bed and threatens to scream and thus ruin his career and marriage if he refuses her a check for $20,000. The contrast is obvious and typical. Gold-digging exists in the earlier films but it is practised by minor characters who are shown in a bad light. If it is done by a likable character such as Bebe Daniels in *42nd Street* she hates what she has to do. Miss Daniels finally refuses to lean on a rich old man any more and chooses to be poorer but honest. By 1934 the Warners musicals view blackmail and prostitution (the essences of 'gold-digging') amorally.

A generally idealistic attitude towards the redistribution of capital is seen in *42nd Street* and *Gold Diggers of 1933* as well as *Footlight Parade*. In *42nd Street* the old, rich Abner Dillon has money, but his money is doing nothing. Marsh has the talent to use his money to provide entertainment for an audience and jobs for a cast and crew of two hundred while making himself a profit. In *Gold Diggers of 1933* it is emphasized that Brad (Dick Powell) is doing a good thing in putting up the $15,000 for the show because it will provide so many people with jobs. This point is made even in *Dames*. Horace (Kibbee) has been blackmailed by Joan Blondell into backing Jimmie's show. Horace wants to stop the show and snarls at Jimmie (Dick Powell), 'You scoundrel – it's my money.' Jimmie responds, 'It *was* your money. . .and you've put a lot of people to work with it. . .you're a credit to your country.' The implication for the American capitalist is quite clear: he *can* be useful, but only if he does what the director (Cagney, Baxter, Roosevelt) wants him to do.

It is a critical commonplace to refer to the 1930s musical as 'escapist.' Andrew Sarris echoes this received wisdom in his *The American Cinema*: 'Berkeley's vitality and ingenuity transcended the limits of his sensibility and he bequeathed to posterity an entertaining record of the audacity of an escapist era.'[11] In July 1933, Cy Caldwell writing in *New Outlook* complained that *Gold Diggers of 1933* wasn't escapist enough:

> This laugh-filled, heart-warming musical comedy romance would be thoroughly delightful from beginning to end if the producers had thrown away the last reel, which unwinds the woes and tribulations of 'My Forgotten Man,' who went to the war and then to seed, causing untold anguish to the lady who sang of his troubles, while we were treated to flash-backs of marching soldiers, wounded soldiers and discharged soldiers who slept in doorways and retrieved cigarette butts. A veteran myself, I can take most war films cheerfully on the chin, but I want none of them in musical comedies, where they certainly

do not belong. For downright offensiveness and bad taste, that last reel wins the Croix de Garbage. . .[12]

It seems both critics misjudge musicals because they are fundamentally mistaken about their nature. Even though the concept of 'escapism' is vague, we can probably say that it is not very relevant to a discussion of these Warners musicals. The terms idealistic, political, and ritualistic are far more relevant. Or, to put it another way: if Mickey Mouse cartoons are 'escapist' and the ritual of the Mass is 'escapist', musicals have much more in common with the escapism of the latter than that of the former.

But rather than being 'escapist' in any sense it seems to me that the great Warners musicals are essentially political. Basic to the collectivist nature of these musicals is their ritualized form. The quintessential symbol is the Berkeley dance number. The urge of the dances and the film is towards cooperation and collective effort. Individually, Berkeley's dancers would amount to little. When, as he occasionally does, Berkeley isolates chorus girls with the camera, or has their faces follow each other filling the screen, the dances are least effective and border on being foolish. But when he has them working together, each atomic unit contributes to an effect larger than perhaps any of them could imagine. As has been indicated, we need not search far for the political sources and implications of this idea. Roosevelt had recently created a new spirit if not a new reality. He cared about the 'little man.' No matter how minor his part everyone had something to contribute. Roosevelt was a kind of political Busby Berkeley; or Berkeley was the terpsichorean metamorphosis of Roosevelt. The 'little man' could trust Roosevelt as the individual chorus girl could trust Berkeley to see that their effort was not wasted, to see that each had his part to play. It takes only a little imagination to see Berkeley's stars and flowers and circles (photographed from above) as symbols of an harmonious nation. Not of course the nation as it was in 1933, but the nation as millions believed and millions more hoped it could be.

The image of a political leader as a large-scale Busby Berkeley is certainly ambiguous. The thrust of such an image is undoubtedly toward collective effort and subjugation of the will of the individual to the overall pattern dictated by the leader. But does this imply the ideal represented for Ruskin by the Middle Ages, or a socialist-communist ideal, or a Hitler-Franco type fascist dictatorship? I'm not sure how to answer this. Perhaps there is no one answer. In any event the temper of America in early 1933 as reflected in the Warners musical was undoubtedly towards some kind of collectivism. Some important American political figures, speaking between Roosevelt's election and inauguration, supported this conclusion. Alfred E. Smith's implication is clear enough: 'In this depression we are in a state of war. The only thing to do now is to lay aside statutes and do what a Democracy must do when it fights.'[13] At the same time Norman Thomas warned, 'The cry will go up for a dictator. He will be of the demagogue type and he will speak with the voice of Huey Long.'[14] Perhaps if Roosevelt had been a Hitler or Stalin he could have had the blessing of the majority in the United States. As we know, he was neither, and as we also know the Warners musical film was an ephemeral phenomenon – spawned during the Presidential campaign of 1932 and, in its full vitality, not outlasting the next year.

Notes

1 Jack Salzman, ed. *Years of Protest* (New York, 1967), p. 84.
2 *Ibid.*, p. 10.
3 *Ibid.*, p. 12.
4 *Literary Digest*, CXVI (1 July, 1933), p. 5.
5 Douglas Newton, 'Poetry in Fast and Musical Motion,' *Sight and Sound*, XXII (July–September, 1952), p. 36.
6 *Ibid.*
7 Cy Caldwell, 'To See or Not to See,' *New Outlook*, CLXII (November 1933), p. 43.
8 Newton, *op. cit.*, p. 35.
9 John Baxter, *Hollywood in the Thirties* (London and New York, 1968), p. 62.
10 'Screen,' *Newsweek*, I (17 February 1933), p. 28.
11 Andrew Sarris, *The American Cinema* (New York, 1968), p. 172.
12 Cy Caldwell, 'To See or Not to See,' *New Outlook*, CLXII (July 1933), p. 43.
13 *Newsweek*, I (17 February 1933), p. 5.
14 *Ibid.*

4 · Robin Wood: 'Art and Ideology: Notes on *Silk Stockings*'

Film Comment, vol. 11, no. 3, May–June 1975, pp. 28–31

Hollywood has a genius for characterization through significant detail. We often learn more about a cowhand from the way he wears his gun than from the dialogue; screwball comedy types its characters very early by revealing their sense of humour (or lack of same); in the musical no attribute is more important than a sense of rhythm. Not only dance, but its very components (rhythm, movement, grace, rapport) carry a message of their own which often seems to rise above the narrative aspects of a film. Many critics have commented on the energy of the dance, but none has succeeded as well as Robin Wood in locating the meaning of dance within a larger context. After laying out a clear picture of the surface ideological project of Rouben Mamoulian's *Silk Stockings* (a process which permits him to seize the various ways in which dance serves as a thematic motif in the film), Wood proceeds to inquire into an aspect of the dance which seems irreducible to the ideological confrontations previously described: somehow the musical numbers of *Silk Stockings* have a vitality which causes them to transcend the film's apparent ideological project. This supplementary nature of dance, its ability to attract even the most recalcitrant of spectators through a never-ceasing excess of energy, is surely one of the characteristics which has helped the musical to weather more than one critical storm.

The strategy of Wood's argument, it may be noted in passing, is one which deserves to be employed more widely in analysis of the musical. Beginning with a rapid summary of the influential study which *Cahiers du Cinéma* devoted to John Ford's *Young Mr. Lincoln*, Wood proceeds to show that this fundamental approach to classical narrative, while applicable to the musical, by no means exhausts its meaning. In a sense the gap between narrative and number, one of the most common surface attributes of the musical, is the very type of rift which the *Cahiers* analyse with such success in Ford's film. Yet the musical tends constantly toward a transcending of that gap, moving as it does toward a moment when narrative and number merge into one, or, as in Wood's analysis, to a point where the energy of the dance bursts out of the ideological parameters which seemed to contain it. A similar strategy underlies more than one other article in this collection, for the musical refuses to be contained by the traditional terminology and concepts of classical narrative analysis. Where the typical Hollywood example of classical narrative emphasizes dialogue, the image track, and transparent presentation of the diegesis, the musical regularly privileges dance or song, subordinates the image to the soundtrack, and foregrounds the process of producing the diegesis. There comes a moment in most musicals when a traditional component reveals a supplementary energy, an independent source of power and value which – at least momentarily – permits the spectator to enjoy the illusion of having escaped from the world of classical narrative, and thus from that of ideological definition. This will not be a popular argument in certain circles, for some will say that Wood has been taken in by the very ideology which he sees the musical as transcending. Nevertheless, Wood's careful delineation of the supplementary nature of dance (and by extension of song) goes a long way toward explaining the particular exhilaration which for decades kept audiences returning to the musical, in spite of the genre's banality, artificiality, and overt ideological posturing.

One of the most stimulating and valuable developments in recent film criticism has been the concern with ideology – particularly with the ideological content of Hollywood films, with the notion that the films are 'determined' (or, at the very least, affected) at all levels by an ideology (definable, roughly as 'bourgeois-Capitalist,' but with specific inflections and emphases peculiar to America) so deeply entrenched as to be largely taken for granted, hence unnoticed and unchallenged, by film-makers and audiences alike.

As a preliminary, it is important to note certain problems that arise from the current usage of the term 'ideological.' First, one is often in some doubt as to its precise force – is the term descriptive or derogatory? Some 'advanced' criticism tends to capitalize on this uncertainty, concealing a charge of condemnation beneath an appearance of scientific description.

Second, the notion of a national (or generally operative) ideology, while indispensable, itself raises problems which are not always clearly recognized. As soon as one confronts it with particular artists and particular works, one comes to realize that every individual has his own personal ideology characterized by its own specific inflections and emphases. At times, the notion of a general ideology comes to resemble the 'structure' (in effect, a grotesque parody) that Peter Wollen draws from the films of Howard Hawks in *Signs and Meaning in the Cinema*. Each individual film relates to the structure; none corresponds to it; and there is a consequent danger that the particularities of local realization in which (and *only* in which) the life of a work of art is manifest will be blotted out in favor of a monstrous parody-abstraction.

Third, the question of the possibility of distinguishing between ideology and fundamental human drives needs to be very carefully examined. Marxist criticism often seems to suggest that *everything* is ideologically determined – yet it also talks about 'liberation.' Presumably, there is something to be liberated which isn't merely ideological; hence there is a tacit assumption that fundamental (universal) drives exist. Yet much current film criticism seems dedicated perversely to denying the most fundamental drive of all, on which all significant art (and all significant life) depends: the phenomenon of human creativity. It seems to me at times that Marxist critics are bent on repressing precisely those qualities they should be trying to liberate, if 'liberation' means anything.

One also encounters a blanket assumption that everything that isn't demonstrably Marxist is 'bourgeois-Capitalist.' Representational art, for example, is often treated as the product of bourgeois ideology, the means whereby bourgeois society reassures itself as to the 'reality' of its world. Yet the earliest known works of art, the cave-paintings, were indisputably representational.

One can distinguish three main phases in the development of ideological awareness and its effect on criticism (though the three are not clearly consecutive, and all currently co-exist). First, there is the total *lack* of awareness that simply takes the Hollywood film, its forms and conventions, at face value, that is to say shares its ideological assumptions. Specific films can of course be criticized adversely from this position, but only on their own terms. For example, the critic may object to an 'implausible' happy ending, without grasping that plausibility is itself an ideologically determined convention.

Second, there is what might be called the naive Marxist position or blanket rejection – a position discredited by the more sophisticated developments in recent Marxist criticism, though still occasionally encountered. This position sees the Hollywood cinema as *simply* the means whereby American Capitalist ideology imposes and perpetuates itself, and finds little more to do beyond crudely demonstrating ideological determination.

The third phase is enormously more complex and sophisticated, taking many different forms, and interwoven with the current interests in semiotics and structuralism. It is accordingly very much harder to sum up succinctly; the work of *Cahiers du Cinéma* and *Screen* in recent years suggests the complexities involved. The premise is that many Hollywood films (they turn out, in the event, to be by and large those already established as significant by way of more traditional critical procedures) are valuable by virtue of the ideological tensions and contradictions they contain. (Or fail to contain – there is a tendency to value films for what traditional criticism would regard, if it perceived them, as failures of realization.)

The underlying assumption (if one may speak of a single assumption underlying so wide a range of criticism) seems again somewhat ambiguous. At times it appears to be that an ideology as monstrous as the 'bourgeois-Capitalist' must inevitably expose its own internal rifts and contradictions, which would imply that these rifts could be perceived and analyzed in any bourgeois-Capitalist work, irrespective of quality. At other times, it appears to be that the rifts only become manifest when some strong, defined presence (such as that of an individual 'author', bringing with him his own set of 'codes') intervenes in what was basically an innocuous ideological project.

The classical example of this critical position is the celebrated 'reading' of John Ford's *Young Mr. Lincoln* by the editors of *Cahiers du Cinéma* (available in an English translation in the issue of *Screen* for Autumn 1972); no one seriously interested in the development of a critical approach to Hollywood can afford to ignore it. One senses, lurking somewhere behind this article (and necessarily suppressed), the quandary of critics who, before the events of May 1968, had developed certain very strong critical allegiances – those associated with the old *Cahiers* championship of the Hollywood cinema – and were then confronted with the fact that the objects of their enthusiasm were the products of a system they felt compelled to regard as politically discredited. They had the choice of rejecting those products or finding devious ways of arguing for their acceptability. This would explain, for example, how it was possible for the pre-1968 *Cahiers* Pantheon to be taken over more or less intact and (in evaluative, as opposed to interpretative, terms) unquestioned.

Of these positions, the first and third seem to me capable of producing useful and illuminating insights (obviously, of very different kinds) into Hollywood films; yet neither completely satisfies me. Without feeling that I can solve all the problems that arise, I want – through an examination of a representative Hollywood film – to suggest at least an approach to them.

Silk Stockings (Rouben Mamoulian's musical version of *Ninotchka*) offers itself as a convenient example precisely because its ideological project appears so clear, indeed blatant. I am also drawn to it because it strikes me as a sadly underestimated, unjustly denigrated film – Tom Milne's enthusiastic and eloquent defense of it in his Cinema One book on Mamoulian seems to be unique – and because I am not at all familiar with Mamoulian's work, so am unlikely to be diverted into auteurist sidetracks.

When *Silk Stockings* first appeared, the response (in England at least; and I would be surprised to learn that things were much different on the other side of the Atlantic) was markedly and almost unanimously hostile. The overt objection to the film (common in the case of re-makes) was generally that it vulgarized a nostalgically venerated original. *Ninotchka* had Garbo and the Lubitsch touch; *Silk Stockings* had Cyd Charisse and a series of deliberately vulgar musical numbers.

It is true that Charisse's performances – except when she is dancing – seldom transcend the barely adequate. Wisely, she was not asked to reproduce Garbo's famous laughing scene; but whenever she is given one of the familiar Garbo lines ('The arrangement of your features is not entirely repulsive'), the effect is somewhat jarring on those for whom the ghost of Garbo's delivery lingers in the background.

I don't think, however, that the hostility to *Silk Stockings* is explainable in such simple terms. It is not true, for instance, that its satire on Communism is cruder than *Ninotchka*'s; it is rather a matter of altered circumstances. In 1939, Communism could still be a subject for 'daring' but flippant bad-taste humor (Billy Wilder was, after all, one of the authors of *Ninotchka*'s script). By 1957, irrespective of one's political stance and of one's attitude to McCarthyism, it was no longer a subject for flippancy, and it is doubtful whether even the Lubitsch touch could have charmed away the feeling of rampant bad taste. Certainly, *Ninotchka* survives because of Garbo, Lubitsch, and Wilder/Brackett. But King Vidor's *Comrade X* (1940), which was also very highly regarded when it came out, is now barely watchable; its anti-Communist satire, once chic, now seems merely infantile. The fault of *Silk Stockings* was not so much that it coarsened the satire of *Ninotchka* as that it reproduced it too faithfully.

Critics were also antagonized, one guesses, because Capitalist ideology is presented so blatantly in *Silk Stockings*; the offense lies in making manifest what 'good taste' would conceal. In Godard's *British Sounds*, the speech by the ultra-right-wing, National Front-type young man derives its power to offend not from its being presented as representative or typical in the usual sense, but precisely from its naked exposure of monstrous implications one would expect to be concealed, or slurred over, or at least understated.

No one will wish to claim for *Silk Stockings* that degree of deliberateness or of political awareness, yet the film works on a level of sophistication that warns one not to dismiss its vulgarities as merely mindless. The concept of 'good taste' so favored by liberal critics often amounts to little more than the concealment or disguising of ideological issues, so that the spectator isn't forced into awareness of their implications.

I discern in *Silk Stockings* four main ideological impulses, linked yet partly separable, listed in descending order of explicitness or obviousness:

1 The film's surface project, which could be summed up as 'You're better off under Capitalism.' The assumption is that all Communists would really rather live in Capitalist societies if they could, or if they knew about all the benefits from experience. The benefits are presented primarily in the form of material possessions, with a strong emphasis on luxury goods – perfume, champagne – the familiar Hollywood emblems of romance, success, and wealth. With this goes the upholding of beauty (Paris at night) against utility. Even on this simple, overt level, the film periodically produces elements or emblems that make the satire double-edged or ambiguous. An example is the absurdly dressed-up poodle in the restaurant which Charisse objects to as 'useless' and Fred Astaire defends as 'amusing.' The connotations of poodles in American movies are, after all, primarily farcical-satirical; here the dog – de-animalized, prettified, constrained – inevitably stands for the sillier excesses of Capitalist society.

2 Less explicitly, but even more pervasively, the film is concerned with the ideological role of woman in Capitalist society – with woman-as-object, the mere embodiment of male wish-fulfilment. As a Communist, and with the sexually neutral title of Comrade, Charisse poses a threat to male supremacy; she must therefore learn in the course of the film to be a 'real woman,' and learn that that is what she *really* wants to be. The ideological project here is expressed most blatantly in her song to Astaire, 'Without Love,' sung literally looking up to him as she lies on the floor. The song is concerned with woman's function as 'a pleasure,' and culminates in the lines: 'For a woman to a man is just a woman/But a man to a woman is her life.'

The richness of the film arises partly from the way in which the notion of woman-as-object is satirized in the overtly vulgar musical numbers involving Janis Paige, particularly 'Satin and Silk,' which at once enacts and parodies the idea that a woman's function is to be 'a pleasure' for the male. The ideological project here, in fact, is somewhat called into question by the film's clear preference for Charisse as against Paige – the grounds for the preference being both the generic definition of the Paige role as comic support and its thematic definition as parody of the woman-object image.

One notes also the weight that is allowed Charisse's protest against the ludicrous musical film Astaire is producing, a moment which draws together a number of the ideological-thematic threads of the film. The musical itself parodies the mindless vulgarity and silliness of standard Capitalist popular entertainment. In it, Paige plays the Empress Josephine (with 'titillating thighs'), her number reinforcing the woman-object parody. The score is a debased version of the music of the Soviet composer whose defection provided the starting-point for the action. Charisse's protest (which we are allowed to take unexpectedly seriously) is provoked partly by her recognition of the way Astaire has manipulated her and ignored her own feelings and commitments.

3 The validation of 'entertainment' as against 'art.' 'Entertainment' – as something to be passively absorbed rather than actively participated in, dedicated to the discouragement of awareness – is a central 'bourgeois-Capitalist' concept and one inherent in the Hollywood musical as a genre, surfacing in the case of individual films as an explicit concern. The overt, if often only superficial, anti-intellectualism of a number of Hollywood musicals – including some distinguished ones, such as *Funny Face* and *The Band Wagon* – is obvious (and is one of the reasons why I have always had difficulties with this particular genre). Art, both classical and avant-garde (with Jack Buchanan's production of *Oedipus Rex* in *The Band Wagon* nicely combining the two), is belittled and ridiculed because it is potentially disturbing and subversive and because it demands active concentration. Entertainment gives people what they 'really want' – the kind of temporary escape and distraction that prevents their dissatisfactions from reaching articulation.

This particular ideological project is neatly epitomized in the 'That's Entertainment' number in *The Band Wagon*, which explicitly reduces all cultural achievements indiscriminately to the same level of innocuousness. (Cyd Charisse's ballet-dancing in the same film can be presented straight, partly because she is a woman and ballet is regarded as a feminine art, partly because ballet here is decorative rather than disturbing, hence poses no challenge to the entertainment concept.) The blatancy of this is concealed beneath an appeal to debased democratic principle: Entertainment is anti-élitist because it is what *anyone* can appreciate without much effort.

(I should stress that these remarks are not to be taken as dismissive either of the genre or of individual films. Much film criticism and film teaching today is concerned, quite rightly, with opposing the effective operation of the Entertainment concept as a 'bourgeois-Capitalist' strategy; to reveal Entertainment as, frequently, disguised art. I am aware, specifically, that there is far more to be said about *The Band Wagon* – that its ideological anti-intellectualism is but one element which is countered and qualified by other aspects of the film, for example the presence of Vincente Minnelli as director.)

In *Silk Stockings* the validation of Entertainment is also partly undermined. A leading plot-thread is the conversion of the Russian composer's music (which is presented, rather awkwardly, as combining the highbrow with the Communist-utilitarian) into the score for an American musical; and one encounters the assumption that Borodin and Tchaikovsky were important composers because they supplied melodies for popular American songs. On the other hand, the tendency of Entertainment to trivialize and vulgarize is quite explicitly commented upon by the hilarious 'Josephine' number; by the composer's outrage (which is treated as not at all unreasonable, and left unresolved and unmollified); and by the seriousness of Charisse's protest. One regrets that the ending of the film fails to find a satisfactory way of resolving these ideological tensions – it prefers to forget them.

4 The opposition between an inhibiting, depersonalizing system and freedom, self-expression, spontaneity. Dance is crucial here, and provides the vindication of transforming *Ninotchka* into a musical, dancing becoming not mere decoration but a leading thematic motif. Charisse's liberation comes when Astaire lures her into dancing. (Her learning to dance corresponds to the moment at the end of *Alphaville* when Anna Karina learns to say 'I love you.') The implicit theme of dance-as-liberation, however, recurs throughout the film, starting from the splendid 'We Can't Go Back to Moscow' number. Crucially, the emphasis in the *mise en scène*

is on *individual* movement, in which even non-dancers like Peter Lorre find some physical means of expression.

A statement at this point from my own personal ideology: I find the first three of these projects (leaving aside for the moment the ways in which they are disturbed or undermined by certain elements) ideologically unacceptable, the fourth wholly admirable. Yet in the film, while the fourth is not simply or comprehensively identifiable with the other three (producing further tensions), it is also not clearly separable from them.

The beautiful Charisse solo number, for example, gives unified expression to all four simultaneously. She surrenders to the various allures of Capitalistic luxury, dressing to transform herself into the object of male desire, and thereby incidentally providing an archetypal Entertainment number. At the same time, the grace and freedom of physical movement (both of dancer and camera) throughout the sequence movingly express the casting off of repressive constraints.

Further, this expression of freedom through dance, while ambiguously linked to 'Capitalism' as opposed to 'Communism' (the quotation marks indicate these as concepts presented in the film rather than as realities existing outside it), is shown later not to be simply dependent on it. The other big number from which Astaire is absent ('The Red Blues') is the film's supreme expression of vitality through physical movement. It uses 'Capitalist' popular music, and retains (if somewhat ambiguously) the characteristic anti-intellectualism of the musical, opposing the dance to the static delivery of political utterances during the two intrusions of the orthodox Communist, when all movement abruptly freezes. (The effect can be read as anti-intellectual or simply as anti-repressive). Yet the dance is naturally dominated by the woman (Charisse), dressed in plain clothes and quite devoid of the emblems of 'Capitalism.' Indeed, freed from 'Capitalist' trappings, she appears arguably *more* beautiful and *more* vital and unconstrained than in her earlier solo number.

One might argue (keeping in view the opposed parodies of 'Capitalism' and 'Communism') that the film implicitly proposes a third ideology, necessarily rather vaguely defined, but based on values of freedom, spontaneity, movement, which is set against both the ideologies that are defined explicitly. Some attempt is made to balance the two discredited ideologies: the degenerate commercialism of the *Josephine* musical against the exploitation of Russian ballet and Russian films as cultural propaganda. But one must note that the two 'false' ideologies are not – could not be – presented on equal terms. We are encouraged to laugh unambiguously at 'Communism,' while our attitude to 'Capitalism,' even at points of the most extreme satire (the Janis Paige numbers), is partly one of complicity. Similarly, the third ideology is decisively and explicitly opposed in the film to 'Communism' but ambiguously related to 'Capitalism.' Inevitably, the 'Capitalist' ideology (and male supremacy) is firmly reimposed at the end of the film. Cyd Charisse is brought back to Paris by Astaire's machinations, the climax of which has her seated in a night club (La Vieille Russie) to watch admiringly Astaire's solo-with-chorus dance number ('The Ritz Roll 'n' Rock') which is a blatant affirmation of the material rewards of Capitalism (though, again, not entirely free from elements of parody that call this into question). She then, after a brief misunderstanding has been cleared up, rather lamely submits to him. Her earlier stand (in reaction against the *Josephine* musical) is forgotten by the film, though not necessarily by the audience. We are left with, at the very least, a sense of dissatisfaction.

There seems to me an alternative way of dealing with the ideological issues posed by *Silk Stockings*, and countless other films. I would suggest – somewhat hesitantly, for it is the sort of suggestion that gets hooted down in contemporary film criticism – that, rather than talk in terms of a 'third ideology,' one might talk of certain aspects partially escaping ideological determination. I would suggest, in other words, that there are indeed certain fundamental drives and needs that are not ideological but universal – drives which certain ideologies can suppress but which no ideology creates – and that such things as freedom of expression, delight in bodily movement, instinctual spontaneity, are among them.

Heretically, and despite Garbo, the Lubitsch touch, and the laughing scene, I enjoy *Silk Stockings* more than I enjoy *Ninotchka* – largely because of the extra dimension given by the musical numbers (or certain aspects of them), a dimension that affects the meaning and values of the film. *Ninotchka* opposes to its simplistically debunked Communism only the materialistic trivia of Capitalism and the dubious charms of Melvyn Douglas. Garbo's emotional awakening, moving as it is, finds no adequate embodiment of values for its satisfaction, so that the satisfaction appears a pretense which the film shallowly fabricates. Cyd Charisse's discovery, through dance, of her individual physical existence opposes itself to both the state-determined automatism of the film's Communism and the woman-object of its Capitalism.

This line of argument has implications that go far beyond *Silk Stockings*. The individual creativity that there finds its concrete expression in dance is expressed more generally in art itself. To enforce the point, however, one needn't look beyond the present example. The vitality of the musical numbers in *Silk Stockings* itself transcends their local ideological functions.

Consider the first number 'We Can't Go Back to Moscow.' Its local function is to establish and celebrate the conversion of the three Soviet emissaries to the material delights of Capitalism, notably champagne and 'available' women; every precise detail can be explained in relation to this function. What transcends the ideological purpose here is the energy of the realization, an energy expressed not merely in the physical movements of the actors but in the inventiveness of the *mise en scène*. (The director of *At Long Last Love* might have learned a lesson here in how to build a musical number involving performers who can neither sing nor dance – including Peter Lorre! But whether Peter Bogdanovich is capable of learning anything of value from his model is becoming increasingly dubious.) It doesn't matter, for the purposes of my argument, precisely who was responsible for the scene's vitality: director, scriptwriter, cameraman, choreographers, actors. The issue of personal creativity is unaffected by the number of possible active contributors. What is important is the communication of creative energies.

The use of abstract words (energy, inventiveness) here is inevitable. I am arguing that Materialism is not enough; that, even when every concrete detail in a given work can be shown to be ideologically determined, the details may be the product of fundamental creative drives that transcend ideology. The prevailing ideology, in other words, may determine (to varying degrees according to the artist's level of awareness) the forms in which the drives find embodiment, but it can't account for the drives themselves.

That is why it is possible (and common) to respond with intensity to works which are ideologically quite alien to us; why I, an atheist, can be deeply moved by the St Matthew Passion; or why I can respond equally to *Klute* and *Tout va bien*. Beneath the apparent contradictions and incongruities is a creativity which is universal in spirit and generally communicative, however its local manifestations are determined. It is essential, today, to reinstate and defend (even, or particularly, in the field of collaborative art) the concept of individual creativity – a reality which certain Marxist critics are striving to suppress by denying its existence.

A part of the interest and richness of *Silk Stockings* lies (as with *Young Mr. Lincoln*) in its internal tensions and contradictions. If, for example, the element of parody of Capitalist ideology represented by the Janis Paige numbers, or the challenge to the image of woman-as-object represented by the Cyd Charisse dances, were absent – if there were no more to the film than the simple 'Capitalism good-Communism bad' opposition on which it is nominally built – its interest would be severely diminished. Yet the film's creative vitality (like that of *Young Mr. Lincoln*) cannot reasonably be reduced to its ideological contradictions. The inventions of the Cyd Charisse solo, for example the 'silk stockings' dance – are almost entirely 'within the ideology.'

The *Cahiers* reading of *Young Mr. Lincoln*, for all its insights, ends by making the film's potential rewards seem somewhat meager. It is not that the 'gaps and dislocations' in which the writers find its interest are irrelevant to its creative energies, but they are also not simply identifiable with them. The attitude to Ford as an artist is curiously ambiguous or evasive. His centrality to the film is implicitly acknowledged, yet his contribution is treated as though it were merely incidental – or accidental – to the film's quality. Indeed, the ambiguity or evasiveness extends (necessarily, I think) to the concept of quality itself. In a sense, the quality of *Young Mr. Lincoln* is taken for granted (the film is introduced as a 'classic'); yet its classic status is scarcely validated by the argument presented.

The day after I read the piece I happened to watch a TV *Tarzan* episode with my children. Gradually, and fascinatingly, it became apparent that very much the same sort of gaps, dislocations, and suppressions were discernible there. I was grateful to the *Cahiers* editors for revealing this – the *Tarzan* episode suddenly acquired an interest it had previously lacked (without acquiring any artistic value). Yet in retrospect it became clear that the status and quality of *Young Mr. Lincoln* as a work of art was left unproven and unaccounted for; and it could only be accounted for, I believe, in terms of individual creativity.

The evaluation of works of art must always be a complex, delicate, and tentative business. Ideological issues cannot be irrelevant to it, yet no work can be justly evaluated on purely ideological grounds. Crucial, it seems to me, is the concept of creativity as at once transcending ideology, even when its concrete forms and details are ideologically determined. That is why it can transcend time and space, so that to listen to the music of Bach, or watch the films of Mizoguchi, can be an enriching experience however alien their cultural determinants; and why it is still permissible (and necessary) – the united efforts of Marxism and semiology to the contrary – to talk of 'genius,' of 'personal expression,' and of 'individual creativity.'

5 · Lucy Fischer: 'The Image of Woman as Image: The Optical Politics of *Dames*'

Film Quarterly, no. 30, Fall 1976, pp. 2–11

In recent years the position of women in Hollywood films has attracted increasing interest. Molly Haskell, Marjorie Rosen, Joan Mellen and many others have heightened our awareness of the limited role accorded to women within the Hollywood paradigm. Most of these analyses have been of a thematic nature, conducting an informal census of the types of role, character, and complexity allotted to actresses. Genres or directors portraying strong women in varied professional roles receive high grades; those who restrict women to the home or turn them into whimpering weaklings fail to get a passing mark. So sexist is the musical, however, that it is rarely even mentioned: from *42nd Street* to *Saturday Night Fever* women serve primarily to provide man's pleasure (as servant, as sex partner, as spectacle). Certainly there is grist here for the feminist mill. Probably no single American entertainment genre so stereotypes woman as does the backstage musical.

The merit of Lucy Fischer's article is to have seen past that simple fact. Instead of analysing the roles women play in Berkeley musicals, Fischer analyses the way in which the camera constitutes Berkeley's women. Her results thus surpass the level of content analysis espoused by many feminist critics, showing instead how woman's position is inalterably tied to certain structural relationships implied by the Berkeley films. Others have concentrated on a particular image of woman; Fischer fastens on the term 'image' itself in order to show how Berkeley makes woman into an *image* both produced and consumed by man. Man is thus both the camera which creates cinematic art and the eyes which consume it, while woman must be content to be frozen into an image, a projection, an exhibition which can be validated only by the male eye. By thus analysing not woman's social function but her identity with part of the cinema-viewing situation, Fischer structuralizes feminist criticism, thus making its discoveries available to a wider range of applications. If we know that Hollywood heroines always cower when attacked we still know very little about the unconscious processes which inform our view of woman's position within society. Knowledge that an important class of Hollywood films identifies woman with the film image itself, however, can lead to new understanding of sexual interaction. The notion of woman as image pulls together numerous aspects of mid-twentieth-century society: from clothes, make-up, and other beauty products, to conventions of advertising and sales of eyeglasses. Cultural analysis succeeds only when it finds similar structures in society and its texts, thus illuminating each through the other. In this sense Lucy Fischer's article is eminently successful, a model for future analysis.

Nevertheless, a *caveat*. It should not be assumed that the structure which Fischer isolates in *Dames* and other Berkeley films permeates all musicals. The spectator is not always forced into the male position of eyeing a female spectacle on-screen. Indeed, an entire class of musicals, those which tend, like Minnelli's *Meet Me in St. Louis*, to portray the reaffirmation of a threatened matriarchy, transform the viewer into a member of that matriarchy. Constantly on the move, man tries to escape from the film frame but is brought back by the women of the family. Were we to adopt Lucy Fischer's methodology for such films we would certainly come to conclusions differing from those which she reaches apropos of *Dames*.

> I never had the intention of making eroticism or pornography. I love beautiful girls and I love to gather and show many beautiful girls with regular features and well-made bodies. It is the idea of spectacle which is expressed in 'What do you go for?' What do you come to do, why do you go to a spectacle? It is not the story, it is not the stars, nor the music. What people want to see are beautiful girls.
>
> –Busby Berkeley[1]

In the proliferation of literature on the status of women in film the most common critical strategy has been that of distilling from the cinematic narrative an abstract 'image' of women in film. Thus, from the reverential treatment accorded to the Gish persona in the films of D.W. Griffith, Marjorie Rosen extracts the image of woman as posed on a Victorian pedestal. From the relationship of the Doris Day character to her male protagonists she posits a vision of woman as militant crusader for chastity. To characterize the adolescent film heroines of the fifties she conjures the image of Popcorn Venus.[2] Similarly, Molly Haskell compares the malign erotic presence of Rita Hayworth in *Lady from Shanghai* to that of a mythological siren, and reads from the machismo sexuality of contemporary cinema the image of woman as rape victim.[3]

In approaching the production numbers of Busby Berkeley, however, we encounter cinematic texts of another order. For rather than present us with a realistic narrative from which we must decoct a feminine 'image' Berkeley's plastic abstractions present us with the essence of image itself – a vision of female stereotypes in their purest, most distillate form.

Berkeley's *mise en scène*, in fact, has a comic propensity to literalize the very metaphors upon which critics like Rosen and Haskell have seized in their characterization of the portrayal of women. While Griffith treats Lillian Gish as though she were on a pedestal, Berkeley, in *Broadway Serenade*, situates Jeanette MacDonald physically upon a pedestal. While some directors shroud their virginal heroines in an aura of sexual impenetrability, Berkeley, in 'Pettin' in the Park,' shrouds Ruby Keeler in a suit of metal armor. While films of the fifties cast women metaphorically in the role of Popcorn Venus, Berkeley, in *Fashions of 1934*, casts them literally as the goddess and her galley slaves. While certain stars have filled the screen with the sense of mythical sirens, Berkeley, in 'By a Waterfall,' fills the screen with the presence of mermaids themselves. Finally, as Molly Haskell finds the image of rape inscribed in the content of contemporary films, so one finds in the style of Berkeley's 'through-the-leg tracking shots' implications of the sexual act transposed to the rhetoric of camera technique.

Thus Berkeley's production numbers provide a spectrum of images of women that range the continuum from Reverence to Rape. On this level Berkeley's *oeuvre* comes to constitute a definitive text upon the subject – an illustrated catalogue whose elegant pages display the cinematic image of woman in all its varied embodiments and incarnations.*

A privileged work in this respect is *Dames* (1934), a film whose very title seems to propose it as germane to a discussion of women in cinema. What distinguishes *Dames* from other works in the Berkeley repertoire is the manner in which its production numbers (with their symbolic discourse on the feminine stereotype) are implanted within a narrative that deals directly with the same thematic issues. The dramatic episodes of the film were, of course, directed by another man – Ray Enright. But it is, nonetheless, intriguing to examine this Centaurian construction and disclose the ways in which its discrete segments inflect upon each other and

---

* In my analysis of *Dames* I will intentionally sidestep several issues which are none the less important but too complex to examine within the confines of a textual reading of the film. I introduce them here as a series of relevant questions: Can a film like *Dames* be judged aesthetically, independent of its underlying ideology? How exactly do films affect cultural attitudes? How do cultural attitudes affect films and our responses to them?

create a rather curious cinematic text. In its hybrid totality *Dames* constitutes an eccentric treatise addressed to three interlocking aspects of the portrayal of women in cinema: (1) the nature of the image of women in film; (2) the character of the relationship between the female screen presence and the male spectator and/or director; (3) the attitude of the Hollywood industry toward the position of women in the commercial film medium.

The feminine mystique and cinematic technique

While conventional film narratives situate their female personae in a realistic universe, the Berkeley production numbers posit their existence in the realm of pure imagery. The space in which his sequences transpire does not conform to that of the concrete external world. Rather, it is abstract, and in its fluid chain of spatial metamorphoses, essentially ambiguous. From this perspective it becomes the perfect décor for fantasy, and often the narrative prologues explicitly locate the numbers in a character's consciousness. 'I Only Have Eyes for You,' for example, proposes itself as an oneiric meditation occasioned by Dick Powell's having fallen asleep on the subway.

But beyond the motivational ploys of the framing stories, it is Berkeley's cinematic technique which renders screen space as quintessentially fantastic. Often the numbers unfold in a void, black space whose dimensions are unknowable. The mechanics of concealed cuts transport us magically from one locale to another, creating a geography unnavigable by the human body. In 'I Only Have Eyes for You,' a cut-out face of Ruby Keeler falls away to reveal 'behind' it a ferris wheel of costumed girls. In actuality, the sites are connected only by a splice and the implication of spatial relation is merely an illusion. Spatial paradoxes emerge as well. In 'I Only Have Eyes for You,' we leave Keeler on the exterior rim of the ferris wheel in one shot, only to discover her on its interior surface in another. Movement in the numbers likewise declares itself synthetic, as images rotate, girls fly up to the lens of the camera, or advance forward propelled by Eisensteinian jump-cuts.[4]

If the geography of the numbers is unchartable, their temporality is unmeasurable; and it is as far removed from the flow of normal time as is that ebony vacuum from the coordinates of conventional space. The constraints of causality are similarly dissolved. Thus in 'I Only Have Eyes for You,' the external world responds to Dick Powell's obsessional fantasies and a crowd of people can be made to simply 'disappear from view.'

Given Berkeley's *mise en scène* as the potential environment of fantasy, with what particular visions of the female image is it populated?

One approach to the question entails an examination of Berkeley's formal technique and the manner in which certain myths concerning women are inscribed in the seemingly value-free level of plastic composition. One should keep in mind the obvious fact that excepting their narrative prologues the production numbers of *Dames* exclude the presence of men. They are, in fact, elaborate corporeo-plastic constructions of women's bodies 'composed' in particular décors. Clearly those compositions are more than just pictorial; and from their physical arrangements of the female form can be read covert assumptions about the female 'norm.'

We might begin with the very concept of *stereotype* which on one level denotes 'having no individuality, *as though cast from a mould.*' Ironically, this very notion of uniformity constitutes a stereotype in the depiction of women in film. One thinks of female screen personae in terms of *types* with a reflex that is not so automatic in the case of males. We have, for instance, the 'blonde bombshell,' the 'femme fatale,' the 'vamp,' the 'gamine,' or the 'sex goddess.' These are not 'career' specifications as are the masculine labels of 'gangster' or 'cowboy,' but rather categories of sexual proclivity and physical demeanor. Indeed the entire history of cinema can be seen as constituting an ongoing fashion show of popular female 'styles.'

This sense of the feminine screen persona as conforming to a particular type is nowhere more apparent than in the chorus-lines of Berkeley's production numbers. Part of the humor of the numbers, in fact, arises from our perception that the women look remarkably alike. This notion is eventually catapulted into another realm entirely in 'I Only Have Eyes for You,' where women are not merely similar but disconcertingly identical. Berkeley clearly prides himself on this stylistic penchant. He speaks in an interview of a particular day of hiring in which he auditioned 723 women to select only three:

> My sixteen regular girls were sitting on the side waiting; so after I picked the three girls I put them next to my special sixteen and they *matched just like pearls*. (Italics mine)[5]

Ultimately this conception of female as stereotype is embodied within the *mise en scène* of Berkeley's work, particularly in the production number also titled 'Dames.' There, as though to demonstrate the precise matching of the Berkeley girls, he lines them up behind one another until their multiplicity is subsumed in an image of apparent unity. 'Dames' also contains a sequence emblematic of woman's alleged conformity to an external image: in depicting a row of show girls making up before their dressing-table mirrors, Berkeley deploys yet another row of women to represent their reflections. One thinks of Molly Haskell's statement on this issue and the way that Berkeley's iconography tends to literalize it. For in speaking of the genesis of feminine cinematic stereotypes, she refers to how the Gish persona was succeeded by a 'long line of replica mirror-image virgins.'[6]

Although Berkeley's relish of the chorus line takes on a transcendent quality, its presence is, after all, a convention of musical comedy. But his mode of engaging it is not, and it is on this level of stylistic innovation that more significant attitudes towards women emerge. What happens in most Berkeley numbers (and quintessentially in 'Dames') is that the women lose their individuation in a more profound sense than through the similarity of their physical appearance. Rather, their identities are completely consumed in the creation of an overall abstract design.

Furthermore the configurations of those designs can clearly be read for meaning. The perpetual arrangement of girls in circular format seems closely associated with symbols of female sexuality. The objects which the chorus line forms are equally tendentious. In 'Dames' the girls delineate the sentimental boundaries of a heart. And in 'The Shadow Waltz' in *Gold Diggers of 1933* they outline a shapely violin being bowed – a metaphor that any Freudian analyst would be proud to unpack. Thus in the Berkeley numbers the notion of women as sexual *objects* takes on a deviously witty relevance.

The chorus-line patterns tend as well to literalize the notion of two-dimensional feminine screen portrayal. If there is any match for the 'flatness' of the Ruby Keeler character in the Enright narrative it is clearly the show girls in 'Dames' whose bodies are pressed into black-and-white patterns, employed interchangeably with animated designs.

This reduction of the female form to biotic tile in an abstract mosaic is not devoid of overtones of power. It tends, in fact, to literalize the stereotype of the male director as potent Svengali who transforms the dull but malleable female form into an alluring screen presence. The words of von Sternberg seem particularly applicable to Berkeley's cinematic technique:

> It is the nature of woman to be passive, receptive, dependent on male aggression . . . In other words she is not normally outraged at being manipulated; on the contrary, she usually

> enjoys it. I have plenty of evidence to assume that no woman, as opposed to male, has ever failed to enjoy the possibly mortifying experience of *being reorganized in the course of incarnating my vision of her.*' (Italics mine.)[7]

Even the narrative element of the production number 'Dames' alludes to the sexuality of power: it portrays an all-male theatrical board of trustees which choreographs the careers of show girls from behind the scenes.

Privileged in the canon of female stereotypes is the conception of woman as decoration, a notion which has had its supreme manifestation in the history of film. Once more, in the iconography of the Berkeley sequences we find this cliché in its rarefied form, unencumbered by the obfuscations of a plot. For the function of the women in a number like 'I Only Have Eyes for You' is essentially plastic, and their status is equal to that of the décor. They are, in fact, simply elements of the total *mise en scène* – facets of its comprehensive ornamental structure. Even the frills of their white organza dresses seem to tell us that they are, after all, pure 'fluff.'

Relevant to this impression is the curious fact that Berkeley girls did not (and, often, *could* not) dance – a phenomenon which accentuates our perception of their role as visual embellishments. As Berkeley himself unabashedly confesses:

> I never cared whether a girl knew her right foot from her left so long as she was beautiful. I'd get her to move or dance, or do something. All my girls were beautiful and some of them could dance a little, some of them couldn't.'[8]

In a number like 'I Only Have Eyes for You,' the women's gestures (swaying back and forth or undulating the folds of their gowns) clearly do not function as choreography. Rather they serve as kinetic designs which interact dialectically with the complex trajectories of the mobile décor and the moving camera. But the awesome proficiency of Berkeley's mechanical décor tends to underscore the technical incompetence of the Berkeley girls and concretize the image of women as essentially passive. The sets of 'I Only Have Eyes for You' are elaborate preprogrammed machines for action which transport the girls through dizzying cycles of aimless, repetitive movement. What heightens this sense of passivity is the zombieism of the Berkeley girls, a quality that they exude beneath the surface of their opaque, dissociative grins. The Berkeley girls, in fact, seem to extend passivity virtually into catatonia and propose the image of female as ambulatory Surrealist mannequin.

Ultimately what becomes apparent from a reading of Berkeley's *mise en scène* is the way in which he generates an image of woman as 'image' itself. This portrayal proceeds on multiple levels. She is represented as image in terms of her embodiment of cultural stereotypes, and as image in her posture of conjured male projection. But the presentation of these first two conceptions depends upon the establishment of a third, and that is Berkeley's obsession with the status of woman as *film image* – as plastic, synthetic, celluloid screen object. Von Sternberg once said of Marlene Dietrich that 'she was a perfect *medium* . . . who absorbed his direction and . . . responded to his conception of female archetype.'[9] While von Sternberg perhaps offered this rhetorically, Berkeley has embraced it literally. For through his articulation of woman as film image she becomes quite concretely a medium – one which in its pliancy can be molded to the configurations of the Berkeley imagination.

All these varied senses of woman as image seem encoded within the iconography of 'I Only Have Eyes for You.' It is, first of all, a sequence whose feminine imagery is diegetically situated within the realm of Dick Powell's fantasies. Its references to women and advertising (the subway posters for Society Cosmetics and Willards for the Hair) furthermore invoke the cultural clichés of surface beauty and vanity. But what is most important in the sequences occurs with the magical dissolves on the advertising posters (transforming each model's face into that of Ruby Keeler) and with the fluid bridge from the final poster to the huge Ruby Keeler head adrift in a black amorphous space. For through those shot transitions we move from the domain of extra-filmic senses of the female image to the possibilities of its embodiment in cinematic imagery itself.

During the course of the number Berkeley proceeds not only to catalogue those possibilities in formal terms but, ironically, to create a fabric of imagery that comments on his very act of creation. One thinks, for example, of a final segment of the number, comprised of an elaborate chain of process shots. First, we see Ruby Keeler step into a mock-up mirror frame, which becomes reduced in scale and supported by a base consisting of small Ruby Keeler figures aligned in apparent unity. Eventually the entire 'mirror' is grasped by the hand of a large Ruby Keeler figure who enters from off-screen left. What we have here, of course, is a pictorial allegory – one which dramatizes the employment of women through cinematic processes to present and support a stereotypical image of women. But the most evocative trope of the number comes in the form of the giant, jigsaw-puzzle vision of Ruby Keeler's face. What we see is an obedient cluster of three-dimensional women who proceed to cover their bodies with a two-dimensional photographic representation (a process which, significantly, is accomplished by lifting their skirts above their heads). What is most intriguing, though, is the form that photograph takes. For it comes to us in the guise of a jig-saw puzzle – a fragmented version of an image that must be sequentially assembled. In his choice of this conceit Berkeley has again generated an iconography metaphoric of the portrayal of women in film. For it is a portrayal which, after all, involves the constitution of a giant synthetic image through the assemblage of interlocking pieces which we commonly refer to as 'shots.'

'Sweet and hot'

In addition to translating certain stereotypes concerning women into the figurative discourse of cinematic imagery, Berkeley's *mise en scène* proposes a particular vision of female sexuality. In order to disclose this, however, it is necessary to locate Berkeley's production numbers within the narrative framework of Enright's *Dames*, and to situate *Dames* within the historical context of film censorship.

The Hollywood production code officially came into being in 1930; but since there were no adequate enforcement provisions it remained for some time merely an advisory document.[10] In the early thirties, public criticism of film content mounted and, according to Richard Randall in *Censorship in the Movies*, the year 1934 (the release date of *Dames*) marked 'the turning point of self-regulation':

> American Catholic bishops formed the Legion of Decency to review and rate films. At the same time they threatened the industry with a general boycott by Catholic patrons if the moral tone of films did not improve. This pressure resulted in the MPPDA's [Motion Picture Producers and Distributors of America] formation of the Production Code Administration (PCA) as a quasi-independent, self-supporting body charged with enforcing and interpreting the code.[11]

Evidently the power of the MPPDA and the PCA was based on their domination by the five largest companies in the industry which, in turn, controlled 70% of the film theaters.

In this historical perspective the plot of *Dames* seems an ingenious parody of the censorship of movies. From the Legion of Decency, we have the Ounce Foundation for the Elevation of

American Morals. (The constant reference to the organization as the 'O.F. for the E. of A. M.' seems to mock the alphabetics of the MPPDA and the PCA as well). For the censorship of film is substituted the censorship of theater. In keeping with the economic realities of film censorship Ezra Ounce (Hugh Herbert) is portrayed as a millionaire and the opening sequence of the film catalogues the name plaques of the myriad enterprises which constitute his monopolistic empire.

Typically, Ezra Ounce's specific objections to the theater focus on the figure of the show girl. It is the flagrant display of women on the musical stage that he identifies as the source of its moral danger.

Clearly we are to regard Ezra Ounce as a blustering fool, a repressed, adolescent man who mistakes 'good clean fun' for sinful prurience. After all, what goes on on the stage of the theater is to be *so* innocuous as to permit the participation of the antiseptic Ruby Keeler (who plays his niece, Barbara).

But ironically what Ezra Ounce supposedly views on the stage as theatrical numbers within the diegesis of *Dames* are, in actuality, the cinematic insertions of Busby Berkeley. This stylistic dislocation is echoed by a shift in sensibility as well. For while the Enright narrative proceeds to spoof the need for censorship of female sexuality, the Berkeley numbers intercede to present it in more slyly perverse configurations than Ezra could have anticipated (or even perhaps appreciated). This tonal disjunction seems epitomized in the title of the fictional musical comedy from which the numbers emerge, which is 'Sweet and Hot.' For the diegesis of the film would have us believe that what transpires on the stage is naively 'sweet.' But the realities of our viewing experience contradict this and assert that what Berkeley depicts on the screen is unremittingly 'hot.'

'The Girl at the Ironing Board,' for example, presents us with what was called in those days a 'specialty number.' The epithet seems peculiarly apt since it unfolds as a comic vignette on the sexual 'specialty' of fetishism. It begins with Joan Blondell voyeuristically peering through the laundry window at a loving couple in a carriage outside. She sings:

Nobody ever has whispered to me
The sweet things a girl loves to hear
Nobody's arms ever twined around mine
Still I'm not lonely for romance is near–
A girl who works at the laundry
Has a dream lover all of her own

A lover, unseen, whose love she keeps clean
With water and soap and a washing machine.

Then, as though the subject of erotic symbolism and fetishistic partialism were not sufficiently overt, she continues:

There is something about your pajamas
That fills me with sweet ecstacy
And because it's part of you
I'm learning to love you
So bring back your laundry to me.

The rest of the number dramatizes the notion of fetish as symbolic substitute for the 'normal' sexual object. We see animated male laundry sing and gesture to her from the clothes-line; she even whisks a pair of longjohns from the pile and dances off with them. At the end of the number she is 'gang raped' by a mass of laundry which slides down upon her from the lines.

In keeping with the fetishism syndrome the number represents the fetish in the context of a series from which Blondell chooses a favorite partner with 'whom' she departs:

> The construction of a series of love objects is exhibited in the [fetishist's] choice of a partner by first imagining a whole row of possibilities and then . . . picking one of them as a favorite.[12]

Significantly, the one aspect of the number that does not conform to the syndrome is the notion of the fetishist as female. Although stereotypes of sexual behaviour are currently under re-evaluation for their cultural determinants, it is nonetheless the case that as late as the Kinsey report of 1953 fetishism was considered an overwhelmingly male syndrome.[13] Thus in 'The Girl at the Ironing Board' we would seem to have a clear case of the imposition of a classically male fantasy on the behaviour of a female screen persona.[14]

Finally, 'The Girl at the Ironing Board' abounds in elements that seem to comment parodistically on the idea of censorship. After its eccentric portrayal of sexuality, the sequence ends on the saccharin note of a chirping bird which sings as Blondell and her laundry walk into the sunset. The Griffith-like sentimentality of this touch is comically false, as disingenuous as the stuffed bird itself which sits on an artificial prop tree.

One thinks as well of the song lyric which speaks of 'keeping love clean' as one views this as a work whose implications had by-passed the process of Production Code laundering. The propriety of the numbers is much like the moral status of Horace

Hemingway (Guy Kibbee) which Ezra Ounce suspects is 'nothing but a snare and illusion.'

From the reviews at the time of the film's release, it seems likely that its implications escaped the public eye, as they had that of Ezra Ounce. An innocuous *New York Times* review of August 26, 1934, for example, described it simply as 'an original combination of comedy and song . . . which is staged very cleverly.'

The Gold Diggers or The Men With the Movie Cameras

But certain things clearly did not escape the public eye and it is precisely to the subject of spectator vision that one must turn to complete an analysis of *Dames*.

The title number of the film confronts the issue most explicitly. It begins with an all-male theatrical board meeting at which various investors argue about the elements which insure commercial stage success. One says: 'I tell you gentlemen, if I'm going to put money into this show I want to be sure that we get the best music possible.' Others interrupt advocating the importance of story or publicity until finally Dick Powell breaks into a song which establishes the economic base of show business on the male desire to look at women:

Who writes the words and music for all the girlie shows?
No one cares and no one knows.
Who is the handsome hero some villain always frames?
Who cares if there's a plot or not, if it's got a lot of dames.
What do you go for? Go see the show for?
Tell the truth – you go to see those beautiful dames.

Then as a horde of show girls enter the board room he expounds on this theme more thoroughly and reveals that the true gold diggers are to be found in the corporate male bureaucracy, and not in the chorus line as generally supposed.

Leave your addresses, my big successes
All depend a lot upon you beautiful dames.
Oh dames are necessary to show business
Dames—without you there would be no business.
Your knees in action, that's the attraction
What good's a show without you beautiful dames.

After this framing episode the sequence erupts into the actual production number. Significantly it emphasizes women's 'knees in action' as the girls' black-stockinged legs are employed to create geometric designs against a pure white floor.

Aside from 'Dames,' however, the theme of vision is referred to in almost every lyric of the score. One song is entitled 'Try to See It My Way'; another (a fantasy of prenatal love) has Powell confessing that he adored Keeler when she 'was a smile on her mother's lips and a twinkle in her father's eye.' There is, of course, 'I Only Have Eyes for You' which alternately represents the love of a woman as optical illusion and optical obsession.

But not only is the act of looking alluded to in the song lyrics of *Dames*, it is invoked in the mode of presenting the imagery of the production numbers themselves. Inscribed in Berkeley's optical stylistics is a virtual discourse on voyeurism and its relation to the female screen presence: the 'Kino-Eye' has become that of a Peeping Tom. This notion is even brought to the literal surface of the narrative as one shot reveals an insert of a gossip column, 'On the Rialto,' whose byline is none other than Peeping Tom.

The implicit thesis of cinema as voyeuristic enterprise (as *spectacle*) is advanced on many levels in Berkeley's production numbers. One thinks immediately of his anecdote concerning his introduction of the close-up into the vocabulary of the film musical. Evidently Sam Goldwyn came on the set of *Whoopee* and questioned Berkeley about his motivation for the technique. Berkeley responded: 'Well, we've got all the beautiful girls in the picture. Why not let the public see them?'[15]

Thus just as Berkeley comprehended the difference between the choreographic potential of theater and cinema, so too he seems to have grasped the difference in their voyeuristic appeal. For the close-up has the power to annihilate the spatial gap which distances the theatrical spectator from the female stage presence.

The number which most clearly transposes the issue of voyeurism into stylistic terms is 'Dames.' Berkeley fills the screen with girls clothed in provocative 'Fredericks of Hollywood' type negligées and has them engaged in the visually taboo pursuits of sleeping, bathing and dressing. As though to shame the camera for its intrusion, however, the lens is continually punished by the withdrawal of sight. A whole chain of such instances occurs in the beginning of the number. In the first such shot, girls run up to the camera and obscure the lens with the fabric of their nightgowns. Then in a masked cut (with attendant change of décor) the fabric is removed to reveal a girl in a bath tub. The girl proceeds to cover the lens with a powder puff which (through another masked cut) is removed by a girl at a dressing table. Eventually the girl takes a bottle of perfume and sprays the surface of the lens. We next see the lens wiped clean, but this time our vision is identified with a particular male stagehand and the lens has become a window through which he watches the show girls approach.

The dialectic of seeing and being prevented from seeing is epitomized in the number's final voyeuristic character, a 'blind' man who sheepishly removes his dark glasses to stare at the show girls who pass on the street. (We should remember that as English legend has it Peeping Tom was, in fact, a Coventry tailor who went blind after peering at Lady Godiva.)

Although Berkeley plays on the notion of camera as voyeuristic tool, he nonetheless conceals its presence. While mirrors figure dominantly in the imagery of the numbers (the 'mirror' of women in 'I Only Have Eyes for You,' and the dressing-table 'mirrors' in 'Dames') they are most often false surfaces which refuse to reflect an image of the camera or of the man who stands behind it.

But the iconography of the Berkeley numbers seems to go beyond engaging the female screen persona as source of mere voyeuristic pleasure. For in addition to the numbers whose effect depends on the presence of *actual* women one is struck by the existence of sequences content with their photographic image.

We might recall, for example, that on the subway in 'I Only Have Eyes for You' Dick Powell conspicuously ignores the corporal reality of Ruby Keeler to embark on a fantasy digression based on her photographic likeness. But the issue seems crystallized in the final sequence of 'Dames.' What we see on the screen is a shot of the Berkeley harem arranged in pyramidal fashion against a complex décor. Imperceptibly, the image of the actual women transmutes to that of a photographic representation. And in a parody of sexual entry, the number ends with Powell's head breaking through the image surface.

Thus what emerges in *Dames* is yet another sense of 'the image of woman as image'. For it is not so much the physical feminine *presence* that is celebrated in *Dames* as much as her synthetic, cinematic *image*. And ultimately the privileged status of that image and its mode of presentation propose it as a virtual *substitute* for woman herself. Von Sternberg had spoken of manipulating the female screen image into a 'visual aphrodisiac.'[16] But in *Dames* it seems, like Blondell's laundry, to have acquired the dimension of a fetish.

Once more we find ironic reverberations of the issue within the Enright narrative. In an early scene of the film, Horace Hemingway goes to visit his millionaire cousin, Ezra Ounce, and with polite duplicity remarks that his daughter, Barbara, sends her love. The following comic dialogue casually ensues, but in retrospect seems to encapsulate the dynamics of the portrayal of women in *Dames*:

Ezra: Barbara sends her love to me? Why should Barbara send her love to me? She's never even seen me!

Horace: She's seen your picture.

Ezra: Well, then . . . *Maybe she's sending her love to my picture.*

Notes

1 Busby Berkeley, 'Rencontre avec le grand "Architecte du Musical," ' *Cinéma*, 103 (Feb. 1966), p. 44.
2 Marjorie Rosen, *Popcorn Venus* (New York: Avon, 1973), paraphrase of material on pages 71, 211, 300ff.
3 Molly Haskell, *From Reverence to Rape* (New York: Penguin Books, 1974), p. 204, 323ff.
4 I am referring to the series of triadic 'jump-cuts' which occur during the coronation sequence in *Ivan the Terrible – Part I.*
5 B. Pike and D. Martin, *The Genius of Busby Berkeley* (Reseda, California: Creative Film Society), p. 64.
6 Haskell, *op. cit.*, p. 49.
7 Josef von Sternberg, *Fun in a Chinese Laundry* (New York: Macmillan, 1965), p. 120.
8 Pike and Martin, *op. cit.*, pp. 51–3.
9 Josef von Sternberg, Introduction to *The Blue Angel – Classic Film Script* (New York: Simon & Schuster, 1968), p. 12.
10 Richard Randall, *Censorship in the Movies* (Madison: University of Wisconsin Press, 1970), p. 199.
11 *Ibid.*
12 Wilhelm Stekel, *Disorders of the Instincts and Emotions* (New York: Liveright, 1952), p. 33.
13 A. Kinsey, W. Pomeroy, C. Martin, P. Gebhard, *Sexual Behaviour in the Human Female* (New York: Pocket Books, 1953), p. 679.
14 The overtones of fetishism in the iconography of *Dames* would seem to go beyond this particular number. In the Enright narrative we have the absurd character of Ezra Ounce who is depicted on several occasions toying obsessively with a series of ceramic elephants. And the image of dozens of Benda-masked Ruby Keeler likenesses in 'I Only Have Eyes for You' has the distinct sense of fetishistic partialism (the necessity for the love object to display particular attributes). Even the precise 'matching' of the chorus girls carries similar implications.
15 Tony Thomas and Jim Terry, *The Busby Berkeley Book* (New York: New York Graphic Society, 1973) p. 25.
16 Von Sternberg, Introduction to *The Blue Angel, op. cit.*, p. 12.

6 · Dennis Giles: 'Show-making'

Movie, no. 24, Spring 1977, pp. 14–25

In *Footlight Parade* the camera tracks between the spread legs of a line of scantily clad chorus girls; in *Yolanda and the Thief* Fred Astaire's hands appear to play not the harp he is holding but the woman who sits behind it, thus making the music appear to emerge from his 'caresses' of Lucille Bremer; in *Daddy Longlegs* Astaire ends up romancing the young French girl whom he has adopted; in *Saturday Night Fever* the disco unmistakably doubles as an opportunity for dance and for sex. Even though the musical labours hard to disguise its interest in sexuality, there can remain little doubt that the genre serves to provide a covert method of conceiving normally undiscussed aspects of intersexual relationships. It is certainly no coincidence that the decline of the musical should coincide with the rise of a new morality and a new openness about sexuality.

Few critics, however, have openly confronted the problem of sexuality in the Hollywood musical. The terms usually used are romance, courtship, and love, when clearly terms like sex, incest, and even rape deserve to be invoked. Dennis Giles is one of the first to take this concern seriously. Where others have pointed up the important parallel between making the show and making the couple, Giles moves directly to the sexual level, reading show-making as love-making. In this way he succeeds where others have failed to establish a structural relationship between the musical's incest motif (most visible in the coupling of young women with older men, often Fred Astaire) and its plot material, which generally turns on the inability of each member of the couple to overcome his/her inhibitions.

Giles's psychoanalytic methodology leads him to conclusions which contrast significantly with the claims of other articles in this collection. In the previous article, Lucy Fischer emphasizes the sexual identity of image and camera: *to show* implies the creation of a female spectacle designed for male consumption. Where Fischer's configuration implies the rape of the (female) image by the (male) spectator's eyes, Giles's approach stresses the castrating effect of the show-making woman on the male initiate, who can enter the show only when she 'retracts her phallus'. Later articles in the collection (Sutton, Altman) stress the role of marriage as a community ritual rather than as sexual coupling. While they see the members of the couple primarily as carriers of cultural categories, Giles goes straight to a primal level, rooted in individual desire rather than culture-specific concerns.

Though some may find Giles's analysis too strong, and his willingness to invoke familiar Freudian patterns too great, it seems to me that 'Show-making' is just what we need at this point in the history of criticism on the musical: an unabashed attempt to discover the underlying sources of our fascination with this seemingly most frivolous of genres. In another article in this collection, Jim Collins points out how one category of dance in the Astaire–Rogers films serves as surrogate sex; Giles goes one step further by placing that surrogate sex into an overall framework, thus establishing for it a function both within the film and in terms of the general film-spectator relationship.

The permanent show

Near the end of *The Band Wagon*, Cyd Charisse tells Fred Astaire 'This show's going to run a long time, and as far as I'm concerned it's going to run for ever.' She is referring not only to the musical revue, staged in the latter part of the film, which ends with the triumphant 'That's Entertainment' number, but also to a more personal phenomenon – the show of love between Astaire and herself. In this concluding statement, Charisse indicates that love is, at its best, a show, and that the relationship between the love show and the stage show (and, by extension, the film show) is so close that each necessarily depends on the other for its failure or success. The two cannot be separated. As far as Charisse is concerned, *The Band Wagon* is 'about' the show in this double aspect – a display which welds two previously warring individuals into a single singing/dancing organism. The show not only abolishes distance but time – it will last, as Charisse declares, 'for ever'.

The moment of perfection finally achieved must be allowed to endure, since only now is each player able to enact his 'true' identity – that of the lover. The trial of show-making has been a process of growth into one's proper role, a role which now must be immobilised by showing it off to the public. Character is stabilised in the showing; the stars (Astaire and Charisse) are now fixed in courses which will be repeated without variation from this night forward.

The permanent show is indeed a cure for the previous drama – its conflict, its agon(y) since the showing arrests the flow of time.

Temporality was previously to be desired, since only in time could the show be developed. But the purpose of the show is to be shown. Any further passage of time is regarded as an evil, since it can only disrupt the harmonies of this moment, only degrade the beauty so precariously achieved. In sum, by virtue of showing the show, the performers pass to a transcendent realm of being. The show bears a resemblance to the state before birth, echoing its timelessness, its ultimate unity of lover and beloved. But it is also a preview of the death state, transforming all the terrors, all the flux of life into a state of permanent being. Yet if showing is a species of dying, it is a benevolent one, killing the players at the height of their powers, at the point of their greatest happiness.

If *poiesis* is an act of 'working' the world, the song and dance film – with its elaborate 'production numbers' – is poetry to the nth power, worked and reworked to reach what some film theorists consider an excessive degree of manufacture. But to others, the glory of the genre is to be found precisely in its excess, its abstraction from lived reality. Thus, Godard called the musical 'the idealisation of cinema', implying that it deals more with essence than appearance or rather transforms essence into appearance through the labour of show-making. To connect Godard's statement with the 'permanent show' of *The Band Wagon*, it is necessary to note that 'idealisation' is not only a process of abstracting the world, but one of freezing it. An idea, in contrast to the flux of apparent reality, is traditionally considered to be immobile, eternal. Like Charisse's show, it runs for ever.

In this study of the show-making musical two questions are posed: how does the show 'show' itself, and what is shown in the showing? It must be emphasised at the start that there is no real boundary between the how and the what. 'Show' is a noun naming the state which ends the process, but it is also the process itself. Like 'dream', it denotes both an action and the product of the action. As Freud felt it necessary to coin the expression 'dream-work' to separate the process from the product, so we will be forced at times to distinguish show-making (or the show-work) from the terminal show.

A basic assumption throughout is that the showing is also a concealing, that something is not only revealed but hidden in the process of show-making. With supreme arrogance, the musical refuses to hide its secrets; like Poe's 'Purloined Letter' its guilt is concealed by means of an open display. We have only to hear the words of the characters, watch them play their scenes, to discover not only the desire but the forbidden deed itself. The crime of the musical is not murder but love – a form of love that we must approach through circuitous routes until we can show it openly.

Identity/denial

At the beginning of *The Band Wagon*, Fred Astaire (Tony Hunter) makes his entrance as a washed-up hoofer. The crowd at the station has gathered to greet a contemporary celebrity, not this has-been. He is the prototypical stranger in town and arrives in New York with more dread than desire. The former star has been given a new lease on life – a prospect of reviving his former glory – *if* (and it is a big if) he can adapt his plebeian talents to an ambitious and 'arty' musical version of *Faust* – the pretension of an ego-maniacal actor/director. Unless Hunter can make the transition, unless he can work effectively in the 'legitimate' ballet style, his career is effectively finished. It is immediately apparent, however, that he and the 'artists' are worlds apart in both training and spirit. Hunter's heart isn't in the project; he is ready to quit.

At this crisis, the Astaire character is taken in hand by Cyd Charisse, as the ballet star Gaby. At first a rivalry, the relationship grows to one of respect, and finally, love. As Hunter's confidence grows with his skill, he gains the strength, first to depose Gaby's lover, assuming his privileged place in her heart and secondly to dethrone the extravagant director and (however reluctantly) to set himself at the head of the incipient show. This show is then thoroughly transformed into the musical we see on the screen. In sum: Tony Hunter the corpse is reborn *via* love into Tony the Tiger; his energy infuses the show with a second triumphant life which echoes his own regeneration; and, as Gaby informs us, this show (and this love) is eternal.

The Band Wagon's first scene – Hunter's arrival – intentionally rouses our expectations only to crush them. It is a shock to see Fred Astaire – usually so much in control of the situation – reduced to a ghost of his former glory. The hero stands ignored on the platform, a victim of the emotional reversal we have just suffered. Our identification with him is achieved at the outset by the device of forcing us to share his mood.

The image of Hunter in forlorn isolation is disturbing only if we know Astaire as the star of previous musicals – the Other Astaire of *Swing Time*, *Flying Down to Rio*, *Easter Parade*, etc. The scene is built on residual characterisation, on our perception that this Astaire is terribly lacking, is not as he should be. The stage is thus set for the renaissance plot which is in so many ways a retrieval of the Astaire of films past.

In *Easter Parade*, for example, Astaire is secure in his customary role as the accomplished dance-master at the height of his powers. There he is the *maestro* with Judy Garland as his nervous protégée who must learn how to dance – to put on the show. Garland's first site in the story (not only her placement in time and space but also her mental set, her mood) is the one occupied by Astaire in *The Band Wagon*. It is a site of pure possibility – the place from which Garland first 'sights' her future. She stands paralysed in the doorway to the public arena where the permanent show can be glimpsed as a lure and a danger. The subject fears not only the possibility of failure but dreads becoming someone else, abandoning the somewhat unsatisfactory, but familiar, *persona* which protects her/him precisely from the terrors of the future.

Early in *The Band Wagon*, the Astaire character absolutely refuses to budge from his home site. 'I am *not* Nijinsky,' he declares, 'I am *not* Marlon Brando. I am Mrs. Hunter's little boy.' This petulant stance – clinging to Mama – effectively kills Tony's show before it begins. The subject must be pushed, prodded to move beyond himself by that catalytic character known to Propp ('Morphology of the Folktale') as the donor, but here the teacher and lover – Cyd Charisse in *The Band Wagon*, Astaire in *Easter Parade*, Gene Kelly in *Summer Stock* and *The Pirate*. The character's function is to serve as guide and example to the stubborn, fearful child, wooing him into the show world. But before we examine how the donor coaxes the child from his fear, it is first necessary to discover why this fear is justified – why Tony refuses to budge.

The novice finds the show-making process terrifying because in this experience it is precisely his *identity* which is at stake. This identity, as Freud and Margaret Mahler ('On Human Symbiosis and the Vicissitudes of Individuation') tell us, is founded upon the memory (both real and imaginary) of a symbiotic relationship with the mother which the child declines to abandon. He fears leaving the comforts of the original unity and, once out of the womb state, seeks to return to the former existence in which he lay immobile, all his needs gratified, protected from the necessity of emerging to combat a hostile world. It is a state prior to the distinction between I and Other which, for the most part, is lost for ever, although it can momentarily be retrieved by the action of Eros (since love, like death, extinguishes the self). To seek to return to the original identity is essentially a wish to give up an identity founded on separation from the parental body, on the knowledge that the self now constituted is unhappily distinct and desiring. Desire is born in the awareness of loss; it is fundamentally a desire to return to home base – to end the dreadful division, to become once more an organ within an organism.

The Astaire of *The Band Wagon* dreads the Other world of the show and the new identity it promises because he has already become Other from the symbiotic nul–identity and does not like it. Cut off from the source, the organ withers and dies. Hunter has been, in effect, expelled from paradise; the double status of being a star and Mrs. Hunter's little boy assured him that not only would all his immediate needs be fully satisfied, but they would be supplied in love – a love that surrounds, encloses and ultimately smothers the subject unless he can be expelled from Eden into a world which tells him: You are no longer who you were, no longer 'one' but a nothing; you have yet to become who you are. As we have seen, Hunter's womb-life is abruptly collapsed in the opening scene of the film. His statement of refusal to enter the show-world ('I am *not* Nijinsky', etc.) is both a denial and a recognition of the loss of the symbiotic identity with the mother, and, further, of the need to achieve an Other self, since every denial must utter the very thing it seeks to deny and, by speaking of it, affirm its existence. There is no 'no' in the Id – that seething cauldron of desire – where, Freud tells us, 'the laws of contradiction do not apply.' In the same statement, our hero recognises the necessity of becoming an Other, wishes to return to the womb, and denies that he ever left it. He explicitly states only the denial, yet in the remaining plot of *The Band Wagon* enacts both the necessity and the opposed desire. In this musical, indeed, there is no law against contradiction. Tony Hunter's desire to retrieve Eden – stardom and Mama – is satisfied, paradoxically, by doing exactly what he here refuses to do; he casts (throws) himself into the show, there to construct not only a theatrical role, but a second identity.

Eros/the maestro

Tony Hunter's dread of the future takes the form of the protest – 'I can't do it', echoing Judy Garland's lament in *Easter Parade*. The best way to define the function of the donor is to say that he is the one who can do it. But the concept – the action – is hardly as simple as it sounds. The donor is the canny one *par excellence* – the individual who has mastered all the tenses of the archaic verb to can. The canny one bears the power of penetration into Earth and/or Woman worlds beyond the site in which one familiarly moves. He not only journeys within, but lives to tell the tale. He has opened the channel of communication between home and alien worlds, and can now pass between the opposed regions at will. The power – and the knowledge – of the one who can is essentially his ability to pass to and from the uncanny (*unheimlich*, literally unhomelike) site and, as donor/teacher/lover, this individual can guide the passage of a selected protégé into the hidden kingdom. He stands on the threshold – an achieved hero – either guarding or 'showing' the mysteries; he is both priest and magician, stamped irrevocably by mark or manner with Other-worldly powers. He appears as Dante's Virgil, who knows both Hell and Paradise; as Tiresias, who has lived as man, woman and snake and now, as teacher, displays the scar of blindness; as St Peter, who holds the keys to The Kingdom; as Carlos Castaneda's Don Juan; as The Professor – Sigmund Freud – who opens 'the royal road to the unconscious' through the interpretation of dreams. And I submit that this wizard is also the Gene Kelly of *The Pirate* – actor and buccaneer – who seduces Judy Garland into the theatrical kingdom, Cyd Charisse of *The Band Wagon*, and the Astaire of *Easter Parade*.

Consider, for a moment, Astaire as the *maestro*. As Paddy Whannel has observed, Astaire's dance functions both as an initiation and a seduction of his female partner. The girl is gradually drawn into the space Astaire creates by his first graceful steps. She is moved emotionally and physically – to join him in his spatial conquest. And it *is* a conquest, for in the dance Astaire converts the turf of Others (a ship's engine room, a shoeshine parlor) into his own domain. He possesses the place, then strongly leads the girl into it; she moves from the role of spectator to that of junior partner (by invitation only) in the firm of Astaire and Company. The innocuous question, 'May I have this dance?' is meant absolutely literally when asked by Astaire. From the start, the dance belongs to him, and once the girl accepts his invitation to share it she, too, is possessed by the *maestro*. This 'typical' Astaire role – reversed so completely in the opening of *The Band Wagon* – is a concrete example of the donor's activity as teacher, guide, and lover, although we suspect that this donor takes more than he gives. Implicit in these scenes is the suggestion that the girl is Astaire's by right, since, after all, it is he who has ushered her into the privileged region (his realm) or into the dance – has freely chosen to share his magical powers inside with a creature of the outside.

As the case of the typical Astaire has demonstrated, the canny one is master of a passage which is, in the widest sense of the word, a sexual passage. Or, rather, erotic (since more is at issue here than carnal love alone). The phallus is the image of Eros, for, as Plato reminds us, he is the winged god who must be able to rise, linking previously separate bodies and minds by carrying them to the heights of ardour. This antique sense of Eros as the potent force which forges new unities and of the phallus as the emblem of the power of penetration and passage is retained today by psychoanalysts of the Freudian tradition. I follow their lead (and Plato's) in stressing that the dance master of the musical *knows* the Other Kingdom of the show in the biblical sense – erotically. The canny one can do it all – the making and the showing – can make the passage to the uncanny realm, can show the student/beloved its splendours, can make the beloved, can *make love and make it show*.

Parent/child

The *maestro* is more than a sexual partner, more than a teacher. In the role of parent, both functions are combined. The role is still an erotic one, in the sense already described, since it involves a passage to Other realms of being. The lover – hero of the sexual passage – now acts as a guide in the child's outward journey, serving as the exemplary being whose every step is to be imitated. In all senses (world mastery, sexual power) the parent has been where the child will go.

In his speech 'I am *not* Nijinsky . . .' Hunter/Astaire recognises himself as a rebellious child resisting all pressures to grow up. He can grow out of the enjoyment of his own helplessness into the show world and an Other identity only if the act of standing out poses as a *return* to the lost unity of mother and child. Thus, the first step in the growth of this petulant child is the exchange of mothers. When Hunter learns to dance, to make the show, he is no longer 'Mrs Hunter's little boy', but Gaby's darling child. The ballet star presides over his passage to potency so that, once Tony achieves full phallic status, she can discard the parental role for a fully sexual one. At the moment, however, she already has a lover – a fully-fledged adult who lives naturally in the ballet world which Tony is expected to enter. She is no virgin, but an experienced lover. The father of the show (the extravagant director) naturally delegates the raising of Tony to Gaby's mother, little dreaming that the child will grow up to depose him. In *The Band Wagon*, the 'father' of this classic Oedipal triangle is enacted by two individuals. The split weakens the paternal role, allowing Tony's eventual castration of both the mother's lover and the boss of the show to be accomplished with ease. That Tony *can* 'grow up' to potency is demonstrated very early in *The Band Wagon* by his dance in the shoeshine parlour; his conquest of alien space there serves as a promise that he will, when the time comes, be fully able to master the show. But to demonstrate in detail how the parent/child relationship is essential to the show-making process, we must consider its function in two other films.

In *Easter Parade*, Judy Garland plays the child to Astaire's benevolent father. Learning to dance seems at times like learning how to walk as Garland strives to live up to Astaire's expectations, fails and tries again. Astaire laughs off the mis-steps, soothes Garland's wounds, assures her she can make it into the place he already inhabits. But the child soon tires of childhood and desires to pass to the terminal status of lover/beloved. The parent here balks at the attempted transition. By refusing to give up his fatherly manner, Astaire disavows Garland's ambition. Discouraged by Astaire's reluctance to change roles, Garland becomes sloppy in her new role as show-maker. For her – and this is the point – show-making must be accompanied by love-making to guarantee the success of either endeavour. Once Garland confesses the problem, Astaire promptly reforms. That the final show is a tremendous success is in no small part due to Astaire's accession to an explicitly sexual role. Just in time for Easter, the parent is reborn as lover – Eros rises from the dead.

The child role in *Easter Parade* seems made to order for Garland; part of her appeal – in legend and on film – is precisely her childishness. Her capacity for bright-eyed wonder, her incredible vulnerability, even her tantrums are exploited to the hilt in *The Pirate*. She is there presented (by her then-husband, Vincente Minnelli) as an over-protected child of the backlands. Cut off from the world and from men, she has been brought to the capital to make her social and sexual debut. She comes to this Caribbean *port* (a doorway) in order to be married, having previously been absolute in her innocence – equally ignorant of love-making and show-making. Into this threshold situation leaps Gene Kelly, willing and able to push the girl into womanhood.

In a scene which speaks pre-rationally, directly, bypassing the mediation of the concept, the spectator is *attuned* (Heidegger's phrase) to the mood of Garland's psyche. Unable to voice her desires, she stares transfixed at the ocean as it pounds against the sea-wall. In the attack of the waves and the turmoil of their retreat, she seems to displace her yearnings, to realise their power, and perhaps their danger. An Other watches her gaze; it is Kelly, tuned in to her attunement to the sea. (The question of who speaks is here a complicated one: apparently, the sea speaks of Garland to Kelly, the watcher, who stands in for the spectator, who is expected to 'identify' with Kelly, who identifies with Garland, who identifies herself with the sea.) For Kelly (playing Serafin, the actor with the name of an angel), the vision is an invitation to release Garland's desire, to tear down the sea-wall, allow the waves to sweep her away. Serafin invites Mañuela (Garland) to his acrobatic magic show, hypnotises her by use of a mirror, and lets her see (and express) her Other self, so long repressed. Under his spell, Mañuela confesses her desire to be carried off by the pirate Macoco – raper of cities, ships and presumably women. Serafin proceeds to enact this dread personage, providing the fuel for Mañuela's extravagant visions of fire and destruction and setting up the incredible complications of the comedy which follows. Under Serafin's tutelage, Mañuela learns both how to distinguish fantasy from reality and how to act, to put on the show.

Mañuela's triumphant entry into the show world is staged at the point when she learns that Serafin is not, in reality, the pirate he pretends to be. While she has previously been wholly the object of Serafin's aggressive sexuality, it is now Mañuela who assumes the active stance. Stripping the role from the pretender, Mañuela takes the stage, acting out a spectacular show of rage. The unmasked actor is ridiculed, physically assaulted, proves inept in his defence. The end of the display of mock hatred finds the two actors – now equals – in each other's arms, confessing their mutual love.

The point is not only that love-making follows hard upon show-making and, indeed, is *produced* through the show, but that the parental role of the *maestro* must necessarily be abandoned at the stage when the child proves that she is now capable of 'making it' – when she crosses decisively into the Other (adult) world of the show.

Regression/castration

So far in this analysis of show-making musicals, a movement of emergence – and growth – has been stressed. But this assumption of skill and power, the passage from potential to actual being, is properly the student's movement, and not that of the donor who guides him. The Spanish word *rumbo*, signifying both course or direction and a lavish show (hence rumba, the spectacular erotic dance) is an apt description of Garland's progress in *The Pirate* and *Easter Parade* (also in *Summer Stock* and *A Star is Born*). It is appropriate, too, to Astaire's course of regeneration in *The Band Wagon*. The direction is forward – the *rumbo* of the musical is a linear thrust into alien regions of being which are conquered, assimilated into the self. Indeed, *The Pirate* might well be subtitled with Freud's slogan of manifest destiny 'where it (Id) was, there I (Ego) shall be', asserting Garland's ultimate mastery of the forces seething behind the seawall. But opposed to this progressive *rumbo*, a movement of regression can also be discerned. It appears most clearly in the story of the *maestro*, but is visible in the acts of the student as well. Yet both movements, progressive and regressive, aim towards the goal of the permanent show.

To the *maestro*, the Other kingdom is wholly familiar, deprived of its Otherness. He has already made the passage to virgin territory, and knows it fully. Unless he attempts to find and penetrate an endless series of unknown regions (Don Juan) he must be doomed to repetition of an act which has lost most of its danger and its savour. The presence of a student or child provides for the past-master an innocent with whom he can identify, making the journey seem a new one. His own story is over; there can be a plot for him only if he is reborn through his emotional investment in the child. To begin again, to make a fresh start – this ambition of the *maestro* is properly seen as a regression back to his childhood.

The guidance of the donor is retrogressive because this achieved hero, having no further place to go, can only circle back to identify himself with the student, who now acts in his place. The identification is only partial, however. The student knows that the *maestro* has been there before and is thus different from himself. In order for the two to be lovers (the aim of the musical plot), they must first be equals. The growth of the student/child to adult status will not alone accomplish a democracy; the child's progress must be accompanied by the regress of the adult, e.g. the *maestro* must be castrated.

The scene from *The Pirate* in which Mañuela first puts on her show narrates, in effect, the castration of the Gene Kelly character. The *maestro* is mastered; the god is deposed. Mañuela tears Serafin from his place in the skies (dancing on a tightrope high above the streets, swinging from the masts of tall ships – a sea-going tarzan); she reduces him to a moaning heap on the floor – a fallen angel, and/or a flaccid phallus. Castration is the appropriate word, because the actor is deprived of his potency – his show-making ability; he is forcibly displaced from the stage to the passive position of spectator.

Why is castration necessary? For the simple reason that the show-making plot seeks to accomplish a love show between two individuals who have until this point enjoyed a parent/child relationship. Because sexual love between the two is prohibited by the incest barrier, the parent is deprived of his parental powers at the same time that the child sheds his childishness. Both abandon their previous roles and assume an Other *persona* in order to consummate their love. The show-making musical must end with the spectacular triumph of Eros – a real or metaphorical 'wedding'.

Only in *The Pirate* is castration a violent act; Kelly actually pretends to have been killed in the fight with Garland. But Charisse in *The Band Wagon* and Astaire in *Easter Parade* voluntarily submit to the limitation of their powers, exchanging roles with little protest. At first glance, to prove the castration thesis apropos *The Band Wagon* would seem to be a difficult task. In the usual sense of the word, only the male is castrated (or threatened with it), while Cyd Charisse, though a parental figure, is most obviously female. Is castration here merely a metaphor for the act of sexual surrender? If so, the term seems so general as to lose all meaning. Can the mother be castrated? Regarding *The Band Wagon* the answer is yes, not only because the growth of the child deprives the mother of her power over him, but also because Charisse plays a quite special kind of parent – the phallic mother.

The mother who possesses a phallus is a personage both envied and threatening to Astaire's little boy. Not only is Charisse fully at home in the Faust project which he dreads to enter, but she is secure in her star status, while he has lost his. Her physical stature, her powerful legs, her mastery of the show-at-hand all tend to lend her virility in the eyes of the fragile, disconsolate Astaire. She possesses all that he lacks – skill, assurance, power in the show-world. Charisse is, indeed, something of a man-eater, perhaps a *vagina dentata* (an aspect again stressed by Minnelli in *Two Weeks in Another Town* and recognised by Kelly/Donen in *Singin' in the Rain*). She is cast in *The Band Wagon* as Astaire's teacher/mother, but is clearly self-sufficient without the child – she does not need him to complete her being. Astaire has reason to believe that their relationship will be difficult at best. While he hopes to be accepted as an adult, it is questionable that he will ever be welcomed as a powerless child.

But Charisse retracts her phallus, loses her frightening aspect. The mothering relationship flourishes, until finally Charisse dispenses with her material phallus (her lover) in favour of Astaire. If in *The Band Wagon* we look in vain for scenes of the female castration of the male, or the student of the parent, it is because the parental *maestro* is in this case a woman of virile aspect who must castrate herself in order to pass to the culturally approved role of the vagina – the wholly feminine beloved who can possess a phallus only as a gift from the man. This man is now Astaire, who has proved his potency by deposing Charisse's lover and boss (Charisse's 'husbands', Astaire's 'fathers') from their place in her heart and her show. Only when Astaire takes over both properties – show and woman – is the stage set for love. *The Band Wagon* can thus be seen as a film in which the usual male-dominant/female-subordinate roles are initially upside down. Its plot reverses this situation, establishes a 'normal' sexual relationship (culturally speaking) – one which is certainly more comfortable for Astaire, who is more accustomed to being the master than the child.

Primal fantasy/primal scene

At this point in our story, both *maestro* and student, parent and child have made the passage to the uncanny realm of the show. Each is now the canny one who has learned how to tap the forces uncovered by his passage, how to control them to make the show. As the artist, like the manufacturer, is commonly understood to own the thing he 'makes' (this is the basis of copyright law), so the show-maker can be said to possess the show-world he has built (remember here how Astaire gains possession of the floor and the woman by dancing). In addition, a successful penetration of a wholly Other world is almost always understood as establishing a claim to ownership (the basis not only of colonialism, but masculine supremacy as well). But there is another side to the Faustian saga of conquest just outlined. In each action of making/penetrating, the canny one not only possesses the Other kingdom – the woman, the love and the show – but is possessed by it. Eros has been unleashed in the act, and he is not a slave but a god. Any show which harnesses erotic power eventually discovers itself to be a runaway project, without brakes. The witch who hopes to control the demonic forces with which he consorts is yet their plaything; the actor on the show stage becomes possessed by the previously imaginary Other he impersonates. Our maker – Charisse, Astaire or Kelly – is also made in the passage to the love show; the one who passes is yet a passenger, is 'carried away' by it all.

To be possessed is desired in the theatre; possession is indeed an aim of the show-making process. The student of the show is trained to control his voice and his body until their movements become natural, even instinctual. The performer hopes to reach a stage at which the watchful, correcting functions of the mind can be disengaged, a point where the show spontaneously flows from the soul (or the Id) much as the surrealist goal was to write 'automatically' the unfiltered text of the unconscious. The act of *poiesis*, Plato reminds us, is dangerous (to the edifice of public morality, hence the State) precisely because it taps savage, subterranean forces. The artist at his most poetic is swept away (as by the waves of *The Pirate*), and this utter abandonment of the self to the Other is properly madness, according to the philosopher.

In the musical film, the show is more than words – it is embodied in the rhythmic contortions of the dance. The madness – the fantasy – moves from the mental realm to the physical one; it invades and controls the body of the dancer much as erotic passion passes 'naturally' from the head to the loins to action on the bed. We can therefore consider the musical to resemble the form of madness termed 'conversion hysteria', in which the body seems to take on a life of its own, independent of the conscious will of the subject, but is, in reality, merely the instrument of an unconscious drama which has passed from its normally invisible psychic sphere to materialise 'on stage' in the body through actions seen by all.

In short, the dance is symptomatic – a somatic manifestation of an interior agon. The play of muscle against muscle is the physical expression of a conflict of dread and desire. But it must be remembered that a symptom may also be a form of satisfaction of an instinct which could otherwise find no outlet, could not show itself. The symptom shows not only a psychic conflict but also the make-shift solution to the problem. It is 'sick' or 'mad' only insofar as 1) it prevents the subject from leading a 'normal' life (which is to say that we are all relatively sick) and/or 2) it is only a substitute for the 'real' satisfaction of the forbidden desire. To Freudian thought, the symptomatic show is a false, distorted reply to the originating desire; it is not a truthful showing but a misleading fiction which nevertheless demands to be 'believed' for the duration of the show. The permanent song, dance and love show which resolves the musical happily ever after can satisfy the raw desires only by drastically revising them. Yet this terminal lie issues from an astonishingly naked presentation of the original desire, later repressed in the show-making process. In the case of *The Band Wagon*, *Easter Parade* and *The Pirate* (and doubtless other musicals as well) the founding desire – the incest wish – is satisfied by the show, but only after the plot has converted both child and parent into the radically different characters of consenting, unrelated adults.

'In every case', J. McDougall (*International Journal of Psychoanalysis*, 53) writes, 'the [hysterical] symptom tells a story. Once decoded, the story always reveals the hero to be a guilty victim of forbidden wishes who has met a set-back on the pathways of desire. His symptoms might be said to result from the combined effects of his unconscious fantasy life and the structures of his ego defences.'

Our final reading of *The Band Wagon* plot is therefore as follows. The Astaire character begins, still under the spell of his mother, regarding himself as 'Mrs Hunter's little boy'. Forbidden from loving his real mother, he constructs a fantasy: accepting Cyd Charisse as a substitute mother, he grows phallic powers, metaphorically kills the father (director) of the show and Charisse's actual lover, preparing the way for a merger of the theatrical show with the love show. But since Astaire's 'ego-defences' still state quite clearly, 'Thou shalt not love thy mother', he can step into the shoes of the deposed lover only when Charisse deprives herself of her parental status by suffering auto-castration. The show of love can now be consummated.

This story sounds 'fantastic' precisely because it achieves a sexual possession of the mother which can occur only in the fantasy of the theatrical show. As I have tried to show earlier, constructing the show necessarily involves exchanging one identity for another, and then being lived by the role. In addition to this conscious exchange of identity, however, we can posit an unconscious exchange designed to satisfy a desire which has been repressed but not erased. This desire now irrupts in the context of the show, true to its original aim. The fiction that the mother is no longer the mother is constructed only to evade regression via a process of substitution; desire is not fooled by the mask but flows straight to the original mother – stage centre – who now moves rhythmically with her son in the love dance. Like all fantasies, this show is timeless. It will run 'for ever'.

There is another way to view the primal fantasy just described – no longer as a participant, but from the position of one off-stage. In this case, the individual accepts the show as all it pretends to be – the love show between two (unrelated) adults. The role of child has been displaced by the show-work from the stage to the spectator. The show is, after all, played for his benefit, awakening his desire, promoting his vicarious pleasure as he imagines himself in place of one or both of the lovers. He is the classic witness (and the subject) of the primal scene which psychoanalysis finds to be repeated, disguised and elaborated *ad infinitum* in the dreams of its patients; it is the scene in which the incestuous desire (and all later fantasy) is permanently rooted. The child watches the *show* – the show of his parents, whom he loves, with whom he is so firmly identified. He watches, afraid to interrupt the show, but yearning to cry, 'Enough!' This child is the ultimate spectator of the film show which he is unable to stop; the action on the screen is wholly beyond his control. The child can do nothing but watch (in secret, in silence, immobilised – ever paralysed – in his spy-place) the mysterious movements of those beings – the parents – who only now are clearly seen to live in an Other world, wholly beyond his reach of comprehension.

An examination of three representatives of the show-making subgenre of the musical has revealed that their story recounts, revises and sublimates an incestuous plot wherein the child is able to sexually love the parent through the triple strategy of 1) 'growing up' to (phallic) potency 2) castrating or otherwise deposing the parent's previous lover, and 3) depriving the parent of his/her parental status (another form of castration). The show-making musical is thus a primal fantasy – a mythical satisfaction of forbidden desire inspired by the child's witnessing of the scene of his parents' intercourse; which primal scene is re-presented in the theatrical situation itself, the spectator taking the role of the child who watches the love show from his secret place 'off-stage'.

Afterword

In *Three Essays on the Theory of Sexuality*, Freud asserts that 'anyone who looks down with contempt upon psychoanalysis from a superior vantage-point should remember how closely the enlarged sexuality of psychoanalysis coincides with the Eros of the divine

Plato.' In the above essay, I consider the Musical as the story – and finally the *show* – of Eros. The Musical is erotic in the Greek sense of the term – a sexuality that rises from the loins to invade and transform the domain of politics and *poiesis*. The common Greek image of erotic force is the winged phallos because, as Plato reminds us in *The Phaedrus* (252b), 'through the power of winged Eros, men possess the power to become like gods', to free themselves from the constraints of the everyday lived-world. The erotic drive is not only the passion to 'make' the other, but an assertion of dominion over the raw material of the world; it is the passion to 'remake' reality in the image of desire.

Not only does the musical relate a love story, but this erotic narrative is profoundly *anti-realistic*; as expressed in the passion to transgress and transcend all 'natural' boundaries of cinema. Eros must, according to Plato, 'reach for the skies', or the passion betrays itself. Or, according to Godard, the genre must *idealize* cinema, or it is nothing.

'Show-making' was originally written in 1975–6. But, a 1979 screening of *The Band Wagon* has convinced me that I overstressed the 'phallic' aspect of the Cyd Charisse character while neglecting her own fear of the show-making process.

I owe Patricia Mellencamp a debt of gratitude for alerting me to this over-emphasis. Despite the caveat, I firmly reassert the principle that the musical deploys a conquest plot which seeks to annul the temporal process in order to display the *permanent show* of love. It denies the decay of erotic passion. The pre-Fosse musical drives towards the moment of metaphoric orgasm in order to freeze the moment of jouissance into a permanent text of pleasure.

7 · Raymond Bellour: 'Segmenting/Analysing'

Quarterly Review of Film Studies, vol. 1, no. 3, August 1976, pp. 331–53

The following article by Raymond Bellour is potentially one of the most fruitful to be included in this collection; yet at the same time it proves to be one of the most frustrating. By proposing radically new approaches to the musical film it simultaneously suggests new paths and invites argument. Since the early days of structuralism, film critics have understood the importance of textual segmentation to any application of semiotic theory. In particular, Christian Metz laid the groundwork for further investigation in two articles, a theoretical treatise entitled 'La grande syntagmatique du film narratif' (*Communications*, 8, 1966) and a practical application to Jacques Rozier's film *Adieu Philippine* (*Essais sur la signification du cinéma*, vol. I). Since those articles, published over a decade ago, only sporadic efforts have been made to modify or further develop Metz's model. Bellour's segmentation of *Gigi* is thus a welcome addition to an all-too-neglected field. Nevertheless, I regret Bellour's decision to treat the image as sovereign, thus turning the soundtrack into a somewhat neglected secondary factor. Yet I remain delighted that this segmentation should give me the opportunity to analyse a film in such a carefully controlled, well-delineated context.

Bellour's careful segmentation permits him to isolate numerous altered repetitions, which he terms 'rhymes'. These rhymes, he claims, lie at the heart of the functional mechanisms proper to the Hollywood film. This insight, to my mind, is an essential one. Unless we can sense the way in which films, and especially the Hollywood variety, invite the spectator to make specific commutations based on highly apparent repetitions, then we shall never be able to understand the methods by which cinema makes meaning. Here again, however, I find myself frustrated by the very power and wide-ranging nature of Bellour's insight. I want to see the rhymes codified, identified, and compared (as indeed I have tried to do in my own article later in the collection). In a similar fashion, I am delighted by Bellour's comments on the way in which narrative is generated by the creation of dissymmetry within a context of symmetry. Instead of neglecting those segments which don't quite fit into a symmetrical arrangement, the critic is freed to consider the dynamic role which their very anomalous nature ascribes to them. But do all filmic texts handle the problem of dissymmetry in a similar fashion? Bellour treats *Gigi* as a transparent example of classical narrative, while I am convinced that the musical regularly undermines the conventions of classical narrative on which its narrative portions are so heavily dependent.

Rarely does an article provoke me to so many types of basic disagreement. The important articles are not those which we can agree with and file away, but those which gnaw at us, which push us to redefine our own thought, which challenge us to the point of disagreement. Raymond Bellour's 'Segmenting/Analysing' is such an article.

---

1 1/47

The film opens. Paris, the Bois de Boulogne, the Avenue des Acacias. The choryphaeus (commentator) of the musical comedy (Honoré) introduces himself and in a voice that is part-song, part-speech, states the theme: 'Little Girls': a theme immediately focused by the appearance of its instigator: 'This story is about a little girl in particular. . . Her name is Gigi.' Gigi passes by and slips away, opening up the theme to the narrative which borrows her name.

The film ends. The theme is taken up again: same set-up, same place, same shot. But now, behind the commentator a couple comes into view, moving in a different, mythical, time, a time apparently outside the narrative since it constitutes the solution of the narrative's enigma: Gigi, accompanied by her husband, Gaston.

Classical cinema (especially American classical cinema) depends heavily on such 'rhyming' effects. They carry narrative difference through the ordered network of resemblances; by unfolding symmetries (with varying degrees of refinement) they bring out the dissymmetry without which there would be no narrative. The classical film from beginning to end is constantly repeating itself because it is resolving itself. This is why its beginning often reflects its end in a final emphasis; in this, the film acknowledges that it is a result, inscribing the systematic condition of the course it follows by signing with a final paragraph the operation which constructs it throughout.

In this instance the repetition-resolution effect has a specific, but very common, character and this is its whole strength; it operates on a broad scale and very precisely, *from segment to segment*, that is, from one major narrative unit to another, from one major syntagmatic unit to another.

But what actually is a segment for the purposes of analysis? This comes down to asking first: with what kind of truth and applicability does the *grande syntagmatique* endow the definition of the segment and the reality of analysis?

2 On the 'grande syntagmatique'

Much has been written about the *grande syntagmatique*: for it, against it, based on it. The work for has perhaps been excessively subservient. That against has recently lacked intellectual generosity and imagination. I shall not recapitulate. But at the same time I shall assume familiarity. However, I shall need to retrace the line which carries it in the thinking of Christian Metz, in order to set my own procedure in context.

The constitution of the *grande syntagmatique* combines two complementary lines of thought, determined by the logic of discovery. This is in 1966, just two years after the impetus provided by '*Cinéma: langue ou langage?*'[1] On the one hand it is necessary to demonstrate by means of *a* code, i.e. *this* code, that *some* code is involved; in other words that codicity is no less effective in cinema than in other fields and that it is possible to try to master it and activate it there. Something no classification, taxonomy, 'montage table', etc. . . had been able to demonstrate, either because they were too formal, or not formal enough. In this sense, the *grande syntagmatique* is a theoretical operator: it actualises the concrete possibility of a semiology of the cinema because it brings its virtualness onto a material level. Moreover, this specific code seems, from both the logical and historical viewpoints, to be pre-eminently suited to illuminating the cultural make-up of film as the basis of a fiction, using a closed series of commutable syntagmatic types.

The interacting pressure of these two lines of thought explains how Metz was able to yield, though only in part, to the immediately punctured illusion of having 'found' THE code of cinema. Very soon, indeed almost at once, the *grande syntagmatique* ceases to be THE code, to become quite simply a (specific) code among others (an assertion *Language and Cinema*[2] goes over again and again to the point of dizziness on the level of codes). But the shadow of ambiguity is valuable. For while the *grande syntagmatique* may be one code among other codes which juxtapose and cross it, it envelops them and is superior to them in the proper sense of the word: that is, manifestly, as the consequence and condition of the fiction.

On the other hand, from its origins, or almost so, the *grande syntagmatique* was the object of a patient and rigorous self-criticism on Metz's part. It is therefore constantly deepened by contradictions turned on itself, in step with a logic of still improbable effects, which in a sense undermines the direct positivity of the code, but augments its potential pressure. From the first *Essais*, Metz confronted three basic objections. First, the gap between the autonomous shot and the seven other syntagmatic types; the sequence-shot (as the name indicates) through a kind of spatio-temporal expansion proves to contain the possibilities of seven other types; it thus imposes the need for a genuine bipartition of the initial chart[3]. Then in the seven other types, the discrepancy between the 'hard' and 'soft' types (which emerges in a concrete form in the syntagmatic analysis of *Adieu Philippine*). For example, between the bracketed syntagma and the non-diegetic insert on the one hand, said to be 'clear configurations, "recognised" with certainty and no possibility of error'; and on the other hand, the ordinary sequence and the scene, said to 'have fairly fluid contours so that it is sometimes difficult to draw them out of the mass and isolate them from the general filmic flux.'[4] (I would add to these a vacillation, first between the scene and the sequence, then between successions of scenes and/or sequences and weak instances of the episodic sequence, which sometimes raises questions.) Finally, the third and in my view most important point: 'The set of problems posed by the fact of alternation' which the two complementary forms (one a-chronological, the other chronological) of parallel and alternate syntagma are powerless to resolve.

> The solution would seem to assume that a rigorous semiological theory be established in order to account for *two facts* that are both pronounced in films though neither of them has yet been satisfactorily explained: (1) the phenomenon of what one might call the *transformation of the insert* (an autonomous segment with a single insert can easily be 'transformed' into an autonomous segment comprising multiple inserts and thus into an alternate type. . .(2) the distinction between *true alternation* (which establishes a narrative 'doubling' in the film) and *pseudo-alternation* (which may be reduced to a mere visual alternation within a unitary space or else derives simply from the fact that the *filmed subject* itself assumes a vaguely 'alternating' aspect within a certain relationship).[5]

Finally a third line of thought deriving logically from the other two: through the methodological investigation carried out by *Language and Cinema*, the code becomes genuinely a code; in other words, radically detached from the filmic text for which it is simply an abstract exponent, actualised there in the concrete form of the autonomous segment.[6] In an article written soon after, this concern prompted Metz to establish the triple criterion of demarcation for the autonomous segment in the 'diegetic film' (actually put into operation by Metz with his syntagmatic analysis of *Adieu Philippine*): 'The analyst of the classical film is justified in considering as a single autonomous segment any passage in the film which is not interrupted by a major change in the course of the plot, by punctuation, or by the abandonment of one syntagmatic type for another'.[7] The autonomous segment is thus consciously set off to the side of the text, in the direction of its obligatory intercodicity and of textual analysis.

All this has meant that today, Metz thinks (as I know from talking to him at length) that a new version of the *grande syntagmatique* is possible. (If so, why not do it, you may ask. Quite simply because science exists only as borne by a desire and desires are displaced – as Freud discovered. Only the imaginary realm of science believes that one always insists on finishing – in a limited period – what one has begun.) The new version of the *grande syntagmatique* would need to break down the positivist illusions frequently linked to the beginnings of any formalisation. It would thus more surely guard against the new positivism which the evolution of linguistics might tend to project onto film theory, by seeking simply to replace the structural model by the generative and transformational model. In safeguarding itself against both, the new version could combine the advances they have made. It would be wary of the plurality of levels which prohibits a strictly Chomskian model from ever rejoining its object, film, in the singularity of its textual system. Cinema will never be a language, nor film a grammar. It is not by chance that Nicolas Ruwet's poetic and musicological analyses owe as much if not more to the structural model as to the generative and transformational. But on the other hand, the new version of the *grande syntagmatique* would need to reinforce the level of abstraction in order to stamp out definitively any flattening structural effect, or any descriptive application between code and text, thus correcting earlier inadequacies. It would thus need to constitute a body of spatio-temporal matrices, where the present syntagmatic types, together with their complements and necessary modifications, would be arranged into an ordered series. Then the surface level, that is, the level of textual actualisation, would alone merit the name autonomous segment, presenting analysis with the constantly renewed singularity of a precise decomposition of the filmic chain.

This very special situation of the *grande syntagmatique* as a problematical, incomplete code, on the one hand prime and primary, on the other, a code among others, seems to have had two opposing results in the field of specific film analyses. Numerous works have developed in the direct line of the *grande syntagmatique*, either applying it literally, or occasionally seeking to perfect it by trying to diversify, enrich and lend flexibility to one or other of its types (but still necessarily remaining within the bounds of Metz's self-critique, which implies its transformation). These works thus reasserted the determining stability of this code, its capacity for historical and stylistic induction and its specific, practical (descriptive) and analytical instrumentality in the textual study of the large narrative units.[8]

On the other hand a number of textual analyses developed within the movement to establish a semiology of cinema and with a more or less explicit reference to Metz's thinking found themselves, not ignoring, but skirting the test of the *grande syntagmatique*. For some this was doubtless because they only placed themselves on the level of the segment (or fragment) in order to concentrate on the work of its smaller units. Or because they started from a segment or a number of segments (or fragments) in order to evaluate their function in the productivity of the textual whole.[9] But this detour extends even to analyses bearing on a film as a whole and thus more or less consciously situated within the perspective defined by Metz as that of the global textual system. I have in mind, consciously bringing together works of very varied nature and intention, *Foetus astral*, by Jean Monod and Jean-Paul Dumont,[10] the collective work of *Cahiers du Cinéma* on *Young Mr. Lincoln*,[11] the book by Claude Bailblé, Michel Marie and Marie-Claire Ropars on *Muriel*,[12] Stephen Heath's long study on *Touch of Evil*[13] and my own analysis of *North by Northwest*.[14] The detour is all the more notable in the last two examples in that the analyses (in other ways very different) depend on a segmentation: a primitive or semi-primitive segmentation which justified Stephen Heath's note following his découpage: 'The segmentation here operates at the level of the narrative signified according to the simple criteria of unity of action, unity of characters, unity of place: it has no analytic status other than that of allowing reference to the film as narrative.' I ought to have added that note to the découpage tables in my own study, were it not obvious that, like Stephen Heath's, they constantly brushed up against the *grande syntagmatique*, without seeking to constrain it and above all, without risking being constrained by it.

This is the risk I should like to take here, because of what it seems to me that it can teach us. Starting from the *grande syntagmatique* and going well beyond it, I will concentrate on the systematic modelling of the narrative units of the classic American film. Perhaps as a *genre* film, which is profoundly coded, *Gigi* shows this modelling better than others. But I remain convinced that, within the irreducible arrangement of each of its textual instances, such a modelling process governs the majority of the films of American high 'classicism.'

This beginning of an analysis of *Gigi* does not aim to fill any gap between the present state of the *grande syntagmatique* and a second, as yet, virtual state. Analysis could no doubt situate that gap and consider it in terms of its own logic. But no more. Here therefore, the *grande syntagmatique* is fully applied (that is, with all its 'lacks') as the operator of the analysis: given first, the descriptive logicalisation it effects on its own level; then, the syntagmatic reference it opens up in the analysis by its capacity to instigate a generalised syntagmatic segmentation. As we shall see, segmentation is a *mise en abîme*, a 'plumbing of depths', a process which has no end theoretically – which does not mean that it has no meaning, in fact that is its whole meaning. Through the differential play it sets up between various levels, segmentation allows us to experience the increased plurality of textual effects.

But the present analysis is only a beginning and within such limited bounds it is by definition far more the setting in place of an analytical framework, a setting in perspective, than analysis itself. I have limited myself to a major extent (but on the level of the smaller units, minimally) to the recording of the differential rhyming and repetition effects which structure the development of the narrative. Their fundamental determining role in the constitution of the classical film at the level of the fragment, the segment, or the film as a whole has been shown by earlier analyses.[15] To me it seemed striking to make them stand out within the crossing of levels at work here. I could obviously not do much more than categorise and list these rhyming effects; what I could not do was produce them in the logic of their textual progression, the material work of their traversal: analysis is not reducible to its framework. Imagination, mine and yours, has to give back to the elements I have broken down, the space that constitutes and is constituted by them; in other words, their textual volume.

3 Segmental

The syntagmatic breakdown of *Gigi* which reveals 47 autonomous segments in the image track of the film (1 to 47 in the summary table) calls for a number of observations.

(a) The extreme redundancy between the three demarcatory criteria demonstrates a high degree of classicalness.

(b) In this sound and musical film, the image is sovereign on the level of syntagmatic demarcation. The instrumental or vocal numbers are lower or equal to the segmental limits, with one exception – Gigi's song ('I don't understand the Parisians') straddles segments 9 and 10, so creating a kind of autonomous sound segment. The voice and dialogue are strictly subject to the phenomenality of the image, its temporal outline. As far as the music is concerned, while its fades occasionally do not coincide with the fades of the segmental demarcation, overall and in relation with the song, it simply reinforces the stability of the autonomous segments of the image. The *grande syntagmatique* of the image-track in the classical film, because of the power specific to the diegesis, is clearly something like THE code – the one which permits the rest.

(c) This strict application of the *grande syntagmatique* ran up against two difficulties:

(i) On the fringes of the scene/sequence vacillation (not generally very strong here) two hesitations in the breakdown: between segments 10 and 11, and within the very long segment 30. A (relatively) slight impression of continuity led me to mark a segment in the first instance. In the second I hesitated over a sequence/scene/sequence tripartition (found as a/b/c in the sub-segmentation).

(ii) The impossibility, in a film which includes no alternating syntagma on the significative level, of giving an account of the alternations (where does the true begin or the pseudo end?) which more or less structure numerous segments: 1, 8, 13, 15, 17, 21 (an episodic sequence which is at the same time an alternate syntagma, but lacks simultaneity between the two temporal series, like the alternate syntagma of *Adieu Philippine*, which Metz used as a basis for raising the question of alternation), 24, 25, 26 (in which the segmental level loses a true scene between Honoré and Mamita), 30, 35 (a bastardised episodic sequence whose first two episodes are a kind of summary of an alternate syntagma) and 47.

The autonomous shot, despite its frequency (9 segments), brings few complications – here again the classic model is in full play.

This breakdown demonstrates two conditions essential to the development of the textual logic.

(a) First the high number of repetitions and rhymes which, within the mirror effect of segments 1–47, operate *from segment to segment*. Not through their syntagmatic forms of course. At this level, the syntagmatic type is simply one pertinence among others, although profoundly different: as a specific exponent of the textual surface it affects, it is the form in which pertinences of varying stability (places, characters, actions, musical or sung motifs) are inscribed in the cinematic signifier, their disposal within each segment being what conveys the narration from segment to segment.[16] In this sense, what I am here calling segmental (i.e. the textual surface delimited by different forms of autonomous segments) corresponds to the level Metz calls 'suprasegmental' in terms of codic units.

One has only to refer to the summary table to recognise the operations taking place, the repetitions, scored by differences, between segments

4 and 37	15 and 41–42
6, 16 and 20	19, 27 and 32
7 and 31	23 and 46
8, 28 and 29	24, 25 and 26
14 and 40	36 and 39.

(b) From segment 36, certain of these operations touch a large number of the final segments of the film (37, 39, 40, 41–42, 46, 47). Such concentration is worth noting: it shows how, through its segmental outlines, the film resolves itself by repetition, through a kind of generalised condensation of the narrative which, on the formal level, conveys it to its ending.

But these chains of repetition-resolution effects are inscribed within the bounds of autonomous segments only to break them down in multiple ways. For if the classical film tends, as Metz saw clearly, towards the sequence (the autonomous segment)[17] far more than towards the shot, it does so at the cost of an equally profound tendency to inscribe the segment within a system of narrative commutation with units which are both superior and, above all, inferior to the segment, with a bearing well beyond the divisions of the filmic chain.[18] These two major movements simultaneously attract and repel, contradict and complement each other. This is what makes it both necessary and difficult to distinguish them: their (decomposable) merging, which turns the film into the space of a generalized segmentality, is the condition which transforms the filmic surface into a textual volume.

4 Supra-segmental/infra-segmental

On the one hand the classical film thus tends towards units which can be superior to the segment (supra-segment or macro-segment), even though they very often coincide with it. Both ordinary and specialised language refers to these as 'sequences'; they often correspond to 'units of scenario'.[19] They are generally determined by a kind of global unity of space, place and action. In *Gigi* this is the case with segments 24, 25 and 26, all situated at Trouville in the course of the same day and involving the same characters (thus constituting a kind of episodic supra-sequence). It is also the case, in a very different way, with segments 12 and 13, the one denoting, by means of an extremely rapid autonomous shot, the front of the Palais de Glace (neither Gaston nor Gigi are visible, but we know that they are walking towards the building and that they are going to go in); the other, the scene which unfolds inside the rink. But unity of place is not an imperative, if the narrative movements prove too dissimilar in spite of the transitions which bind them; it thus seems more correct not to combine segment 27 (XVI) where Alicia persuades Mamita to accelerate Gigi's education and segments 28 and 29 (XVII) which are devoted to the educational sessions. The supra-segment is a kind of unified minor dramatic mould which is what justifies its also being able to cover several different locations in succession. Hence segments 3, 4, 5 and 6 (III) which preside over the meeting of Gaston and Honoré, or segments 30 and 31 (XVIII) and 43, 44, 45 and 46 (XXVI), which present in one block Gaston's contradictory reactions to Gigi's transformation.

The determination of the supra-segment is obviously less rigorous than that of the autonomous segments because it is not determined by any cinematic specificity, but derives solely from the pressure of the textual system. It is therefore to a profound degree subject to the singularity of each film; and it depends on analysis which gives it an intermediary function between the segments and the large film sections (A, B, C, D, E here) which distribute the dramaturgy of the narrative. Its interest, like that of any découpage operation, is primarily descriptive and involves circumscribing the rhyming effects which unite or superimpose themselves on those of the autonomous segments. Through a kind of internal tautology, the segments grouped into a supra-segment rhyme among themselves all the more strongly within this new unit. An operation which in one sense adds little, but is nevertheless striking since it concentrates the rhyming effect in the narrative succession. This is so in the case of segments 24, 25 and 26 at Trouville mentioned earlier, which group three 'sequences' supported by the same characters; likewise segments 28 and 29 which bring together into one 'education' syntagma the two episodic sequences in Alicia's apartment. But the most eloquent are clearly those large-scale rhymes which are established across the film from supra-segment to supra-segment: the one clear example relates to the two 'Maxim's' sets, which unite segments 14 and 15 and segments 40, 41 and 42, in VIII and XXV respectively. There are other effects at work between sets, but their nature is more partial and is determined by the complementary test of sub-segmentation.

For in this film, as in the classical film generally, it is clearly on the level of the units lower than the segment that the multiple echo-play, which structures and constrains the progressive resolution of the textual system throughout, is systematised in a much broader way. At this lower level, let us consider what I shall call *elementary* sub-segmentation; i.e. the sub-segmentation which defines two or more successive times within the continuity of the same segment, each circumscribing a small scene. I mean this in the dramatic, not syntagmatic sense, obviously.

It will be recalled that Metz invoked a third criterion to determine the demarcation between two autonomous segments: 'a major change in the course of the plot'. The criterion is clearly imprecise: what is a major change? But this is to pose the question badly. For demarcation in terms of the 'plot itself'[20] is nearly always obvious: the absence of the two other criteria almost automatically entails the transparence of the third. This stems from the fact that the classical film defines its segmental units by a series of breaks in the signified of temporal denotation: only a major change in the course of the plot can manifest the break when it is not done by punctuation or variation in treatment. The imprecise criterion is therefore the sure one. Through a kind of tautological proof, a narrative change which entails no segmental mark can only be a 'minor' change; but in return, the minor change will often be far less minor than others which are nevertheless sanctioned by segmental demarcation, precisely because the change introduced into the course of the plot by the other two criteria would not exist without them (except in cases of redundancy of course, and these are always numerous). Consider for example the mutation introduced into the narrative by the appearance of a character (major or minor as the case may be) and inversely, the slightness of the change denoted by the demarcation through punctuation between the autonomous shot of the facade of the Palais de Glace and the scene inside which follows. In other words, segmental découpage determined by the multiple inscription of the signified of temporal denotation in the filmic signifier only half coincides (occasionally more, occasionally less) with the unfolding of the plot and the succession of narrative actions. Hence a series of dissociations which open the way to an operation of sub-segmentation.

The episodic sequence (and the same would be true of the bracket syntagma) has a particular privilege in this context, arising out of the precise demarcation of each episode. This demarcation is effected again (but at a lower level, as a 'sub-segmentation') by the diegesis itself, in most cases by internal punctuation (for the sake of consistency, let us call it a sub-punctuation). On the one hand episodes are thus almost always linked together (as are the segments in certain supra-segments) by a succession of rhyming effects, as in the case of the various episodes of segments 14, 21, 28 and 29.[21] On the other, a certain episode may establish rhyming effects over a distance with some segment or sub-segment. This is how the overall rhyme linking segments 14 and 20 takes its precise shape: the fourth episode of segment 14 (14d), in which Liane and Gaston enter Maxim's, is repeated by segment 40, where Gigi and Gaston enter in their turn.

Inversely, the criteria of sub-segmentation in the other segments are determined outside any specific inscription in the cinematic signifier. Their indisputable indeterminate character should not be taken as a cause for hesitation. True scenes are constituted nevertheless. They rest on disjunctions provoked by characters' entries and exits, particularly emphatic in this *genre* film and strongly marked by the dynamic of theatrical representation. The locations, actions, instrumental and vocal motifs, clearly all give powerful support to the stage scene effects organised between characters. But they do not have the same degree of pertinence: the instrumental or vocal motifs, because their limits are almost always inferior or equal to the segment, only partly coinciding with that of the sub-segment; the actions, because they are not truly divisible into segments in the same way and tend to be diluted in the overall mass of narrative signifieds; the locations, because the temporal form which distributes them is already the precise object of the *grande syntagmatique*.

Scenes thus appear, opening up multiple networks of rhymes.

Right from segment 1, the fifteen shots which succeed each other before Gigi appears show Honoré in the position of commentator (1a), as he will be again in the first episode of segment 14 (14a); then again in sub-segment 34b, after the disappearance of Gaston. In the same way in segment 32, the disappearance of Gigi in shot 154 opens a brief scene between Mamita and Gaston which responds to the one which preceded it in segment 7 and the one which succeeds it by the same means in sub-segment 30b, before being renewed in segment 31.[22]

On the other hand, the sub-segmental divisions allow the establishment of new commutations on the basis of intermediary sets between the sub-segment and the segment, the segment and the supra-segment. Thus the first 'education' set which overlaid segment 8 and sub-segment 9a following it finds its full echo in supra-segment XVII (28 and 29). In the same way the very long sub-segment 30c, sub-segment 43b and the short segments 44 and 45 mark with a very sharp repetition effect Gaston's two departures and returns, which prelude his decision first to keep Gigi, then to marry her. In this way an overall rhyme is established between sub-segment 30c and segment 31 on the one hand, and segments 43, 44, 45 and 46 on the other; supra-segment XXVI in other words. This last rhyme serves to increase in a major way the condensation which brings together in the final section (E) a series of earlier elements from the four other sections. Space does not allow for a demonstration of the subtle way in which condensation, in this last example, only touches segment XXVI from the starting point of the earlier effect which condenses (pre-condenses) supra-segments XIV and XXVI in supra-segment XVIII. But to make the text's productive return on itself fully readable, it would be necessary to go much further into the decomposition of its elements: i.e. it would be necessary to sub-segment the sub-segmentation.

5 (Sub-supra) segmental/textual

For sub-segmentation goes much further than this. Up till now I have channelled it into scene effects, corresponding to one or more shots; and in the first case, always either to very long shots (like 34b) or to the more specifically determined units in the episodic sequence.[23] I have, moreover, simply brought out successive dissociations in terms of a linearity which sometimes corresponds exactly to the truth of the text, but more often only in part, mimicking its truth with a representative approximation which is neither altogether false nor altogether true.[24] This is the reason for my qualification of that first sub-segmentation as *elementary*.

Complex sub-segmentation goes much beyond this. It might be called *micro-segmentation* – indicating a movement, which is the progressive work of textual and analytical pressure. For here there is no longer anything which corresponds to the precise distinction between segmentation and sub-segmentation. Before segmental demarcation there are only degrees of narrative expansion. This is why complex segmentation does not have anything to do with the limits of the shot, even though the play that is set up with the demarcatory boundary of the shot in turn constitutes a textual pertinence and a stylistic index.

Here I can only give two very summary examples of this movement.[25]

(a) *Segment 33*. Shot 302 shows Gigi in her room (this décor appears here for the first time); she is alone, stretched out on the bed, stroking her cat and she gets up to open the door to Gaston within the continuity of the same shot. This beginning of a scene is soon matched by a true scene, the long autonomous shot of segment 38, in which Gigi is singing in her room, holding her cat in her arms. The simplicity of this arrangement shows clearly the way in which the film proceeds through the varied duplication of its successive elements. Moreover it completes the condensation effect operating between the fifth section of the film and the four others: from segment 37 to segment 47 there is none which does not repeat a moment, a segment, or a sub-segment, from the four others, scored by the variation which carries the film to its end.

The three quite unequal sub-segments which follow (b/c/d) are inscribed along three axes which, because the sub-segmentation is not developed, only emerge incompletely: the first, which covers almost the whole of the segment (302–307), is inscribed in the series of scenes between Gigi and Gaston; the second, determined by Mamita's appearance in shot 308, is inscribed in the series of multiple scenes or scene-fragments between Gigi, Mamita and Gaston (in particular, it ushers in the dramatic and equally very brief 43a); the third, after Gigi has rushed to her room, is inscribed by means of a second internal split in shot 308, in the series of scenes, peaceful and dramatic by turns, which bring together Mamita and Gaston.

(b) *Segment 47*. Here again, internal splitting of the shot brings out three minuscule sub-segments in the last two shots of the film: (a) in shot 348, Honoré is singing, leaning on a tree in close medium shot; (b) in shot 349, Gigi and Gaston advance at a slant across the lawn and go towards a cab which they climb into, followed by the camera which then loses them to rejoin (c) within the continuity of the same shot, Honoré in the same fixed frame of the preceding shot.

This final example gives a clear indication of how the progressive decomposition of the dramatic instances of the filmic chain, opened up by the decomposition of the *grande syntagmatique*, leads of itself and more or less inevitably towards internal analysis of the segments on the one hand and on the other, towards a comparative analysis of the segments which echo each other. It can be seen that the final segment, which displays a clearcut classicism, is constructed on an a/b/a alternation which reproduces that of the initial segment of which it is the resolution: in both places, it is clearly between Honoré and 'the rest' that a narrative alternation is established. But at the start it is done in 21 shots which would need to be broken down; for example it would be seen that neither the first nor the last shot shows Honoré, and that the last shows Gigi alone, because the narrative is beginning; in the final segment it is accomplished in two shots which both show Honoré and in between the two Gigi, but with her husband Gaston.

At this micro-systematic level, analysis encounters the increased dispersion and constraint of the specific codes (codes of camera movement, looks, scale of shots, etc. . .) deployed within and throughout the macro-systematic code of the *grande syntagmatique*. Analysis meets anew with the voluminous pressure of the textual system, the full organic play of its differential repetitions. For example, the segmental analysis thus increased, operating from segment to segment as from supra-segment to sub-segment, would end by constructing, on the basis of the multiple scenes 'at Gigi's', the immense paradigm of entries and exits (there are others, but this is the most obvious) sustaining the micro-systematic structuration of the narrative units of the film (the large, medium and the less large, which, as Metz clearly saw, are still remarkably large precisely because they are the smallest).[26]

6 Segmental/familial/conjugal

To conclude, let me note a final, fundamental effect, proper to many American classical films, whereby the textual volume multiplies and closes off doubly the field of its own expansion. The systematic accumulation of symmetries and dissymmetries throughout the filmic chain, decomposed by the work of a generalised segmentation, constantly mimics and reproduces (because the one produces the other) the schema of family relations which founds the narrative space.

Gigi on the one hand, Gaston on the other, are two children brought up, in accordance with their sex, by a substitute mother (Mamita) and a substitute father (Honoré). A triple dissymmetry is inscribed in this symmetry, which pledges Gigi and Gaston to each other from the outset.

(a) One man, Honoré, corresponds to two women, Mamita and Alicia, in the role of adoptive substitute parent.

(b) A genealogical gap makes Gaston Honoré's nephew and Gigi the grandchild of Mamita and grand-niece of Alicia.

(c) A clear difference in age between Gigi and Gaston reproduces this genealogical gap, making one already a man, the other still a child.

The mutual feeling between Gigi and Gaston is crystallised in the supra-segment (XV) at Trouville. These three segments (the analysis lacked the opportunity to go into this point) are partly constructed on a narrative alternation which juxtaposes Gigi and Gaston on the one hand, and on the other, Honoré and Mamita, who meet in the film for the first and last time. They seem to be bound by an old love and go so far as to evoke the marriage which might have united them. This retrospective marriage clearly simply serves to reflect the as yet potential marriage of Gigi and Gaston. But it suggests much more than that. At this precise moment, the bar of dissymmetry jumps from one generation to another, with the help of a single reply. When Mamita tells Honoré with an insistence of no use to the plot, but necessary to the symbolic level: 'Gigi is my grand-daughter', Honoré's gallantry, which is structural in the proper sense, prompts him to reply: 'Grand-daughter, no. Daughter.' What clearer way of indicating that the children they have not had are obviously those they have both adopted, whom the film is to unite in marriage. In this way, an incest fiction, so favoured by the classic-romantic imagination, is established. The dissymmetry obviously reappears, like Alicia, who is absent from this four-term structure. But the dissymmetry of the structures serves what it hides and allows to be resolved: thanks to a discrepancy in age, Gigi is to recover in Gaston the substitute for a father even more strangely absent than the mother who is heard singing as a voice-off, and Gaston recovers in Mamita the obvious substitute for a mother of whom not a word is spoken.

This then is the story the film tells us, within a narrative which makes of the segmental the textual condition for a happy slide from the familial into the conjugal, and so assigns itself as an object the resolution of Oedipus. This is the effect of textual production which I tried to grasp in terms that were both different and rigorously complementary, in an analysis of Alfred Hitchcock's *North by Northwest*, as an effect I called 'symbolic blockage'.

Section	Supra-segment	Seg-ment	Place	Sub-segment	Characters	Shots	Syntagma	Music	Action
	0	0	Titles over engravings			x		Champagne Gigi	
A	I	1	The Bois	a	Honoré	1–15	sequence	'Bois' theme	Honoré introduces the Bois de Boulogne and himself: the bachelor stockholder and a lover of women.
				b	Honoré Gigi	16–21		'Little Girls' theme/by Honoré	He praises little girls and introduces Gigi, playing with some friends. She passes behind him and goes off through the Bois.
	II	2	At Gigi's (ext./int.)		Gigi Mamita	22–24	sequence	Mother's singing voice-off	Gigi arrives at her grandmother Mamita's and is reminded that it is the day of her visit to Aunt Alicia.
	III	3	Paris At Gaston's (ext.)		/Honoré/	25	autonomous shot	'Little Girls' variation	A cab crosses a square and stops in front of a luxurious building.
		4	At Gaston's (int.)		Gaston tradesman valet	26	autonomous shot		His uncle's visit is announced to Gaston Lachaille. He finishes dealing with a few matters and goes out.

Section	Supra-segment	Segment	Place	Sub-segment	Characters	Shots	Syntagma	Music	Action
		5	At Gaston's (ext.)		Honoré Gaston	27–28	sequence		The meeting between the uncle and the nephew who go off in a cab across Paris.
		6	Paris		Honoré Gaston	29–40	scene	'It's a bore' theme, then sung by Honoré/Gaston	Honoré praises the charms of life (Paris, wine, women, high society). Gaston responds that everything bores him and stops the cab.
	IV	7	At Gigi's (ext./int.)		Gaston Mamita	41–48	scene		Gaston arrives at Mamita's. They talk about Gigi. Gaston is astonished by the 'lessons' Alicia is giving her.
	V	8	At Alicia's (ext./int.)		Alicia Gigi	49–64	sequence		Gigi arrives at Alicia's running. The lesson is on how to eat ortolans. Conversation on marriage.
		9	At Alicia's (int.)	a	Alicia Gigi	65–67	scene		Lesson (continuation): jewels, cigars. Conversation on love and art. Alicia leaves.
				b	Gigi	68–71	scene	'The. . .	Gigi inveighs against the Parisians and love and goes off.
	VI	10	Le Jardin des Tuileries		Gigi	72–75	sequence	. . . Parisians' by Gigi	Gigi continues singing as she crosses the Tuileries and ends up sitting on a bench.

		11	Le Jardin des Tuileries		Gigi Gaston	76–82	scene		Gaston arrives in a cab, recognises Gigi ('Gaston, do you make love all the time?') and teases her as he takes her along to the Palais de Glace where he is meeting Liane d'Exelmans.
	VII	12	The skating rink (ext.)		/Gigi Gaston/	83	autonomous shot	waltz	The façade of the Palais de Glace
		13	The skating rink (int.)		Gigi Gaston Liane skating teacher	84–90	sequence	waltz	They enter and sit down. On the rink are Liane and her skating teacher. Gigi finds her common and vulgar and leaves suddenly. Liane joins Gaston and reminds him that they are to meet Honoré at Maxim's. They leave.
B	VIII	14	At Maxim's (entrance)	a	Honoré (+x)	91	episodic sequence	Maxim's theme	Honoré introduces Maxim's and praises it.
				b	Baron de la Cour. Girl.	91–92		Maxim's theme chorus in speech/song	The Baron de la Cour enters with a 'belle'.
				c	Honoré. Girl	92–93		,, ,,	Honoré enters with a 'belle'.
				d	Gaston Liane	93–94		,, ,,	Gaston enters with Liane.
		15	At Maxim's (room)		Gaston Liane Honoré	95–105	sequence	'She is so gay tonight', by Gaston	At the table, Liane is in high spirits, Gaston gloomy. 'She is not thinking of me.' Honoré asks Liane to dance. Liane grows more and more exuberant. Gaston increasingly bad-tempered.

Section	Supra-segment	Seg-ment	Place	Sub-segment	Characters	Shots	Syntagma	Music	Action
	IX	16	At Honoré's (int.)		Gaston Honoré Manuel	106–121	scene	'It's a bore' by Honoré/Gaston, then Manuel	Gaston arrives at his uncle's to announce that Liane is being unfaithful with the skating master. Honoré takes him to Honfleur where the couple are hiding, to settle the affair in a gentlemanly way.
	X	17	At Honfleur (ext./int.)		Honoré Gaston Liane skating teacher	122–134	sequence		Honoré and Gaston arrive at an inn and surprise the couple. Gaston offers the man a thousand francs to disappear and says goodbye to Liane who faints.
		18	Newspaper		(Gaston Liane)	135	autonomous shot		A front page with a photo of Liane. 'Sugar Prince breaks with Liane d'Exelmans.'
	XI	19	At Alicia's		Alicia Mamita	136	autonomous shot		Alicia and Mamita comment on Liane's 'suicide'.
	XII	20	At Honoré's		Gaston Honoré Manuel	137	autonomous shot		Gaston arrives at Honoré's and is congratulated by Honoré on his first suicide; he dissuades him from shutting himself away and advises him rather to live it up.

C	XIII	21	At Gigi's (int.)/	A	a	/Gigi/ (Gaston)	138	sequence	Gigi's hands hold an illustrated programme: 'Gaston Lachaille opens Pré Catelan for a gigantic party.'
			Pré Catelan	B	b	Gaston Honoré	139–141		Honoré enjoying himself at a table with several girls while Gaston yawns.
			At Gigi's (int.)/	A	a	/Gigi/ (Gaston)	142		Gigi's hands hold an illustrated programme: 'Who will be Gaston Lachaille's Queen at the battle of flowers?'
			The Bois	C	c	Gaston	143–144		In a flower-covered float, Gaston, looking bored beside a girl.
			At Gigi's (int.)/	A	a	/Gigi/ (Gaston)	145		Gigi's hands hold an illustrated programme: 'Two thousand guests invited to Gaston Lachaille's masked ball.'
			At Gaston's (int.)	D	d	Gaston Honoré	146–148		Honoré looks for Gaston in the costumed crowd and finds him slumped in a corner on a couch.
			At Gigi's (int.)	A	a	/Gigi/ (Gaston)	149		Gigi's hands hold an illustrated programme: 'Gaston Lachaille invites the opera company home.'

Section	Supra-segment	Seg-ment	Place	Sub-segment	Characters	Shots	Syntagma	Music	Action
	XIV	22	At Gigi's (int.)	a	Gigi Mamita Gaston	149–154	scene	'Little Girls' whistled by Gigi	The bell rings. Gigi gets up and opens the door to Gaston. Mamita is preparing a cassoulet in the kitchen. Gaston decides to put off his party and sends Gigi with an apology.
				b	Mamita Gaston	155–156		Mother's voice off	Mamita and Gaston talk about Honoré.
		23	At Gigi's (int.)		Gigi Gaston Mamita	157–175	scene	'Champagne' by Gigi, Gaston, Mamita	Gaston and Gigi play cards. Gigi makes him promise that if she wins he will take her with him to Trouville. She cheats and wins. Gaston is furious but gives in, agrees to take them. They sing and dance with Mamita as they empty a bottle of champagne.
	XV	24	At Trouville The beach The sea		Gigi Gaston Girl Man Honoré Mamita	176–183	sequence	'Champagne'	While Gaston and Gigi frolic in the water, Honoré is about to pass a note to a girl when he catches sight of Mamita on the beach, greeting him. He puts away the note and a man goes into the girl's cabin.

		25	At Trouville Tennis	Gigi Gaston Girl Man Honoré Mamita	184–194	sequence	'Champagne'	Honoré arrives on the tennis court. The girl, dressed to kill, is solemnly playing with her admirer on one side. On the other, Gaston is playing with Gigi, who is running about like a mad thing under the amused eye of Mamita.
		26	At Trouville The terrace The beach	Gigi Gaston Girl Honoré Mamita	195–223	sequence	'I remember it well' by Honoré/Mamita	Gigi and Gaston on the beach with a pair of donkeys. Mamita watches from the terrace, laughing. Honoré is about to follow the girl as she comes into the hotel when he catches sight of Mamita and goes to sit beside her. They evoke past love at length. Night falls. Gigi and Gaston return, dragging the donkeys.
D	XVI	27	At Alicia's (int.)	Mamita Alicia	224–235	scene		Alicia warns an amazed Mamita about Gaston's likely passion for Gigi and persuades her to speed up Gigi's education before the return of Gaston who has left for Monte-Carlo.

Section	Supra-segment	Seg-ment	Place	Sub-segment	Characters	Shots	Syntagma	Music	Action
	XVII	28	At Alicia's (int.)	a	Alicia Gigi	236	episodic sequence	'Little Girls'	The lesson in manners: how to serve coffee, which Gigi spills.
				b	,, ,,	237			Lesson in manners: how to walk, how to sit down. Not very successful.
				c	,, ,,	238			Lesson in manners: tasting wine, on which Gigi gets tipsy.
				d	,, ,,	239			Lesson in manners: choosing a cigar, which Gigi snaps in two.
		29	At Alicia's (int.)	a	Alicia Mamita Gigi mannequin couturier	240–246	episodic sequence	'Little Girls'	Presentation of a dress, which Mamita and Gigi like, Alicia doesn't like.
				b	Alicia Mamita Gigi etc. . .	247–250			
				c	Alicia Mamita Gigi etc. . .	251-254			A second dress, which Mamita and Gigi like, Alicia doesn't like.
				d	Alicia Mamita Gigi etc. . .	255–256			A third dress, which Mamita and Gigi don't like and Alicia chooses.

XVIII	30	At Gigi's (int.)	A	a	Gigi Mamita Gaston	257–268	sequence	 'Little Girls'	Gigi tries on the dress and is aghast. Gaston arrives at Gigi's. She rushes straight into her room and returns in a white dress. Gaston, who doesn't accept the metamorphosis, loses his temper and leaves, then returns to invite Gigi to tea at the 'Reservoirs'. Mamita is against it and Gigi goes back to her room.
				b	Mamita Gaston	269–275		'She is a babe', by Gaston	Mamita explains to Gaston that she cannot let Gigi go out with him alone. Gaston loses his temper, insults Mamita and leaves.
		From Gigi's back to Gigi (ext.)	B	c	Gaston	276–289		'Gigi' by Gaston	He walks across Paris as far as the Tuileries, where he met Gigi earlier, and returns. When he left, Gigi was only a charmless child; on his return, a girl with whom he is in love.
	31	At Gigi's (ext.)			Gaston Mamita	290–291	scene		He rings and asks Mamita to receive him.
XIX	32	At Alicia's (int.)			Alicia Mamita	292–301	scene		Mamita reports to Alicia Gaston's proposal on keeping Gigi: a private apartment, a car, etc.

Section	Supra-segment	Segment	Place	Sub-segment		Characters	Shots	Syntagma	Music	Action
	XX	33	At Gigi's (bedroom)	A	a	Gigi	302	sequence	'I remember it well'	Gigi comes out of her room to open the door to Gaston.
			At Gigi's (living room)	B	b	Gaston Gigi	302–308			Gigi refuses Gaston's proposals, bursts into tears when she learns that he loves her.
			At Gigi's (living room)		c	Gaston Gigi Mamita	308			Mamita rushes in, Gigi runs to her room.
			At Gigi's (living room)		d	Mamita Gaston	308			Gaston says Goodbye to Mamita and leaves.
	XXI	34	At the restaurant		a	Honoré Gaston	309–311	scene		Gaston arrives in a restaurant where Honoré is having lunch and explains his disappointment to him. Honoré consoles him and invites him to join him that evening with 'Michèle' at Maxim's.
					b	Honoré	312		'Poor boy', by Honoré	Honoré congratulates himself on having reached an age where conflicts like this don't matter.
	XXII	35	On the telephone	A	a	Mamita	313	episodic sequence		Mamita telephones in tears.
			At Alicia's	B	b	Alicia	314			Alicia puts down the telephone and has a cab called.
			In Paris	C	c	(Alicia)	315			A cab crosses a square in Paris.

		36	At Gigi's	Alicia Mamita Gigi Gaston	316–325	scene		Alicia arrives at Gigi's and reproaches Mamita for her clumsiness. Gaston rings, he has received Gigi's letter. She comes out from her room for a moment to tell him that she would rather be unhappy with him than without him and returns to her room. Gaston goes out. The two sisters look at each other.
E	XXIII	37	At Gaston's	Gaston Jeweller	326	autonomous shot		Gaston chooses a jewel for Gigi.
	XXIV	38	At Gigi's (bedroom)	Gigi	327	autonomous shot	'Say a prayer for me tonight' by Gigi	Gigi mentally prepares herself for the evening she is to experience.
		39	At Gigi's (int./ext.)	Gigi Alicia Mamita Gaston	328–329	scene		Gigi emerges from her room in an evening dress. She kisses Alicia and Mamita, opens the door to Gaston's ring and they go out.
	XXV	40	At Maxim's (entrance)	Gigi Gaston	330–331	sequence	Maxim's theme	Gaston and Gigi enter Maxim's and move to a table.
		41	At Maxim's (inside)	Gigi Gaston Honoré	332–335	sequence	'She is so gay tonight'	At the table. Gigi applies Alicia's lessons to perfection: the coffee, the cigar, and the jewellery. They get up to dance, as they pass greeting a surprised Honoré who recognises Gigi.

Section	Supra-segment	Seg-ment	Place	Sub-segment		Characters	Shots	Syntagma	Music	Action
		42	At Maxim's (entrance hall)			Gigi Gaston Honoré	336–337	sequence		Gaston offers Gigi his gift. Gigi exclaims like a real woman of the world over the beauty of the diamonds which she offers to the room to admire. Gaston is angered and leaves, dragging her to the exit.
	XXVI	43	From Gigi's (ext.)	A	a	Gigi Gaston Mamita	338	sequence		He drags Gigi by the hand up the steps. Gigi throws herself tearfully into Mamita's arms. Gaston goes back down the
				B	b	Gaston	339–340			steps and walks across Paris.
		44	Les Tuileries			Gaston	341	autonomous shot	'She is a babe' 'Gigi'	He passes in front of the Tuileries fountain, stops, and turns back.
		45	Towards Gigi's (ext.)			Gaston	342–344	sequence		He retraces his steps and goes slowly up Gigi's stairway.
		46	At Gigi's (int.)			Gaston Gigi Mamita	345–347	scene		Mamita and Gigi are sitting up. Mamita goes to open the door to Gaston and begs him to avoid a scandal. Gaston asks Mamita for Gigi's hand. She rushes into his arms tenderly.

XXVII	47	The Bois	Honoré Gigi Gaston	348–349	sequence	'Little Girls' by Honoré	Honoré sings. Gigi and Gaston appear and leave in a cab. Honoré goes on singing.
Repeat		Ending on painting		a shot			

Notes

1 Translator's note: This celebrated work by Metz first appeared in *Communications* in 1964, as one of his *Essais sur la signification au cinéma*, initially published in a variety of journals. *ESC* volume I, appeared in book form in 1968 (Paris: Klincksieck). The English translation by Michael Taylor appeared as *Film Language: a semiotics of the cinema* in 1974 (New York: OUP). *ESC* II was published by Klincksieck in 1972.
2 Translator's note: *Langage et cinéma*, Larousse, Paris, 1971. English translation by Donna Jean Umiker-Sebek, *Language and Cinema* (The Hague: Mouton, 1974).
3 *Film Language*, p. 134; *ESC*, II, pp. 203–4.
4 *ESC*, II, p. 206.
5 *Film Language*, p. 164, note.
6 ' a purely logical entity which, by itself, does not take place in the film; . . . in this code of the large syntagmatic category, the distinctive units do not consist of filmic segments, but of sorts of abstract exponents each of which is attached to a filmic segment' (*Language and Cinema*, pp. 201–2). 'The autonomous segment is not a unit of the "film", but a unit of the systems of the film' (Ibid, p. 190, note 8).
7 *ESC*, II, p. 129.
8 I have in mind here the works of Adriano Aprà and Luigi Martelli on *Viaggio in Italia* ('Premesse sintagmatiche ad un'analise di *Viaggio in Italia*', (*Cinema e Film*, 1–2, Spring 1967); Jean-Claude Bernardet on the Brazilian film *São Paulo, sociedade anonima* (Metz, *A significacào uo cinema*, São Paulo, 1972); Jan Toft on *Battleship Potemkin* (Christian Metz og Eisenstein, *Exil*, VII, 1, October 1973); Genevieve Jacquino on the didactic film (forthcoming); Francis Ramirez and Christian Rolot on the films of the modern French comedy school (forthcoming): and the more partial utilisations of the *grande syntagmatique* by Roger Odin on a part of Grémillon's *Gardiens de phare* ('Sémiologie et analyse de film-lecture de codes', *Travaux de linguistique*, II, 1972, Editions de l'Université de Saint-Etienne); and by John Ellis on *Passport to Pimlico* ('Made in Ealing', *Screen*, vol. 16, 1, 1975) and Stephen Heath on *Touch of Evil* ('*Touch of Evil*' in the same issue).
9 For example, Kari Hanet, 'The narrative text of *Shock Corridor*' (*Screen*, vol. 15, 4, 1974/5) and Thierry Kuntzel, 'Le travail du film 2' (*Communications*, no. 23, 1975).
10 Paris: Christian Bourgeois, 1970.
11 *Cahiers du Cinéma*, no. 223, Aug.–Sept. 1970.
12 Paris: Galilée, 1975.
13 Already quoted.
14 'Le blocage symbolique', *Communications*, no. 23, 1975.
15 '*Les oiseaux*: analyse d'une séquence', *Cahiers du Cinéma*, no. 216, Oct. 1968; 'L'évidence et le code', *Cinéma: théorie, lectures*, Klincksieck, Paris, 1973; 'Le blocage symbolique', *Communications*, already quoted.

16 Only the punctuation mark, when it is demarcatory, constitutes a pertinence of the same order as the syntagmatic type, because it participates in a specific code (the straight cut is obviously part of that code when it is substitutable for the punctuation mark). Cf. *ESC*, II, pp. 122–4.
17 'It seeks not the shot, but the sequence, which is a permanent concern and problem: actions, epochs, landscapes, must be distributed and organised over the totality of the film: regroupings both superior to the shot (= unit of shooting) and inferior to the *work* (the maximal unit) must be established.' *ESC*, II, pp. 120–1.
18 In their syntagmatic analysis of *Viaggio in Italia*, Adriano Aprà and Luigi Martelli have very carefully noted the need for complementary segmentations: one at the superior or 'structural' level, constituting units which they call *cine-periodo* (after the cine-phrase adopted by the Russian formalists), the other at the inferior level, called 'grammatical' (through an odd abuse of words current for a few years in Italy). But in spite of everything they remain essentially with Metz's autonomous segments and compromise their work of decomposition and pre-analysis largely by the distinction they make between the grammatical and the structural which avoids the fundamental problem of the single and plural (i.e. textual) articulation of the different levels of description possible.
19 *Film Language*, op. cit. p. 181.
20 *ESC*, II, p. 127.
21 And all the episodic sequences except segment 35, whose bastardised character I have underlined.
22 At this level, the specific pertinence established between the segments by the differences between the syntagmatic types is displaced in the form of an opposition between segment and sub-segment (with, as we have just seen, the intermediary case of sub-segments constituted by the episodes of episodic sequences).
23 With one exception, 43a. This clearly underlines the way that from the moment the breakdown becomes textual, it is constantly opening up depths. To avoid being inaccurate I did not wish to credit Gaston alone with segment 43 where he brings Gigi and Mamita into one shot; on the other hand, in order to be exact, I ought to have divided sub-segment 43a again into two sub-segments, Gigi-Gaston and Gigi-Gaston-Mamita, which would be perfectly practicable for numerous other scenes.
24 This is quite striking for the set of segments which rest totally or in part on alternations of a more or less structuring kind at various levels. By definition, they impel more strongly than the rest towards an approximation which can only be broken down by a deeper sub-segmentation.
25 The first figures in the summary table along with the other operations, to show that what is involved is always only the same operation displaced. I have not included the second, more complex example which can be described by analysis alone.
26 *ESC*, II, pp. 138–40.

8 · Jim Collins: 'Toward Defining a Matrix of the Musical Comedy: The Place of the Spectator Within the Textual Mechanisms'

When a familiar genre begins to receive critical attention, it commonly inspires remarks of an interesting but overly general nature. This is particularly true of the musical, a genre which everyone knows as a fan but few know as scholar or critic. The 1930s musical, according to these general pronouncements, is an escapist response to Depression conditions; song-and-dance numbers celebrate and express the lovers' joy (thus standing in opposition to the relatively drab narrative sequences); the musical as a genre somehow stands apart from the classical narrative tradition; and overall, musicals are films which involve the spectator to a greater extent than many other Hollywood films.

Now, each of these clichés bears a truth of a sort, but it is an old truth, the truth of a previous critical generation. We are now in a position where we no longer need to be contented with such generalities. In the article which follows, Jim Collins takes each one of those received notions and subjects it to an intense rhetorical analysis. Instead of simply accepting the cliché of the musical's escapism, he shows how the Astaire–Rogers RKO musicals of the 1930s carry out, during the course of each film, a value shift from monetary rewards to amorous ones. We are thus left not with a single general comment about the film's overall tone, but with a sense of the structuring principle which underlies the film's rhetoric. Similarly, Collins eschews the familiar holistic analysis identifying 'dance' with 'joy', in favour of a careful typology of song/dance numbers. This move from pure phenomenology of the dance to a structured rhetorical analysis of the *function* of each dance proves to be extremely rewarding. The clarity of Collins's analysis is especially visible in his critique of Christian Metz's analysis of the rhetorical foundations of classical narrative cinema. By combining insight into song delivery, camera handling, eye contact, and other generally neglected aspects of the musical, Collins manages to demonstrate the limited nature of the Metzian model and its non-applicability to the musical. Again, a general notion (the non-classical nature of the musical) receives careful definition, thus permitting Collins to connect, through further rhetorical analysis, the musical's high coefficient of spectator involvement and its low coefficient of classical narrativity. Taking little for granted, analysing before pronouncing, questioning rather than simply reaffirming, Collins provides multiple examples of analytical techniques which deserve to be applied more widely within the study of the genre.

Throughout the history of film criticism there have been countless studies devoted to the gangster and western genres, but there has been very little serious work done on the musical comedy. It has been considered the most escapist or 'purely for entertainment' of all Hollywood genres, and therefore not considered worthy of critical attention. But little has been said about the nature of this escapism or the undeniable popularity of this particular genre. This paper, then, is an attempt to analyse this escapism through an examination of the dances/songs in a number of films in order to demonstrate the complexity of the textual mechanisms, particularly in regard to the position of the spectator within the text.

The films I have chosen for this analysis are the Fred Astaire–Ginger Rogers musicals made at RKO between 1934 and 1938, *The Gay Divorcee* (1934), *Top Hat* (1935), *Follow the Fleet* (1936), *Swing Time* (1936), *Shall We Dance* (1937), and *Carefree* (1938). They are generally considered synonymous with escapist entertainment. These films are unified not only by Astaire and Rogers as the major stars, but also by an entire production unit headed by Pandro S. Berman as producer, with Alan Scott, Ernest Pagano, and Dwight Taylor as scenarists, David Abel as cinematographer, Hermes Pan as choreographer and Irving Berlin and George Gershwin for the music. These films make a very strong case for a generic, as opposed to an auteuristic approach. The films directed by Sandrich and that directed by Stevens (*Swing Time*) are virtually indistinguishable, so the attribution of authorship must go to the unit rather than any one individual.

To describe the particular matrix or configuration that unifies these films one must go beyond thematic or iconographic definitions and analyse the actual mechanisms of the text. To demonstrate this I will use a typology of the dance/songs in these films. These categories are in no way meant to be exhaustive or mutually exclusive. Instead each category typifies a specific function within the texts. I have used a representative song to head each category:

I 'Shall We Dance' (*histoire/discours*)
II 'The Continental' (glorification of the dance)
III 'Cheek to Cheek' (sexual power of the dance)

I 'Shall We Dance' (*histoire/discours*)

While the Astaire–Rogers films make little direct reference to the economic conditions of the 1930s, the songs continually acknowledge the existence of some sort of difficult situation. What is important about these references is that they are coupled with the offer of the dance as an alternative to despair. The words to 'Shall We Dance' serve as a type of 'hymn' or 'anthem' to the musical and represent perfectly the opposition treated by this category of songs.

Drop that long face, come on have your fling, why keep nursing the blues?
If you want the whole world on a string, put on your dancing shoes.
Stop wasting time, put on your dancing shoes, watch your spirits climb.
Shall we dance, or keep on moping?
Shall we dance, and walk on air?
Shall we give in to despair, or shall we dance with never a care?
Life is short, we're growing older,
Don't you be an also ran,
You better dance little lady, dance little man
Dance whenever you can.

There is exactly the same opposition of depression vs. dance in 'Let Yourself Go':

If you step out on the floor you forget your troubles,
If you go into your dance you forget your woes.
So come, get together, let the dance floor be your leather,
Step as lightly as a feather,
Let yourself go.
Let yourself go, relax and let yourself go,
Relax, you've got yourself tied up in a knot,
The night is cold, but the music's hot,
So come, cuddle closer, don't you dare to answer no sir,
Butcher, banker, clerk, or grocer,
Let yourself go. (From *Follow the Fleet*)

In the set-up for the song 'Let's Face the Music and Dance' Fred Astaire is about to commit suicide because he's lost his fortune, but then saves Ginger Rogers from her own suicide attempt and sings:

There may be trouble ahead,
But while there's moonlight and music and love and romance,

Let's face the music and dance.

Again in 'Slap That Bass' there is the offer of the dance as remedy to difficulty:

Zoom, zoom, zoom, misery you got to go.
Slap that bass, use it like a tonic,
Slap that bass, keep your philharmonic,
Zoom, zoom, zoom, and the milk and honey'll flow.
Zoom zoom, zoom zoom, the world is in a mess,
With politics and taxes, and people grinding axes,
There's no happiness.
Zoom zoom, zoom zoom, rhythm leads your ace,
The future doesn't fret me, if I could only get me
Someone to slap that bass.
Happiness is not a riddle,
When I'm listening to that big bass fiddle. (From *Shall We Dance*)

These lyrics are a crucial aspect of the unique relationship the musical comedy has with its spectator. The repetition of the I/You pronoun structure is indicative of a desire to establish a certain intimacy or rapport with the spectator which is essential to any notion of 'escapism'. The work of Emile Benveniste provides an important distinction that is useful in characterizing this relationship. The I/You pronoun stresses the *discours* rather than the *histoire* quality of scenes. Briefly, Benveniste describes *histoire* as third-person narration that suppresses all marks of *énonciation** and ignores the presence of the reader. *Discours* is narration that utilizes the 'I', thereby continually implying the 'You' and revealing the marks of *énonciation*.[1] Christian Metz has utilized this distinction in reference to film in his article 'Histoire/Discours (note sur deux voyeurismes)'.[2] For Metz, 'the traditional film presents itself as *histoire*. It is, however, discourse if one refers to the intention of the film-maker, to the influences that it exercises over the public, etc.; but the property of this discourse, and the very principle of its efficacity as discourse, is precisely to efface the marks of *énonciation* and to disguise itself as *histoire*.' This distinction is correct in regard to a western or gangster film, but not

---

* *énonciation* — This term refers to the process of creating a given utterance. It cannot be easily translated into 'enunciation' since the English word can refer both to the process and the result, the act of enunciating (*énonciation*) and the enunciated (*énoncé*). The term, in Benveniste's sense, refers to the process that the speaker goes through in constituting an utterance in which he establishes himself as speaker and posits, implicitly or explicitly, a receiver for his message.

entirely in regard to the musical comedy. The Astaire–Rogers films and other musicals that 'put on a show' insist upon showing the marks of *énonciation* in order to create the illusion that the work is a *discours* in the process of creation.

This illusion of 'creation' involves another central element in the rapport between text and spectator. For Metz an essential aspect of the *histoire* quality of traditional fiction film is that 'the film is not exhibitionist. I watch it, but it does not watch me watching it. However, it knows that I am watching it. But it doesn't want to know it.' Again, this may be true of other genre films, but certainly is not true for the musical, where the presence of the spectator is continually recognized and exploited. This recognition of the viewer is stressed in both the *regard* (the look or glance of the character) during the songs, and the use of pronouns in the lyrics. For example, Astaire sings 'Shall We Dance' directly to the audience, and addresses the audience as 'you' – 'You'd better dance little lady, dance little man. . .' He even uses the 'we' in the refrain of the song, which goes beyond even the I/You relationship in creating the impression of intimacy between actor and viewer. In 'Let Yourself Go' the 'you' is used throughout ('If *you* go into *your* dance *you* forget *your* woes'), and then is stressed even further by the final line, 'Butcher, baker, clerk or grocer/ Let yourself go.'

The presence of a spectator is also recognized within the diegetic world of the films. There are frequent shots of the audience and subjective shots from the viewpoint of an imaginary spectator within the diegetic audience. For instance, the first shot of *Swing Time* is a subjective shot from the point of view of the imaginary spectator or 'you' in centre balcony within the diegetic audience, with the rest of the audience clearly visible below, and Astaire on the stage. The same kind of imaginary spectator subjective shot is used again in the 'Top Hat' song in *Top Hat*. In this case the diegetic audience is emphasized even more strongly. Having 'shot' the chorus with his cane, Astaire then aims his cane at the audience and 'shoots'. The next shot is of a group in the audience recoiling from the 'shot'. Again in *Shall We Dance* there is the emphasis on the diegetic audience. While a number is in progress there is a conversation in the audience between Edward Everett Horton and a friend, and the diegetic audience shushes them. A shushing match follows, first with a subjective shot from the audience's point of view, and then a subjective shot from Horton's point of view. The result is that at one point the diegetic audience faces the audience in the theatre and shushes them, so that the audiences are face to face, the diegetic audience itself acknowledging the presence of the viewer.

Another device used to address the viewer directly occurs when the characters address the diegetic audience but, in the process of reframing that audience becomes invisible and the characters talk directly to the viewer. Instances of this technique are too frequent to catalogue entirely, but examples can be found in the 'Shall We Dance' number, the 'Waltz' from *Swing Time*, and 'Let Yourself Go'.

Through these different forms of direct address (*regard*, pronouns, diegetic inclusion, and reframing) the presence of the viewer is recognized and utilized by the text to include the viewer within the world of the film. The audience of a musical comedy is invited to participate directly in the action of the film: 'Put on your dancing shoes, stop wasting time/Put on your dancing shoes, watch your spirits climb.' It is essential that the audience feel included within the text because the very nature of the text glorifies entertainment; if the viewer enjoys participating, he shares in the success of the performance. The viewer is placed in a paradoxical situation – he can experience identification with the characters of the film only if he enjoys himself, but he can enjoy himself only if he experiences identification. This situation is the result of the presentation of the dance or entertainment as all-important. Therefore, not to enjoy oneself is to be part of the dull, drab world that Astaire and Rogers triumph over. The spectator, then, normally a passive witness to a non-discursive narrative, has an active role in the musical comedy because his place as a spectator is essential for the entertainment to succeed.

The musical text is successful not because, as in Metz's description, it is *discours* disguised as *histoire*, but rather it is *histoire* that disguises itself as *discours*. It not only acknowledges the spectator, but creates the illusion that he is sharing the creative process. The following diagrams may be useful in illustrating this distinction:

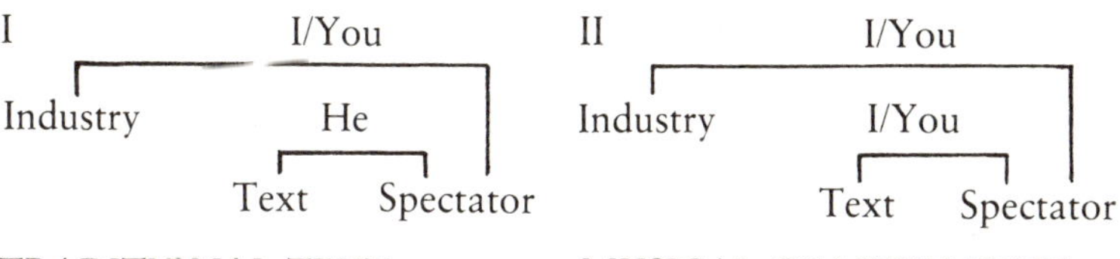

TRADITIONAL TEXT MUSICAL COMEDY TEXT

Both diagrams show the *discours* between industry (Hollywood, film-maker, etc.) and the spectator as the fundamental relationship upon which the text is predicated, and demonstrate the differing forms a text can take to accomplish that relationship. The efficacy of the *discours* in diagram II between industry and spectator is entirely contingent upon the success of the counterfeit *discours* between text and spectator.

The I/You relationship is absolutely essential to these films as ideological mechanisms, particularly as products of the 1930s. The structure typifies what Althusser calls the *interpellation* of the individual within the text. This notion of *interpellation* is crucial to an understanding of the ideological ramifications of the discursive quality of the musical text. For Althusser 'toute idéologie interpelle les individus concrets en sujets concrets' ('all ideology interpellates concrete individuals into concrete subjects').[3] He uses the example of the Christian ideology in which God speaks directly to the subject. For the text to be effective, the reader must believe it is he himself that is addressed in a phrase such as 'And so, I say unto you. . .' There is a structured gap, an opening in the text which allows for the 'calling in' of the reader. The desired reaction for the individual in any ideological text is the reaction 'Oui, c'est bien moi' ('Yes, it's me') in the text. The musical comedy depends on a double recognition by the spectator of himself in the text. Only when this double recognition is achieved can the spectator experience a solidarity with the text and believe that he is essential to the entertainment in progress. It is this function which the first category of songs ('Shall We Dance') must fulfil, disguising the standard *histoire* text-spectator relationship as a bond of *discours*, thus interpellating the spectator into the text as an active and fully entertained 'you'. It is the strength of this bond that makes the dance so persuasive as an alternative to despair.

II The Continental (glorification of the dance)

The second major category of songs, 'The Continental', is a complete glorification of the dance. These songs presuppose the first category 'Shall We Dance' in that they no longer suggest dance as an alternative to despair, but work from the notion that the viewer has already been convinced of the importance of the dance. The placement of these songs within the film reflects this presupposition. They invariably appear in the middle or second half of the film, preceded by at least two other dances. In all but one of the Astaire–Rogers films there is at least one song dedicated solely to the presentation of a new dance: 'The Continental' in *Gay Divor-*

cee, 'The Piccolino' in *Top Hat*, 'I'd Rather Lead A Band' in *Follow the Fleet*, 'Bojangles of Harlem' in *Swing Time*, and 'The Yam' in *Carefree*. These songs are dedicated only to the greater glory of the dance. Their references to other dances reflect the presupposition that the dance is of vital importance. In 'The Yam', for example, we find these references:

I didn't come to do the Charleston,
I didn't come to Ball the Jack.
I didn't come to do the Susie Q,
Or the Bottom they call Black.
I didn't come to do Big Apple,
I didn't come to do the Shag,
But Honey here I am to do the Yam,
'Cause the Yam is in the bag.

In fact, we are even given instructions on how to do the Yam: 'Raise your hand and sway, like you hold a tray.' Both Astaire and Rogers demonstrate how the dance is done. The desire to involve the spectator in the world of the film is visually enacted when Astaire and Rogers take people from the diegetic audience and teach them the dance, so that by the end of the song everyone is 'doing the Yam'.

A subset of this second 'Continental' category includes the dance solos of Fred Astaire in which the virtuosity of Astaire himself is foregrounded. These numbers glorify the dance, but focus on Astaire rather than the production number as a whole. A few examples of these dances are the 'Free For Anything Fancy' and 'Top Hat, White Tie, and Tails' numbers in *Top Hat*, the tap dance to the off-speed record-player in *Shall We Dance*, the dance to the off-screen band playing varying rhythms in *Follow the Fleet*, the second half of the 'Bojangles' number, when Astaire dances the shadows, in *Swing Time*, the golf-swing dance in *Carefree*, and the 'Sing for your Supper' number in *Gay Divorcee*. The significance of these virtuoso performances will be more fully explained in conjunction with the third category, but I mention them here since part of their function is unquestionably the glorification of the dance.

What is so significant about this glorification is that it represents the displacement of value that is central to the mechanism of the musical. The economic success that is so highly considered in the 'real' world is replaced in the fictional world of the musical by success in love and the dance. But it is not a simple replacement of one by the other. The escapism of the musical is accomplished only through a constant reference to the world as it is, and this reference is at the very basis of the value displacement. Not only does success in love and the dance replace economic success, but the two are placed in opposition throughout the films of Astaire and Rogers. For instance, in *Swing Time*, one success is possible only at the exclusion of the other. If Astaire earns too much money he must return to his fiancée, and fail in his love affair with Ginger Rogers. If he does not succeed monetarily he can remain with Rogers, thereby succeeding in love. This opposition is set in motion at the beginning of the film through the hypocritical transformation of the father when he believes that Astaire has missed the wedding because he has been making money. The change of heart demonstrates his attitude toward the importance of money, even over his daughter's happiness. His statement that 'money shows character' has an ironic effect in this situation, because it shows how little character the wealthy have. Therefore, before the adventure in New York has even begun, economic success has been given very negative connotations.

In *Swing Time* economic terms are utilized throughout the film to describe love relationships. In the love strike in the hotel corridor Astaire's placard protests the unfair amorous, rather than economic, treatment he is receiving from Rogers. This 'economy of love' even extends to Rogers's name in the film, 'Penny'. This name is emphasized repeatedly in the song 'Never Gonna Dance'. The first line in the song, 'And so, I'm left without a penny' is repeated throughout the song as 'And so, I'm left without *my* penny'. We find the culmination of this 'economized love' in the combination of Astaire's and Rogers's fictional names, 'Lucky Penny'.

In *Shall We Dance* the same value shift is foregrounded with the two types of success placed in opposition. In this film the opposition is between high classical art as embodied by the ballet, and popular art as embodied by the musical revue. Astaire, despite his status in an aristocratic art, longs to tap dance, and more importantly, to dance with Rogers, a popular dancer. In the song 'Slap That Bass' he says specifically 'Keep your philharmonic'. Twice within the film the popularization or de-aristocratization of Astaire's dance is seen in writing – first in the newspaper headlines 'Jazz-Ballet Merge' and later in the sign 'Broadway and Ballet Merge'. Astaire's final production number is a combination of the ballet and popular styles which represent his internal conflict, with the popular dance winning in the end when Astaire wins Rogers. The notion of success is not abandoned, only the object of value is altered. Instead of winning money, Astaire wins the girl in a contest against his rival, who loses because he is a 'Park Avenue Cluck'.

Given this structure of oppositions, one might expect Astaire's rivals to be businessmen, but an entertainer vs. non-entertainer opposition does not hold true. His rival in *Swing Time* is Ricardo Romero, a singer and bandleader. In *Top Hat*, too, his rival is a creative artist, a designer who very pointedly 'sings'. The key difference is not that Astaire is an entertainer. The difference is that Astaire is a dancer, and Astaire continually succeeds specifically because he can dance. In *Swing Time*, *Carefree*, *Top Hat*, *Shall We Dance*, and *Gay Divorcee* the love between Astaire and Rogers begins when they dance together for the first time. The power of the dance is emphasized even further in these same films when Astaire regains the love of Rogers with a dance in the second half of the film. This 'power' of the dance is perhaps most clear in *Carefree*. In 'Change Partners' Astaire, a psychiatrist in this film, hypnotizes Rogers by dancing with her.

III Cheek to Cheek (sexual power of the dance)

The power of the dance is enormous within the diegetic world of the film because the dance is repeatedly a metaphor for the sexual act. These dances that first bring Astaire and Rogers together constitute a category of dances/songs all their own. These dances glorify the dance, but not as in the first or second categories. In these numbers the dance is not seen as an alternative to despair or as a glorification of itself as a dance, but as a means to sexual intimacy. In 'Cheek to Cheek' Astaire sings,

> Heaven, I'm in heaven, and my heart beats so that I can hardly speak,
> And I seem to find the happiness I seek,
> When we're out together dancing cheek to cheek.

All of these private dances – 'Never Gonna Dance' (*Swing Time*), 'Change Partners' (*Carefree*), 'Night and Day' (*Gay Divorcee*), and 'Lovely Day' and 'Cheek to Cheek' (*Top Hat*) – have certain shared characteristics that set them apart entirely from the other dances. First of all, these numbers are marked by a complete absence of a diegetic audience, a major feature of categories I and II. There is also a total lack of a diegetic orchestra that is usually standard in the other categories. While we usually find a diegetic dance-floor of some sort in this category of dances, there is no diegetic imperative for the dance, such as a public performance. These dances are solely a private performance. Even when they (Astaire and Rogers as a couple) begin to dance on a floor with others, they separate themselves from this public dance-floor, and complete the dance together on a totally different, private dance-floor. This is the case with 'Cheek to Cheek', 'Change Partners', and 'Night and Day'. A public dance-floor is used in 'Never Gonna Dance', but the action takes place after the club is closed, and Astaire and Rogers are totally alone.

As part of this privacy, the *regard* is seldom directed at the audience, and the voyeurism that Metz speaks of in reference to the cinema as *histoire* appears only in these private dances. For instance, in 'Night and Day' the camera is within the room with Astaire and Rogers when they begin to dance together, but then abruptly shifts to a view from outside the room, looking through a curtained window at the dance within. The camera then shifts back within the space of the room, but the viewpoint is literally from under a table, looking up at the couple, the sides and top of the table being visible at the edge of the frame. It is hardly coincidental, then, that the status of the narrative switches radically from a *discours* to an *histoire* quality at the moment of greatest intimacy.

Not only do the lack of diegetic audience and orchestra, along with the camera placement, stress the intimacy of these dances, but the actions of the dances themselves strongly suggest the sexual nature of the dance. At the conclusion of 'Night and Day' Astaire and Rogers come to rest on a chair at the side of the dance floor. Astaire lays her back so that she is in a reclining position, and dusts his hands off lightly to signify that he has accomplished something. There are the same suggestive motions coupled with punctuation in the music in the 'Cheek to Cheek' dance. The music builds subtly throughout the dance until it abruptly stops momentarily. The sudden stop occurs exactly at the moment that Astaire has slung Rogers over and is holding her in a reclining position, in which Rogers drops her head and shoulders back in a gesture of total submission. This total freeze in the action in regard to both the music and the actions of the dancers, occurring when Astaire and Rogers are in such a significant position, creates a symbolic or metaphoric orgasm. Just as the music increased in pace before the sudden stop, after the stop the music is softer and slower paced, and the motions of the dance are much slower.

In *Swing Time* the 'Never Gonna Dance' sequence mixes suggestive dance movements with suggestive pacing and punctuation in the music. The number begins with Astaire singing to Rogers that if he leaves he will not be able to dance again. After he stops singing they begin to dance, re-enacting at first the steps of their first dance-walk together at the dancing academy, and then re-enacting their first real dance together. They begin to dance more and more intensely, and the music begins to change pace accordingly. What is significant in the movement is that after the initial song is sung, the music continues for the dance, but the singing stops. In dances like 'Change Partners' and 'Cheek to Cheek' there is a movement not only away from the public dance-floor to the private, but also a move away from the verbal to the non-verbal as part of the suggestion of the sexual act.

The phallic power of the dancer Astaire is suggested repeatedly throughout these films. In the 'Bojangles of Harlem' number the enormously long artificial legs attached to Astaire unquestionably function as massive phallic symbols. But more importantly, in regard to the structure of dances in the textual system, the dance solos of Astaire discussed as a subset of the second 'Continental' category demonstrate his virtuosity or power. The relation between virtuosity in the dance and virtuosity in sexual relations is accentuated in the misunderstanding between Astaire and Rogers in *Gay Divorcee*. In this conversation Rogers has the wrong impression that Astaire is a gigolo, and not a dancer, so his remarks about bringing joy into the lives of thousands of young girls and giving them satisfaction have only a very shocking effect on Rogers. The scene is purposely comic and the misunderstanding is eventually cleared up, but the idea that Astaire is considered as someone bringing joy into the lives of young girls in a somewhat questionable way remains imprinted on the viewer.

This typology is meant only as a starting point in the study of the textual mechanisms involved in these musicals. The 'escapism' of these films depends upon an entire textual apparatus that insures its own success by 'musicalizing' the world. The musical creates not only the possibility for involvement of the spectator, but also the *desire* for that involvement through its own self-glorification. The importance of the spectator in relation to the structuration of the musical is essential to a more complete understanding of the particular matrix of elements that constitute the musical comedy genre. Genre study must, like the musical, acknowledge the existence of the spectator to ensure its success.

Notes

1 Emile Benveniste, *Problèmes de linguistique générale*, Paris: Gallimard, 1966.
2 Christian Metz, *Le Signifiant imaginaire*, Paris: 10/18, 1977.
3 Louis Althusser, 'Idéologies et appareils idéologiques d'Etat', *Positions*, Paris: Editions sociales, 1976.

9 · Alan Williams: 'The Musical Film and Recorded Popular Music'

By any rational standards, a volume of this kind should contain numerous essays on the interplay between the musical as a genre and the technology borrowed and developed to support the genre's unique structure and function. As the first begotten son of sound technology, the musical has remained more closely tied than any other genre to technological innovation and development, not only in the film industry but in the field of sound recording as well. Invention after invention can be traced to particular formal innovations in the musical (or vice versa): not just particular developments in the quality of sound recording but such independent inventions as the camera crane, the playback unit, the technology for combining animated and photographed sequences, plus scores of special effects. Yet for all this interplay, hardly a word has been written regarding technology's effect on the musical's signifying practice.

Even more surprising is the relative paucity of material available on the musical's use of music. The growing literature on popular song tends (like that on dance) to treat the Hollywood musical as a bastardized derivative form hardly worthy of separate treatment. Film composers (Herrmann, Waxman, Rozsa, Tiomkin, etc.) receive their due, but not composers of songs appropriated by the musical. (Even when those songs were written directly for Hollywood they are for some reason always assimilated to Broadway or Tin Pan Alley, depending on the previous activities of composer and lyricist.) And in a world where the songs themselves receive precious little treatment, it is needless to point out that we look in vain for careful analyses of the interrelationship between sound and image, between diegetic and non-diegetic sound, between the sound track of the narrative and that of the numbers.

Alan Williams's article on the formal and technological aspects of the musical's soundtrack thus comes as a welcome oasis in what is otherwise hardly more than a critical desert. Two insights in particular merit mention, here, for they deserve to be pondered at length in the years to come. (Indeed, I would say that Williams's essay, more than any other in this volume, heralds the form which criticism on the musical genre must take in the future.) The first constitutes one of those seminal thoughts on which critical schools are founded, a notion quite parallel to the characteristic French school emphasis (Baudry–Comolli–Metz) on the visual apparatus: that between 'music' as a general cultural category and the music which we find in the musical lies an unacknowledged but all-important gap, that of recording technology. We cannot understand the position of the auditor in the musical unless we can seize that of the subject as defined by recorded sound. Now, the position of the spectator as defined by the image does not necessarily match that of the auditor as defined by recorded sound. In particular, the sense of intimacy created by close miking contrasts strongly with the long shots with which such close-up sound is often matched. This disparity between image-space and sound-space constitutes a basic characteristic of the musical, yet remains totally unacknowledged by the mass of criticism written on the genre. Second, Williams points out the radical differences which separate the popular song (the musical's basic medium) from late nineteenth-century symphonic music (the idiom of most background music in narrative films). Here too, the ramifications of a simple distinction are astoundingly widespread. In the past the methodology applied to the musical has derived almost entirely from two well-developed and closely related areas: image analysis (*mise en scène*, decor, style, etc.) and narrative analysis (plot, structure, motivation, and so forth). Perhaps in the future critics will follow Williams's lead and increasingly turn their attention to problems of musical form and sound reproduction.

In a brief penetrating article entitled 'Music on the Screen', Maurice Jaubert gives a formulation that I wish to use as point of departure in speaking of the film musical. Jaubert does not define the musical film inductively, as an ideal object, but as contrasted to what he terms the 'non-musical film'. In the musical:

> The director finds in a song the excuse for a lyrical transposition of music into images . . . [T]here are born out of the music images which no longer need to submit themselves to that 'veracity' which the non-musical film insists on so imperiously. Freed from their role as copies of real objects, their expressive power flows out purely in plastic rhythms, strictly united with the music. . . . If we pass now to the non-musical film, whether dramatic, comic, or sentimental, the music, ceasing to dominate, becomes the servant of the image. . . .[1]

Formulated in this manner, such an opposition is too global: in the American musical comedy, specifically, this liberation of the image from the demands of veracity occurs only in musical numbers, which are embedded in a narrative that relies on 'realistic' sound/image relations. One could maintain, in fact, that the alternation between number and narrative is a defining characteristic of the genre.

That the image is only intermittently freed from the demands of veracity is not surprising if we consider that 'veracity' in the cinema (as elsewhere) only *seems* natural – in fact, it is highly codified and conventionalized. This is most easily argued with a counter-example. Kenneth Anger's *Scorpio Rising* includes recorded popular music on its soundtrack without raising issues of dominance or veracity. In that film, image and sound run *parallel*, with frequent points of rhythmic and semantic coincidence; yet the two channels remain separate because a common origin (reference to a diegesis) is never posited – except inasmuch as it is the film-maker who has matched them. Music cannot dominate the image, nor vice versa, since they do not share any common ground on which to do battle.

Such a state of affairs would be foreign to the American musical comedy, where sources other than the soundtrack itself – characters, situations – are continually affirmed. Yet it is almost axiomatic that the musical comedy depart from diegetic realism in its musical numbers. In this respect, the films observe two options: either the sound remains diegetic while the image introduces extra-diegetic material (the classic Busby Berkeley number) or the image remains diegetic while the soundtrack introduces extra-diegetic material (the unseen orchestra on the beach or in a small hotel room). In each case, the space of the musical number becomes *larger* than the space of the narrative. This sense of expansion, however, only occurs as the distortion (but not destruction) of an initially coherent space.

So it is that, in this respect at least, Jaubert's contrast between 'musical' and 'non-musical' operates *within* most musical films. In order for domination to occur there must seem to exist an object or figure to be dominated. In the musical, this something is not merely the image, but the created coincidences of image and diegesis. But there must be a master for this slave. 'Music', in Jaubert's formulation, is too vague. It is not music in general (whatever that would be) that dominates the musical number, but a particular, formally distinct and recognizable type – 'popular' music – which is produced according to particular technological norms or codes – those of the American recording industry. The remarks that follow will attempt to define some of the functions of recording practices and musical forms as employed in musical films. In this, following Jaubert's example, I will proceed comparatively, opposing 'musical' to 'non-musical' (or dramatic) films.

I 'Popular' recording as sonic model

If we accept for the moment that in musical sequences (leaving aside the tricky limit-case of dance-only sequences) music somehow *dominates* the image track (or, rather, dictates the order and rhythm of the visible diegesis, as well as frequently setting semantic boundaries), then an important qualification must be made. It is recorded music that dominates, and certain of its effects follow from how it was recorded. Early musicals, for technical reasons, had to be recorded live, but the practice of pre-recording was quickly adopted, so that numbers were first performed as music, then visuals matched to them. The major reason for this change-over, of course, was the greater clarity of sound achieved in this manner.

But 'clarity' itself is a value imposed by sound recording, one capability of which (microphone distance) is to make sound sources seem as close or as far away as desired. The 'closer' the sound (via microphone placement), the 'clearer', at least in pre-stereo recording practices. The perceived distance between sound source and listener that one senses in live performance may be almost totally eliminated via close microphone placement. In this way, sound recording is exemplary of what Walter Benjamin called the capability of mechanical reproduction to abolish the 'aura':

> The concept of aura which was proposed above with reference to historical objects may usefully be illustrated with reference to the aura of natural ones. We define the aura of the latter as the unique phenomenon of a distance, however close it may be. If, while resting on a summer afternoon, you follow with your eyes a mountain range on the horizon or a branch which casts its shadow over you, you experience the aura of those mountains, of that branch. This image makes it easy to comprehend the social bases of the contemporary decay of the aura. It rests on two circumstances, both of which are related to the increasing significance of the masses in contemporary life. Namely, the desire of contemporary masses to bring things 'closer' spatially and humanly, which is just as ardent as their bent toward overcoming the uniqueness of every reality by accepting its reproduction.[2]

It should be noted that I am most definitely not arguing that *only* close microphone distance produces the 'decline of the aura' in sound recording. In fact, elsewhere, in a work in progress, I will argue that close miking is the very paradigm of sound recording, and that other practices give us not the 'distance' of which Benjamin speaks but rather the *signs* of distance.

What is important here is the difference between the recording of dialogue in the musical film and the recording of musical numbers – particularly the recording of singing voices. Singing voices were recorded at closer distances than dialogue (this reaching a grand climax in films of the 1950s). One explanation for this is that until recently close microphone placement was not possible in studio sync-sound recording. In the music studio, on the other hand, it is what occurs most naturally – 'naturally', since the recording practices most influential for Hollywood music recording were those of the 'popular' recording industry and its aesthetic of clarity and presence.

The clarity of close sound recording, in fact, depends on the abolition of spatial impressions; not only does the sound seem very close, but it also conveys a sense of relative *spacelessness*. (These remarks apply to older, monaural recording practices as developed through the 1950s; the situation is considerably more complicated today.) Thus, the very clarity and closeness of commercial music recording partially violates canons of 'realism' when juxtaposed with a supposedly believable visual image since, except in extreme close-up, the perceived distance of sound source would be much closer than that of the object within the image. To imagine this effect outside the context of the musical, the reader has only to think of any badly dubbed foreign film as an analogue; the voices seem 'too close' and whatever implied spatial environment they do possess does not change, which results in an effect that is frequently comic – though the same procedure seems 'natural' in a musical number.

Even though it is technically feasible to maintain continuity of recording practices between dialogue and music (either by 'distancing' the musical segments via added reverberation or by closely dubbing dialogue), the musical, through most of its history, has not done this. Rather, the majority of films operate via a process of alternation between what are literally two types of image–sound relationships. In dialogue sequences, there is the dominant relation of mutual spatial reinforcement – aural and visual perspective seem to coincide. Of course, they actually do no such thing, since the materials and sense channels involved are so disparate; the weakly coded spatial data conveyed by recorded sound is, for the most part, 'placed' by the more perceptible and explicit spatial hierarchy of visual perspective. But the alternate case, that of the closely miked musical number, demonstrates that, conventional or not, this 'coincidence' can be violated. And, indeed, in musical numbers it does seem to be a case of something like *violation*: the voice of the singer, to take the most extreme case, will remain seemingly just barely behind the screen (where the theatre's speakers literally *are*) while an entire assortment of close-ups, long shots, motionless or not, brief or lengthy, occur on the image track. Immobile, impossibly close sound juxtaposed with mobile and variable visual placement of the spectator: a definite splitting of the viewing-hearing subject occurs in many, in fact in most, musical numbers to some extent.

What 'happens' in *The Band Wagon* for example, when Fred Astaire begins to sing 'By Myself' while walking down a loading platform at Grand Central Station? His voice subtly but abruptly changes, seems to come closer to us (and, in fact, *does* come closer – to the microphone) as ambient noise drops significantly and an unseen orchestra begins to play, slightly more distant than Astaire's voice but still 'closer' than the sounds that went before. The effect is often described as 'magical'. And so it is – but it is the technological magic of stage illusion rather than any primitive sort. The music recording becomes figure to the previous recorded sound's ground. It stands out precisely by the contrast that is so spectacularly demonstrated.

The phenomenological effect is that the visuals become in some way an extension of the song. Astaire's body is not given as point of origin of the music, but rather as *sign* of the origin of music, which thereby seems to emanate from the whole image. In a similar way, Bruce Baillie describes his film *All My Life*, which juxtaposes a recording of the song of the same name with a 360° pan of a field with fence, as 'a singing fence'. But in that film, the effect and its origins are not concealed; in *The Band Wagon*, the 'magic' Astaire is given as extension of the 'real' one.

So it is worth speculating that some of the *pleasure* given by musical numbers might actually be something closer to *pseudo-bliss*, since the effect, so subtle as to pass generally unperceived, is an implicit loss of coherence of the implied spectator. A slight loss, to be sure – an innoculation against bliss (*jouissance*), possibly, rather than the 'real thing' – but important none the less since it seems to be one defining characteristic of the musical film to deliver effects of precisely this sort.

It is worth noting here that not only does this effect of subtle splitting and dominance (because 'closer') of the soundtrack obtain in the context of the musical; it also obtains even if 'real' sound space is co-present. Recording frequently mimics the work of the

Bye Bye Birdie. Hello glitter. From Sidney's brilliant, overstuffed staging of the telephone sequence . . .

. . . to the confetti-specked steps of the State House (see page 34)

Circular motifs as symbols of female sexuality (see page 75)

Twenty Million Sweethearts. The magic of close miking: even though separated from Dick Powell by a glass wall, every woman in the audience hears his voice from close up as if she—like the microphone—were being held in his arms (see page 151)

A characteristic move in the Astaire-Rogers cycle: from the voyeur's distant fascination . . .

. . . to a nearly participatory closeness accompanying the climactic steps: *Top Hat* (see page 144)

Cyd Charisse in *Silk Stockings:* transcendent, energetic, beyond ideology (see page 65)

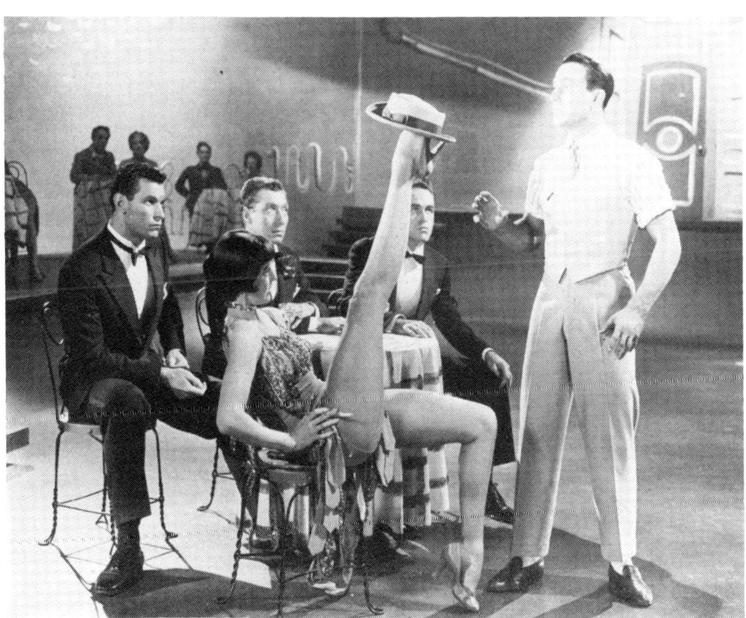

Cyd Charisse as siren, as sorceress, as *vagina dentata:* for Gene Kelly in *Singin' in the Rain . . .*

. . . and for Fred Astaire in *The Band Wagon* (see page 96)

New York as a small town, New Yorkers as a good-natured folk audience drawn onto the Band Wagon by the melody in Fred Astaire's heart—and the shine on his shoes (see page 170)

New Moon (1940). Jeanette MacDonald holds forth on deck for her titled company . . .

. . . while Nelson Eddy and his comrades chant their feelings in the hold below (see page 199)

The musical's often repeated climax: male and female, dark and light, commoner and aristocrat at last united *(New Moon)* (see page 201)

Gigi (pages 201ff)

Role definition

Ia 

Gigi primping

Ib 

Gaston buying

Role reversal

IIa 

IIb 

While Gigi learns the manners of Gaston's world Gaston helps himself to another of Mamita's cookies

Identical sets

IIIa 

IIIb 

Two songs culminate on the same park bench ('I don't understand the Parisians'/'Gigi'). The swans evoke Gaston's discovery that Gigi is no longer an ugly duckling

Parallel sets

IVa 

IVb 

Juxtaposition of similar mirror shots highlights Gaston's and Gigi's divergent attitudes toward love

ears and perceptual system in general. Whereas in everyday life we can listen to one strand of a sonic continuum and ignore the rest (this is the famous concept of 'attention' – however it might be explained), this cannot be done nearly so easily in one-channel recording. What is 'closest' dominates our attention. (This argument is parallel to Munsterberg's argument that changes of distance on the image track seemingly mimic the 'work of the mind'.[3]) So it occurs that this recording practice is not compatible with 'dramatic' sequences in any sort of film, since music so recorded would claim our attention over more (narratively) important speech or sound effects. As a result, close miking of music does not occur (or is substantially weakened by, for example, the addition of reverberation) in narrative films that incorporate but do not privilege musical performances. (There is, however, the important intermediary case of close miking visually justified by the presence of microphones – such as in film noir nightclub sequences.)

II Musical forms: size and shape

But recording practices alone do not explain domination of the diegetic in the musical number. There is also the question of musical form. The musical's most frequently used form (by an incredible margin, even in 'operetta' films) is that of the 32-bar AABA American pop song. In marked contrast, the symphonic score of the dramatic film (until the 1950s) employs shorter musical motifs of one to four measures in length. In Bernard Herrmann's *Citizen Kane* music, for example, the Kane motif is composed of only four notes, and the score's other principal motifs are barely longer.

This difference in size is more important than it might seem on first consideration. The Kane motif (or any other of comparable length) may be heard in its entirety in a few seconds. It can slip in and out of the musical background serving as punctuation device as well as musical characterization. It is not long enough to interrupt (unless desired) a chain of actions visually or linguistically depicted. Motifs that seem to 'rise up' briefly to fill a gap in dialogue or action are frequent in the symphonic scoring of the fiction film. The popular song form, on the other hand, is not nearly so malleable. Although it can be and often is thematized (as we will see below) its length renders it both more obvious – its smallest complete version would last over a minute – and more recognizable as musical entity, since it is more structured both through tonality and repetition. Tonality itself is an aspect of the different musical parentage of music for the 'musical' and for the symphonic score. The traditional popular song is almost always tonally directional; it tends towards a harmonic goal, most often an obvious one. The typical symphonic film score, until the late 1950s, was written in the late romantic musical idiom, a major characteristic of which is, precisely, a relative *lack* of tonal direction and the attendant effects of anticipation followed by 'completion'. Completion itself, a natural characteristic of the closed, harmonically directed popular song form, would be out of place in the symphonic score, whose conclusion in any definite sense must coincide with sequence ends or ultimately with the end of the film, and not with any internally logical musical structure.

Musical form itself is thus concealed by the symphonic film score, this being a logical correlate of its function to follow (emphasize, interpret, specify) rather than rule the diegesis. So it is that most viewers are unaware, even after two or three viewings, that *Kane* or any comparable film has a tightly structured system of musical references. The shortness of motifs in such scores, as well as their comparative lack of harmonic direction, allows their effects to be largely unnoticed, subliminal. Also, any motif can, in general, follow or blend into any other (or into quotation of source music, e.g. folk songs and the like), so that the music can indeed follow the diegesis with ease and efficiency. Thus, even the same procedures of music-diegesis interaction applied on the one hand to the short motifs typical of the symphonic score and on the other to the pop songs used in musical films will have different effects and will be used to different ends. The clearest example of this is probably the practice of thematization.

'Thematization' may be defined as the recurrent association of a recognizable musical entity (diegetic or non-diegetic) with a particular character, situation, or idea. As used in the narrative cinema in general, however, the word 'recognizable' in our definition must be qualified: although the motifs thematized *can* be recognized as distinct entities, for most spectators they are not. Motifs easily go unrecognized both because of their 'size' (smaller than perceived narrative events) and because they are frequently related musically. In *Kane*, for example, the 'Rosebud' motif is an inversion of the 'Kane' motif. (That this is not consciously evident to most viewers presumably strengthens the associational effects of the practice.) Unperceived (but none the less registered), the music may make connections, underline meanings (the various manifestations of the 'Rosebud' motif, as well as its very relation to the 'Kane' motif), provide narrative closure (emphasize a concluding idea, situation, or character), punctuation, and emphasis on the progress of the fiction.

Musicals, on the other hand, tend to treat their songs as entire units – possibly because 'thematized' music in the genre is not merely or even primarily commentative, but rather serves as a means of familiarizing the audience with materials for 'numbers to come'. It is, of course, quite possible to take a bit of a complete, well-structured pop song and turn it into a motif to be used, by excerpting it, weakening it harmonically, and so on. This in fact occurs in an entire sub-genre of the symphonic score, but not, significantly, in the musical. To do this in a musical would be in a sense self-defeating, since it is the very self-sufficiency of musical form which will serve as point of departure for the functioning of numbers.

Footlight Parade offers an example of how far musicals typically go in the process of thematization. The film's score relies largely on four songs, to which correspond four numbers (one a 'rehearsal'): 'Sittin' on a Backyard Fence', 'Honeymoon Hotel', 'By a Waterfall', and 'Shanghai Lil'. All of these songs are also heard as 'background music', generally diegetic, to various dialogue scenes. The rationale is easy: offscreen, the cast is rehearsing various numbers which 'just happen' to filter through walls and doors. It also just happens that characters and songs linked in this way divide into two neat groups: the two pairs of lovers (Cagney and Blondell, Powell and Keeler) are accompanied by 'By a Waterfall' and 'Shanghai Lil', whereas everybody else (avaricious and/or lustful types such as Guy Kibbee, Ruth Donnelly, Claire Dodd, and Hugh Herbert) is associated with 'Sittin' on a Backyard Fence' and 'Honeymoon Hotel', both songs about illicit sex. True love gets love songs, money-and-joyless-sex people get cat yowls and house detectives, and that's pretty much that. The lovers get the down-tempo numbers, the illicit types get up-tempo, pseudo-hot numbers – this totally in keeping with *Footlight*'s simple cultural grid, where hot = sexy and sex is relatively incompatible with love.

Although not all musicals try this hard to be pleasing to devotees of Lévi-Strauss, most of them do seem stuck at the whole-song level of thematization, with two to four songs involved in (by comparison with dramatic film music) relatively obvious references to characters and situations. The references are most frequently based on song lyrics and simple musical distinctions such as up-tempo versus slow, or syncopated versus even-flowing. Because of the appeal to simple cultural-musical codes such as these, songs are not modified much – harmonically, rhythmically, or melodically

– to suit situations in which they occur. On the contrary, this is exactly what occurs in the typical dramatic film score, where a single motif or theme can occur in major or minor, in various tempos, orchestrations, and so on. Since the motifs themselves are not useful in proportion to their recognition-value, it matters little that they shade into one another, appear in various guises, and so on. But the function of music in the musical film is not to go unnoticed, but rather to go so thoroughly noticed and felt (directionality, mood, and so on) that it can assume from and for narrative the function of temporal and often semantic structuration in the number. Narrative may seem to die (or hibernate) in the musical number, but filmic time persists – the time of regularly progressing, recognizable, ordered musical form.

Perhaps for this very reason, from the musical and musico-dramatic point of view 'musical' films are less subtle and interesting than films where music serves rather than dominates. Clichés and exploitation of clichés (e.g. musical parody) abound. Songs that hold our interest solely as songs, today, are a rarity in the film musical, and I do not think that this is wholly because tastes change. The musical, to be successful, did not *need* good songs, merely serviceable songs – songs that could function in some way as authority and anchor for the image-music relationship in musical sequences. It is autonomy and clarity of musical form that seems necessary.

One reason may be immediately advanced for the 'authority' needed by popular songs in the musical film. The songs must impose themselves abruptly and effectively because the music is not continuous. (This seems to be a more important factor in the film as opposed to the stage musical.) This, it strikes me, is the distinction to be made between film musicals and film opera. The film opera, such as Demy's *Umbrellas of Cherbourg*, may use somewhat smaller musical building blocks (forms) and combine them a bit more freely, merely because the implicit assertion 'Here is some music!' need not be made within the diegesis, since music is isotopic to the diegesis. The musical film's alternation between music and diegesis seems both permitted and required by the strong boundaries that popular songs set for themselves. Music and narrative are set up as two terms of a paradigm, and the relative rarity of film operas as compared to film musicals suggests, also, that marketable effects obtain somehow for the alternation.

In guise of a conclusion

And yet, this is the problem: the effects must be termed *marketable*. The musical, for all of its deviations from 'classic' norms, cannot be called a radical or deconstructive genre. What deconstruction (of diegetic conventions) does occur in the genre seems to function in an economy of displacement, wherein one mass-marketed, mechanically reproduced object, the recorded 'popular' song, is valorized at the (temporary) expense of another. Recorded music in the musical comedy seems larger than life because the 'life' it transcends is its own reduced model of the fiction film. If the musical comedy uses filmic diegesis as a straw man, knocked down to affirm the power of music, this occurs in the context of a larger, uninterrogated and mystified project: *entertainment*. Everyone loves a good fight – as long as it stays in the ring where it belongs. But a boxing match is not a revolution, and *The Band Wagon* is not *Nude Descending a Staircase*. Nor, for that matter, is there any reason why it should be.

I would like to conclude with a brief plea for certain directions of work in the area of the musical film. In my discussion I have implicitly assumed that musical numbers are based on popular songs and that these songs are generally sung by a diegetic character. This procedure completely neglects the important category of dream ballets – which are, first of all, *meta-diegetic* (narrated by a secondary narrator within the diegesis), and in which the role of music is in many ways different from that outlined above. It is worth asking whether in a sense most dance in film musicals (except, perhaps, comic dance) is meta-diegetic. Dance itself needs to be discussed in terms of specific steps, the type and length of syntagmatic units, their interaction with music, and so on.

Another area in need of investigation is the history of recording practices (both in general and of musical numbers). At the least we need some working hypotheses – an 'Evolution of the Language of Cinema' for the soundtrack. Lacking this, we should have precise *descriptions* of the soundtracks of selected musicals and non-musicals . . . A last example, which I find particularly appealing, is the comparison of popular music as employed in avant-garde cinema and in the musical – *Scorpio Rising* versus *Jailhouse Rock*, *All My Life* versus *The Band Wagon*. Such thinking demonstrates the existence of alternate modes of sound–image relationships not employed in the musical.

This list could continue indefinitely. What unity it possesses and what for me ties it to the bulk of this article, is that all these areas could best be attacked comparatively rather than inductively. This is the usefulness of a formulation like Jaubert's: one is not obliged to define the musical as ideal type, but rather to procede quasi-deductively, defining the musical at each level by what it is not. I hope to have shown in these pages how such work might begin.

Notes

1 'Music on the Screen', in Charles Davy, ed., *Footnotes to the Film* (London: Lovat Dickson, 1937), pp. 104–5.
2 'The Work of Art in the Age of Mechanical Reproduction', in *Illuminations* (New York: Schocken, 1969), pp. 222–3.
3 See his *The Film: A Psychological Study* (rpt. New York: Dover, 1970), particularly chapter 4.

10 · Jane Feuer: 'The Self-reflective Musical and the Myth of Entertainment'

Quarterly Review of Film Studies, vol. 2, no. 3, August 1977, pp. 313–26

Perhaps the most characteristic aspect of so-called Hollywood classical narrative is the transparency of its language. In the typical Hollywood product everything is calculated to keep us from realizing that we are watching a film. We never notice that the people we are observing consist only of shadow and light, that multiple cameras and microphones have been used in the construction of the image and its soundtrack, that sound and image emanate from different sources. Modernist narrative, on the other hand, is usually associated with the foregrounding of filmic language, multiple levels of narration, and the estrangement of the spectator. Such clichés, long central to the enterprise of narrative analysis, simply will not survive a confrontation with the musical. As Jane Feuer points out, the musical from its very beginnings has been a self-reflective genre, presenting all the alienation devices which we normally associate with Brecht and an aesthetic or Marxist avant-garde, yet the musical shares none of the revolutionary purpose supposedly implied by self-reflexivity. (Alan Williams comes to the same conclusion in the preceding article.) Mobilizing radical technique for a conservative purpose, the musical undermines traditional attempts to identify a specific ideology with a given technique.

Not content to point up the musical's challenge to well-established notions of the limits and elements of classical narrative, Feuer goes on to demonstrate how the musical turns its self-reflective technique to its own purposes, foregrounding its technology only in order to reaffirm its own values better. Critics of the musical complain that it provides entertainment but nothing more. Feuer shows how a group of the genre's best-known films answers that complaint and puts it at least temporarily to rest. Far from simply *being* entertainment, these musicals are *about* entertainment; whatever the spectator's notion of entertainment may have been, these films redefine it in such a way that it cannot help but be positive. By allying forms of entertainment with values previously held by the spectator, or by opposing entertainment to patently false or ridiculous non-entertainment forms, the musical succeeds amply in the process of self-justification. The spectator is thus doubly at the mercy of the film: at first he/she is lured into believing in the film's fundamental honesty because the film admits that it is 'only' a film, yet all the while this particular film is being aligned with a set of values which the spectator cannot help but accept, so that by the end of the film the spectator has been convinced that this product of big business, modern technology, and mass distribution is a downhome blend of spontaneity, togetherness, and singalong sensitivity. By creating its own myth of entertainment the musical succeeds in disguising the crass commercialism of the mass media behind a wholesome front of folk art.

Earlier decades of film criticism were all too happy to forget the embarrassing fact that Hollywood often makes decisions on economic rather than artistic grounds. In recent years, however, more and more critics have successfully introduced the socio-economic facts of film production into their analyses. Feuer's article represents for the musical a pioneering effort in this direction. She shows how the musical manages to make a virtue out of its embarrassing past, how the musical serves as a mechanism to disguise not its own status as a Hollywood product but Hollywood's unmentionable status as a commercial enterprise.

Within the musical film the most persistent subgenre has involved kids (or adults) 'getting together and putting on a show'. *The Jazz Singer* (1927) featured a show business story, and during the talkie boom that followed (1929–1930), a large percentage of the early musicals took for their subjects the world of entertainment: Broadway, Vaudeville, the Ziegfeld Follies, burlesque, night clubs, the circus, Tin Pan Alley, and, to a lesser extent, mass entertainment media in the form of radio or Hollywood itself. Warner Brothers' *42nd Street* (1933) precipitated a second cycle of musicals. The *42nd Street* spinoffs tended to feature a narrative strategy typical of the backstage musical: musical interludes, usually in the form of rehearsal sequences detailing the maturation of the show, would be interspersed with parallel dramatic scenes detailing maturation of the off-stage love affairs. Even a radio story such as *Twenty Million Sweethearts* (1934) took its narrative structure from this paradigm. Perhaps these 'art' musicals fulfilled a need for verisimilitude; perhaps the audience felt more comfortable viewing musical numbers within the context of a show than seeing fairytale queens and princes suddenly feel a song coming on in the royal boudoir. Whatever the explanation for its origins, the backstage pattern was always central to the genre. Incorporated into the structure of the art musical was the very type of popular entertainment represented by the musical film itself. The art musical is thus a self-referential form.

All art musicals are self-referential in this loose sense. But given such an opportunity, some musicals have exhibited a greater degree of self-consciousness than others. *Dames* (1934) climaxes its show-within-the film with an apology for its own mode of entertainment, appropriately entitled 'Dames'. Moreover, the 'Dames' number resolves a narrative in which the forces of Puritanism do battle with the forces of entertainment. It is this victory of what might be termed the 'prurient ethic' over the Puritan ethic that the final show celebrates within the film, and that the 'Dames' number celebrates within that show. In similar fashion, the Fred Astaire–Ginger Rogers cycle at RKO (1933–39) began to reflect upon the legends created in its dancing stars.[1]

Shall We Dance (1937) culminates in a show merging popular dancing with ballet. Yet that merger consists not in an equal union but rather in the lending of youth, rhythm, and vitality to the stiff, formal, classical art of ballet. Once again, a musical film has affirmed its own value for the popular audience.

Dames and *Shall We Dance* are early examples of musicals that are self-*reflective* beyond their given self-referentiality. Historically, the art musical has evolved toward increasingly greater degrees of self-reflectivity. By the late forties and into the early fifties, a series of musicals produced by the Freed Unit at MGM used the backstage format to present sustained reflections upon, and affirmations of, the musical genre itself. Three of these apologies for the musical (all scripted by Betty Comden and Adolph Green), *The Barkleys of Broadway* (1949), *Singin' in the Rain* (1952), and *The Band Wagon* (1953) involve contrasts between performances that fail to please audiences and performances that are immediately audience-pleasing.[2] Performances in these films are not restricted to onstage numbers. Multiple levels of performances and consequent multiple levels of audience combine to create a myth about musical entertainment permeating ordinary life. Through the work of these filmic texts all successful performances, both in art and in life, are condensed into the MGM musical.

To say that entertainment is 'mythified' is to institute a triple play upon conventional meanings of the word 'myth'. Most simply, it means that entertainment is shown as having greater value than it actually does. In this sense musicals are ideological products; they are full of deceptions. As students of mythology have demonstrated, however, these deceptions are willingly suffered by the audience. In *American Vaudeville as Ritual*, Albert F. McLean attempts to explain this contradiction in his definition of myth as:

> a constellation of images and symbols, whether objectively real or imaginary, which brings focus and a degree of order to the

> psychic (largely unconscious) processes of a group or society and in so doing endows a magical potency upon the circumstances of persons involved.[3]

McLean's notion of myth as 'aura' occupies a pole opposite that of myth as 'untruth' in constituting the myth of entertainment.

According to Claude Lévi-Strauss, the seemingly random surface structure of a myth masks contradictions which are real and therefore unresolvable.[4] Art musicals are structurally similar to myths, seeking to mediate contradictions in the nature of popular entertainment. The myth of entertainment is constituted by an oscillation between demystification and remythicization.[5] Musicals, like myths, exhibit a stratified structure. The ostensible or surface function of these musicals is to give pleasure to the audience by revealing what goes on behind the scenes in the theater or Hollywood, that is, to demystify the production of entertainment. But the films remythicize at another level that which they set out to expose. Only unsuccessful performances are demystified. The musical desires an ultimate valorization of entertainment; to destroy the aura, reduce the illusion, would be to destroy the myth of entertainment as well.[6] For the purpose of analysis, the myth of entertainment can be subdivided into three categories: the myth of spontaneity, the myth of integration, and the myth of the audience. In the films, however, the myth makes its impact through combination and repetition. Thus, a single musical number can be highly overdetermined and may be discussed under all three categories.

The myth of spontaneity

Perhaps the primary positive quality associated with musical performance is its spontaneous emergence out of a joyous and responsive attitude toward life. The musical buffs' parlor game which attempts to distinguish Fred Astaire's screen persona from Gene Kelly's ignores the overriding similarities in both dancers' spontaneous stances.[7] *The Barkleys of Broadway*, *Singin' in the Rain*, and *The Band Wagon* contrast the spontaneity of Astaire or Kelly with the prepackaged or calculated behaviour of other performers.

In *Singin' in the Rain*, spontaneous talent distinguishes Don, Cosmo, and Kathy from Lina Lamont. Lina's laborious attempts to master basic English are followed by Don Lockwood's elocution lesson. Don and Cosmo seize upon the tongue-twister to turn the lesson into a spontaneous, anarchic dance routine, 'Moses Supposes'. Spontaneous self-expression through song and dance characterizes the three positive performers: Cosmo in 'Make 'Em Laugh,' Don in 'Singin' in the Rain,' and all three in 'Good Mornin,' which evolves out of their collective solution to the problems of the 'Dueling Cavalier.'

In addition, the impression of spontaneity in these numbers stems from a type of *bricolage*; the performers make use of props-at-hand – curtains, movie paraphernalia, umbrellas, furniture – to create the imaginary world of the musical performance. This *bricolage*, a hallmark of the post-Gene Kelly MGM musical, creates yet another contradiction: an effect of spontaneous realism is achieved through simulation.

The Barkleys of Broadway opposes strained, artificial 'serious' performances to spontaneous and natural musical comedy performances. Dinah Barkley's sparkling costume and demeanor in the title sequence with Astaire ('Swing Trot') contrasts with her subdued garb and sullen demeanor as a dramatic actress. Early in the film we see Dinah truncating her understudy's carefully calculated audition, doing a brief warm-up, and going into a perfectly executed rehearsal of a tap routine with her husband. The rehearsals of 'Young Sarah' (a play about Sarah Bernhardt's *struggle* to become an actress) are quite the opposite. Josh (Astaire), the musical comedy director-performer, is always spontaneous and natural. In the parallel sequence to Dinah's labors over 'Young Sarah,' we see Josh doing a completed number from his new show. 'Shoes with Wings On' presents musical comedy dancing as an involuntary response, like breathing. Dancing is so spontaneous for Josh that animated shoes pull him into performance. The Astaire character never changes; he is presented as an utterly seamless monument of naturalness and spontaneity. Others must adapt to his style. Dinah can succeed as a performer only in a musical setting with Josh. Even their offstage performances stem from a spontaneous responsiveness to ordinary life, as when their dance to 'You'd Be Hard to Replace' evolves out of the natural movements of putting on robes.

Similar oppositions between spontaneous and canned performers structure *Singin' in the Rain* and *The Band Wagon*. Astaire's trademark, 'reflex' dancing, has its counterpart in the 'Gotta Dance' motif which informs Kelly's 'Broadway Ballet,' part of the ultimately successful film-within-the-film. *The Band Wagon* cuts from Tony Hunter's (Astaire's) spontaneous eruption into song and dance at the penny arcade to Jeffrey Cordova in *Oedipus Rex*. The moaning sounds in the background of this production are later associated with the reactions of an audience to Cordova's laborious musical version of *Faust*. We are shown Cordova from the point of view of Tony and the Martons in the wings (almost always a demystifying camera position), as he moves from his curtain calls as Oedipus into his offstage pomposity. Although Cordova's *Oedipus* is said to be successful with audiences *in* the film the extent to which it is demystified for *us* undercuts its status as a successful show. Cordova is characterized throughout the first half of the film by the mechanical nature of his actions and utterances. He continually gives rehearsed speeches such as the one about Bill Shakespeare's immortal lines and Bill Robinson's immortal feet. On the first day of rehearsals, Cordova tells the cast exactly what will happen to them before the show opens. Not until he dances with Astaire (and in Astaire's style) in the top-hat, white tie, and tails soft-shoe number in the second 'Band Wagon' does Cordova achieve true spontaneity as a performer.

Almost every spontaneous performance in *The Band Wagon* has a matched segment which parodies the lack of spontaneity of the high art world. Tony drops Gaby while attempting a lift during the rehearsal of a ballet number for the first show; later in 'The Girl Hunt,' a jazz ballet, he lifts her effortlessly. Tony and Gaby's relaxed offstage rehearsal of a dance to 'You and the Night and the Music' literally explodes on stage at the dress rehearsal. A prepackaged orchestral rendition of 'Something to Remember You By' at the official New Haven cast party dissolves into a vocal version of the same song spontaneously performed by the 'kids' at the chorus party. Spontaneity thus emerges as the hallmark of a successful performance.

The myth of spontaneity operates through what we are shown of the work of production of the respective shows as well as how we are shown it. In *Singin' in the Rain*, we see the technical difficulties involved with filming and projecting 'The Dueling Cavalier,' including Lina's battle with the microphone and the failure of the film when its technological base is revealed to the preview audience. 'The Dancing Cavalier,' in contrast, springs to life effortlessly. The film shows an awareness of this opposition between the foregrounding of technology in 'The Dueling Cavalier' and the invisibility of technology in the 'Dancing Cavalier.' 'The Broadway Ballet' is presented in the context of an idea for a production number, and one of the biggest jokes in the film concerns the producer's inability to visualize what we have just been shown, elaborate and complete. Yet at many other points in *Singin' in the Rain* this awareness is masked, often in quite complex ways.[8] In 'You Were Meant for Me' the exposure of the wind machine figures prominently in the demystification of romantic musical numbers. Yet in a dialogue scene outside the soundstage just prior to this number, Kathy's scarf had blown to the breeze of an invisible wind machine. Even after we are shown the tools of illusion at the beginning of the number, the camera arcs around and comes in for a tighter shot of the performing couple, thereby remasking the exposed technology and making the duet just another example of the type of number whose illusions it exposes. Demystification is countered by the reassertion of the spontaneous evolution of musical films. Perhaps the ultimate in spontaneous evolution of a musical number occurs in *The Barkleys*. At the end of the film, the couple decides to do another musical. Josh describes a dance routine which, unlike 'Young Sarah,' will have *tempo*, and the couple goes into a dance, framed to the right of a curtain in their living room. As they spin, there is a dissolve to the same step as part of an elaborate production number in the new show.

In *The Band Wagon* the labor of producing the first show eclipses the performances. Never do we see a completed number from the first show. Technical or personal problems prevent the completion of every number shown in rehearsal, as when Tony walks out or when Cordova is levitated by the revolving stage. It is not because high art (ballet) and popular art (musical comedy) are inherently mutually exclusive that Cordova's show fails. After all, it is Tony's impressionist paintings which pay for the successful show. Rather, the film suggests that Cordova fails because he has been unable to render invisible the technology of production in order to achieve the effect of effortlessness by which all entertainment succeeds in winning its audience.

Of course spontaneous performances that mask their technology have been calculated too – not for audiences within the films but for audiences *of* the film. The musical, technically the most complex type of film produced in Hollywood, paradoxically has always been the genre which attempts to give the greatest illusion of spontaneity and effortlessness. It is as if engineering were to affirm *bricolage* as the ultimate approach to scientific thought. The self-reflective musical is aware of this in attempting to promulgate the myth of spontaneity. The heavily value-laden oppositions set up in the self-reflective films promote the mode of expression of the film musical itself as spontaneous and natural rather than calculated and technological. Musical entertainment thus takes on a natural relatedness to life processes and to the lives of its audiences. Musical entertainment claims for its own all natural and joyous performances in art and in life. The myth of spontaneity operates (to borrow Lévi-Strauss's terminology) to make musical performance, which is actually part of culture, appear to be part of nature.

The myth of integration

Earlier musicals sometimes demonstrated ambiguous attitudes toward the world of musical theater, perceiving conflicts between success on the stage and success in the performers' personal lives. In *Ziegfeld Girl* (1941), Lana Turner is destroyed when she forsakes the simple life in Brooklyn for the glamor of the Follies. In *Cain and Mabel* (1936), Marion Davies has to be physically dragged onto the stage after deciding to retire to a garage in Jersey with prize fighter beau Clark Gable. But the self-reflective musical asserts the integrative effect of musical performance. Successful performances are intimately bound up with success in love, with the integration of the individual into a community or a group, and even with the merger of high art with popular art.

In *Singin' in the Rain*, the success of the musical film brings about the final union of Don and Kathy. This consummation takes place on the stage at the premier in front of a live audience and in the form of a duet. The music is carried over to a shot of the lovers embracing in front of a billboard of Don and Kathy's images. But the successful show on the billboard is no longer 'The Dancing Cavalier'; it is *Singin' in the Rain*, that is, the film itself. This hall-of-mirrors effect emphasizes the unity-giving function of the musical both for the couples and audiences *in* the film and for the audience *of* the film. In *The Barkleys*, Josh and Dinah are reunited when she realizes she wants 'nothing but fun set to music,' that is, the type of performance associated with the MGM musical. Gaby, in *The Band Wagon*, learns the value of popular entertainment as she learns to love Tony. 'Dancing in the Dark' imitates the form of a sexual act as it merges two kinds of dancing previously set in conflict. The number combines the ballet movements associated with Gaby and her choreographer beau Paul Byrd with the ballroom dancing associated with Astaire. At the end of the film the long run of their successful show is used by Gaby as a metaphor for her relationship with Tony.

The right kind of musical performance also integrates the individual into a unified group just as the wrong kind alienates. *The Band Wagon* traces Tony's repeated movements from isolation to the joy of being part of a group. At the beginning of the film, Tony sings 'By Myself' isolated by the tracking camera; as he enters the crowded terminal, the camera stops moving to frame him against the crowd, a mass that becomes an audience for Tony's antics with the Martons. The arcade sequence repeats this opening movement. Once again Tony overcomes his sense of isolation by reestablishing contact with an audience through spontaneous musical performance. The '?' machine at the arcade symbolizes the problem/solution format of the narrative. When Tony answers the question of how to make a comeback by dancing with a shoeshine man, the machine bursts open and his audience rushes to congratulate him. Another such movement occurs when, after the failure of the first show, Tony finds himself the only guest at the official cast party. 'I Love Louisa' marks his renewal of contact with yet another audience – this time the common folk of the theater itself. At the end of the film, Tony moves from a reprise of 'By Myself' into the final integration – a symbolic marriage to Gaby and to the rank and file of the theater. The myth of integration makes itself felt through the repetitive structure of the film.

Paralleling Tony's movement from isolation to integration and also paralleling the integration of the couple, is Gaby's integration into the populist world of musical theater from the elitist world of high art. We first see Gaby in a ballet performance in which she functions as prima ballerina backed by the corps. At Cordova's, the two worlds are spatially isolated as the representatives of high art (Gabrielle and Paul) and those of popular art (Tony and the Martons) occupy separate rooms. The possibility of movement between the two worlds is stressed by the precisely parallel actions taking place in each room as well as by Cordova's role as mediator between the two rooms (worlds). Cordova prevents a terminal clash between Tony and Gaby by rushing into the neutral space of the front hall and drawing the representatives of both worlds back into his own central space.

Gabrielle begins her integration into the world of popular art through a renewal of contact with the common folk in Central Park, a process which culminates in 'I Love Louisa' with Gaby serving as part of the chorus. Paul Byrd draws Gaby away from the group into an isolated space symbolic of the old world of ballet; the camera frames the couple apart from the mass. The colors of their isolated space – subdued shades of brown and white – contrast with the vibrant colors of the chorus' costumes which have just filled the frame. In leaving this isolated space to return to the group, Gaby has taken the side of the collective effort which will produce the successful musical. 'New Sun in the Sky,' the first number in the new show, again finds Gaby backed up by a chorus, but this time the mood is celebratory – the bright golds and reds as well as the lyrics of the song emphasize Gaby's rebirth. Even the musical arrangement of the song – upbeat and jazzy – contrasts with the more sedate balletic arrangement we heard in that rehearsal for the Faustian *Band Wagon* in which Tony dropped Gaby. At the end of the film, Gaby expresses her feelings for Tony by speaking for the group, the chorus framed in back of her as she speaks.

Everyone knows that the musical film was a mass art produced by a tiny elite for a vast and amorphous consuming public; the self-reflective musical attempts to overcome this division through the myth of integration. It offers a vision of musical performance originating in the folk, generating love and a cooperative spirit which includes everyone in its grasp and which can conquer all obstacles. By promoting audience identification with the collectively produced shows, the myth of integration seeks to give the audience a sense of participation in the creation of the film itself. The musical film becomes a mass art which aspires to the condition of a folk art – produced and consumed by the same integrated community.

The myth of the audience

It follows that successful performances will be those in which the performer is sensitive to the needs of his audience and which give the audience a sense of participation in the performance. Josh Barkley berates Dinah for her performance in the subway scene because 'the audience wants to cry there and you won't let them.' Cordova is more concerned with the revolving stage than with delivering audience-pleasing performances; his canned speeches of solidarity with the cast are undercut by his delivering them with his back to the group, oblivious to their response. Tony Hunter, on the other hand, is willing to leave the self-enclosed world of the theater to regain contact with the folk who make up his audience. 'Dancing in the Dark' is precipitated by observing ordinary people dancing in Central Park.

The insensitive performer also attempts to manipulate his audience. Cordova wants to control the timing of the curtain, the actress's exit pace, and the placing of an amber spot in *Oedipus*. Lina Lamont masks the fact that she is unable to speak for herself either on stage or on screen.

Yet while setting up an association between success and lack of audience manipulation, the musicals themselves exert continuous control over the responses of their audiences. The film musical profits rhetorically by displacing to the theater the myth of a privileged relationship between musical entertainment and its audience. Popular theater can achieve a fluidity and immediacy in this respect that the film medium lacks. The out-of-town tryout, the interpolation of new material after each performance, the instantaneous modulation of performer to audience response – none of these common theatrical practices is possible for film. Hollywood had only the limited adaptations made possible by the preview system and the genre system itself which accommodated audience response by making (or not making) other films of the same type. The backstage musical, however, manages to incorporate the immediate performer-audience relationship into films, thus gaining all the advantages of both media. Musical numbers can be shot from the point of view of a front-row theatrical spectator and then move into filmic space – combining the immediate contact of the theater with the mobility of perspective of the camera. Numbers that begin within theatrical space merge, often quite imperceptibly, into filmic space. Extended musical sequences such as 'Shoes With Wings On' and 'The Girl Hunt Ballet' start within a proscenium frame and then become fully edited filmic sequences, in a tradition stemming from the early Berkeley musicals.

The Band Wagon uses this double perspective to manipulate the film audience's point of view. In 'That's Entertainment,' Cordova and the Martons try to convince Tony that all successful art is entertainment. The number takes place on the stage of an empty theater with the first refrain of the song shot from camera positions that approximate the point of view of a spectator *on* the stage (angles available only to the cinema). Midway through the number, at the point where Tony is convinced, the action shifts to the performing area of the stage and the point of view shifts to that of a spectator in the theater. The film audience sees, from the point of view of a theater audience, the number performed in the empty theater becoming a direct address to the film's audience. The effort to convince Tony has become an effort to convince *us*. In the reprise of 'That's Entertainment' at the film's finale, the point of view shifts from over-the-shoulder shots to frame the performers directly in front of the camera as they ask us to celebrate once again the merging of all art into entertainment, this time in the form of the film *The Band Wagon* itself (an effect quite like that of the billboard at the end of *Singin' in the Rain*). 'Make 'Em Laugh' is much more subtle in shifting points of view. Starting from a subjective shot over Don's shoulder, the number begins as an affirmation of the value of entertainment as Cosmo attempts to cheer up his friend; however, the point of view quickly shifts so that the message is addressed to the film's audience. We quickly lose track of Don's point of view, and the number never returns to it.

The use of theatrical audiences *in* the films provides a point of identification for audiences *of* the film. Even *Singin' in the Rain* emphasizes the responses of live audiences at previews and premiers. Although inserted shots of applauding audiences can be used as a trick similar to television's use of canned laughter, self-reflective musicals tend to use audiences-within-the-film more subtly. In *The Barkleys*, Astaire and Rogers dance 'Swing Trot,' a routine designed to arouse nostalgia for the famous team, under the film's titles. At the end of the number there is a cut to a side angle, and we see the couple taking a bow before a live audience. The audience in the film is there to express the adulation the number itself sought to arouse from the film's audience.

MGM musicals make use of natural, spontaneous audiences which form around offstage performances.[9] 'Shine on Your Shoes' in *The Band Wagon* demonstrates Astaire's ability to adapt his dancing to any occasion and any audience, as he incorporates the shoeshiner into his performance. The spontaneous audience which forms around the duo provides a point of identification for the film audience as well. In 'I Love Louisa' the chorus serves first as an audience for Tony and the Martons's clowning, and then participates in the dance, providing a vicarious sense of participation for the film audience. Audiences in the films suggest a contagious spirit inherent in musical performance, related to the suggestion that the MGM musical is folk art; the audience must be shown as participating in the production of entertainment.

Intertextuality and star iconography can be a means of manipulating audience response. Many of the later MGM musicals play upon the audience's memories of earlier musicals. *The Barkleys* plays on the Astaire–Rogers legend from its first shot of the couple's feet, which echoes the title sequence of *Top Hat* (1935). The couple's reunion performance to 'You Can't Take That Away From Me' harks back to *Shall We Dance* (1937), with the dance itself reminiscent of one of their old routines. Such attempts to evoke nostalgia play on the star system's desire to erase the boundaries between star persona and character, between on-screen and off-screen personalities. *The Barkleys* thus celebrates Ginger Rogers' return to musical comedy after a series of straight dramatic films, suggesting that the only way she can succeed with an audience is by dancing with Astaire in musicals.[10]

Other self-reflective musicals make use of audience response to songs from previous stage musicals or films. Most of the songs in *Singin' in the Rain* were written for the earliest MGM film musicals. *The Band Wagon* takes its music from stage revues of the same period (late twenties to early thirties). In the interim many of these songs had become standards, and the films were able to play upon the audience's familiarity with the lyric. 'Dancing in the Dark,' for example, is used only in instrumental arrangement, thus inviting the audience to participate by supplying the lyric. Two related practices of the Freed Unit – biopics fashioned around a composer's hit songs, and the purchase of a song catalog around which to construct an original musical – depended upon audience familiarity (through both filmic and nonfilmic intertexts) for their effectiveness.

Conclusion

Self-reflective musicals mediate a contradiction between live performance in the theater and the frozen form of cinema by implying that the MGM musical *is* theater, possesses the same immediate and active relationship to its audience. Both the myth of integration and the myth of the audience suggest that the MGM musical is really a folk art, that the audience participates in the creation of musical entertainment. The myth of integration suggests that the achievement of personal fulfilment goes hand-in-hand with the enjoyment of entertainment. And the myth of spontaneity suggests that the MGM musical is not artificial but rather completely natural. Performance is no longer defined as something professionals do on a stage; instead, it permeates the lives of professional and nonprofessional singers and dancers. Entertainment, the myth implies, can break down the barriers between art and life.

The myth of entertainment, in its entirety, cannot be celebrated in a single text or even across three texts. Different aspects of the myth achieve prominence in different films but the myth is carried by the genre as a whole. The notion of breaking down barriers betwen art and life, for example, is more prominent in Minnelli's *The Pirate* (1947) than in any of the films discussed here. It might be said that the elements of the myth of entertainment constitute a paradigm which generates the syntax of individual texts.

Ultimately, one might wonder why these films go to such lengths to justify the notion that all life should aspire to the condition of a musical performance. That is, why expend so much effort to celebrate mythic elements the audience is likely to accept anyway? Answering this question involves an awareness both of the function of ritual and of the ritual function of the musical. All ritual involves the celebration of shared values and beliefs; the ritual function of the musical is to reaffirm and articulate the place that entertainment occupies in its audience's psychic lives. Self-reflective musicals are then able to celebrate myths created by the genre as a whole.

Yet the extremes of affirmation in *The Band Wagon* need further justification in terms of its function for MGM as well as for the popular audience. At a time when the studio could no longer be certain of the allegiance of its traditional mass audience, *The Band Wagon*, in ritual fashion, served to reaffirm the traditional relationship. For the musical was always the quintessential Hollywood product: all Hollywood films manipulated audience response, but the musical could incorporate that response in the film itself; all Hollywood films sought to be entertaining, but the musical could incorporate a myth of entertainment into its aesthetic discourse. As Thomas Elsaesser says, 'The world of the musical becomes a kind of ideal image of the [film] medium itself.'[11]

Nowhere is Lévi-Strauss's notion of myth more applicable to the musical than in the relationship of the genre to the studio system which produced it. Faced with declining attendance due to competition from television, the studio could suggest, through *Singin' in the Rain*, that making musicals can provide a solution to any crisis of technological change. Faced with charges of infantilism from the citadels of high art, the studio could suggest, through *The Barkleys of Broadway*, that all successful performances are musical performances. Faced with the threat of changing patterns of audience consumption, the studio could suggest, through *The Band Wagon*, that the MGM musical can adapt to any audience. *The Band Wagon* ends where the films *That's Entertainment I* and *II* commence, in an attempt to recapture the aura of the 'Golden Age' of the Freed/MGM musicals. It is not surprising that the 'That's Entertainment' number from *The Band Wagon* should have been inserted into the contemporary sequences of the nostalgia compilations. For the ending of *The Band Wagon* already marked the genre's celebration of its own (and Hollywood's) economic death and ritual rebirth.

Self-reflexivity as a critical category has been associated with films such as those of Godard, which call attention to the codes constituting their own signifying practices. The term has been applied to aesthetically or politically radical films which react against so-called classical narrative cinema by interrogating their own narrativity. Thus we tend to associate reflexivity with the notion of deconstruction within film-making practice. The MGM musical, however, uses reflexivity to perpetuate rather than to deconstruct the codes of the genre. Self-reflective musicals are conservative texts in every sense. MGM musicals have continued to function both in the popular consciousness and within international film culture as representatives of the Hollywood product at its best. I hope to have shown that this was the very task these texts sought to accomplish.

Notes

1 See Leo Braudy, *The World in a Frame* (New York: Anchor Press/Doubleday, 1976), pp. 143–47, for a discussion of self-consciousness in *Shall We Dance.*

2 *The Barkleys of Broadway* presents Josh and Dinah Barkley (Fred Astaire and Ginger Rogers) as the Lunts of musical comedy. Dinah leaves musical comedy to do a serious play ('Young Sarah'), and finally learns the lesson that there's no difference between serious acting and musical comedy acting. She returns to do a musical at the end of the film. *Singin' in the Rain* depicts the coming of sound to Hollywood. An early talkie which fails ('The Dueling Cavalier') is remade as a musical which succeeds ('The Dancing Cavalier'). *The Band Wagon* also involves the re-production of a show that flops (a musical version of the Faust story called 'The Band Wagon') into a musical revue which succeeds (again called 'The Band Wagon').

3 University of Kentucky Press, 1965, p. 223.

4 'The Structural Study of Myth' in *Structural Anthropology* (New York: Basic Books, 1963), p. 220. I am also indebted to Lévi-Strauss for other ideas contained in the same essay: first, that a myth works itself out through repetition in a number of texts; second, that myth works through the mediation of binary oppositions.

5 These terms are taken from Paul Ricoeur, *Freud and Philosophy* (New Haven: Yale University Press, 1970), p. 54. Ricoeur uses them to refer to two schools of hermeneutics which nevertheless constitute 'a profound unity.' I find them equally applicable to texts which seek to interpret themselves.

6 The inseparability of demystification from its opposite (remythicization) is best illustrated by *A Star is Born* (Warners, 1954), at once the last bearer of the studio's myth of entertainment and the first of the antimusicals. Even the supposedly Brechtian antimusical *Cabaret* (1972) merely inverts the backstage paradigm, while maintaining its narrative strategy.

7 See Braudy, p. 147 ff. for a discussion of the function of spontaneity in the Astaire and Kelly personae.

8 See David Lusted, 'Film as Industrial Product – Teaching a Reflexive Movie,' *Screen Education* 16 (Autumn 1975) for detailed examples of the mystification-demystification dynamic in *Singin' in the Rain*.

9 Other good examples of 'natural audiences' in the MGM musical include 'By Strauss,' 'I Got Rhythm,' and 'S'Wonderful' in *An American in Paris* (1951); 'Niña' in *The Pirate* (1947); and 'I Like Myself', Gene Kelly's dance on roller skates in *It's Always Fair Weather* (1955). The history of this device in the musical film may be traced from Jolson to Chevalier to Astaire to Kelly and back to Astaire, spontaneity of performance providing the link among the major male musical stars.

10 The extreme example of this phenomenon is *A Star is Born* (1954), the signification of which depends upon the audience's knowledge of Judy Garland's off-screen life as the negation of her MGM on-screen image.

11 'The American Musical,' *Brighton Film Review* 15 (December 1969), p. 13.

11 · Richard Dyer: 'Entertainment and Utopia'

Movie, no. 24, Spring 1977, pp. 2–13

Every society depends on categories which are somehow above all suspicion: people may not be able to define a given practice, but 'they know it when they see it.' Entertainment is one such category in American life. Borrowed from a French term meaning to keep up, to maintain, to foster, or to feed, the term entertainment stresses the hold which certain forms of spectacle have on the spectator. By its very etymology, then, the term entertainment suggests a discursive phenomenon rather than an impersonal narrative form. 'Let me entertain you' = 'Let me hold your interest; let me create a bond between you and me.' The French long ago abandoned the term 'entretenir' to designate various forms of popular spectacle, however. At least since Pascal the word has been 'divertir' – to turn away, to distract, to divert. Far from placing emphasis on entertainment's power to hold the spectator's interest, the French term stresses instead entertainment's tendency to create 'an attack or feint that draws the attention and force of an enemy from the point of the principal operation,' as Webster's would have it ('diversion').

Traditionally, critics have chosen one of these two definitions and ignored the other. Entertainment is either a highly developed form created by past-masters in the art of dialogue, geniuses at sensing the mood of an audience, or it is a drug which lulls the masses to sleep, bribes them with pleasurable dreams, and thus distracts them from the stern tasks which are their true destiny. In fact, these two statements are complementary rather than contradictory, yet rarely have the prejudices aroused by the mere mention of the term entertainment allowed this fact to surface. The widespread nature of this blindness makes Richard Dyer's article all the more important, for where others have simply justified to the faithful (fans or radicals) their prejudice that entertainment is either good or bad, Dyer demonstrates how the musical lies at the intersection of diversion and discourse. A careful and extremely sensitive reading of three diverse films permits Dyer to make some basic generalizations about the value structure of American entertainment. In so doing Dyer is able to construct a model for resolving the most persistent paradox about the nature of entertainment: how can it be that entertainment simultaneously appeals to the spectator by reaffirming his values *and* provides the spectator with those very values? By revealing how and why entertainment works – why it satisfies us at the very same time that it is limiting our interests – Richard Dyer helps us, finally, to remove the category of entertainment from the vault of unquestionable cultural givens and expose it for the scrutiny of us all.

This article is about musicals as entertainment. I don't necessarily want to disagree with those who would claim that musicals are also 'something else' (e.g. 'Art') or argue that entertainment itself is only a product of 'something more important' (e.g. political/economic manipulation, psychological forces), but I want to put the emphasis here on entertainment as entertainment. Musicals were predominantly conceived of, by producers and audiences alike, as 'pure entertainment' – the *idea* of entertainment was a prime determinant on them. Yet because entertainment is a common-sense, 'obvious' idea, what is really meant and implied by this never gets discussed.

Musicals are one of a whole string of forms – music hall, variety, tv spectaculars, pantomime, cabaret, etc. – that are usually summed up by the term 'show biz'. The idea of entertainment I want to examine here is most centrally embodied by these forms, although I believe that it can also be seen at work, *mutatis mutandis*, in other forms and I suggest below, informally, how this might be so. However, it is probably true to say that 'show biz' is the most thoroughly entertainment-oriented of all types of performance, and that notions of myth, art, instruction, dream and ritual may be equally important, even at the conscious level, with regard to, say, westerns, the news, soap-opera, or rock music.

It is important, I think, to stress the cultural and historical specificity of entertainment. The kinds of performance produced by professional entertainment are different in audience, performers and above all intention to the kinds of performance produced in tribal, feudal or socialist societies. It is not possible here to provide the detailed historical and anthropological argument to back this up, but I hope the differences will suggest themselves when I say that entertainment is a type of performance produced for profit, performed before a generalised audience (the 'public'), by a trained, paid group who do nothing else but produce performances which have the sole (conscious) aim of providing pleasure.

Because entertainment is produced by professional entertainers, it is also largely defined by them. That is to say, although entertainment is part of the coinage of everyday thought, nonetheless how it is defined, what it is assumed to be, is basically decided by those people responsible (paid) for providing it in concrete form. Professional entertainment is the dominant agency for defining what entertainment is. This does not mean, however, that it *simply* reproduces and expresses patriarchal capitalism. There is the usual struggle between capital (the backers) and labour (the performers) over the control of the product, and professional entertainment is unusual in that: 1) it is in the business of producing forms not things, and 2) the work force (the performers themselves) is in a better position to determine the form of its product than are, say, secretaries or car workers. The fact that professional entertainment has been by and large conservative in this century should not blind us to the implicit struggle within it, and looking beyond class to divisions of sex and race, we should note the important role of structurally subordinate groups in society – women, blacks, gays – in the development and definition of entertainment. In other words, show business's relationship to the demands of patriarchal capitalism is a complex one. Just as it does not simply 'give the people what they want' (since it actually defines those wants), so, as a relatively autonomous mode of cultural production, it does not simply reproduce unproblematically patriarchal-capitalist ideology. Indeed, it is precisely on seeming to achieve both these often opposed functions simultaneously that its survival largely depends.

Two of the taken-for-granted descriptions of entertainment, as 'escape' and as 'wish-fulfilment', point to its central thrust, namely, utopianism. Entertainment offers the image of 'something better' to escape into, or something we want deeply that our day-to-day lives don't provide. Alternatives, hopes, wishes – these are the stuff of utopia, the sense that things could be better, that something other than what is can be imagined and maybe realised.

Entertainment does not, however, present models of utopian worlds, as in the classic utopias of Sir Thomas More, William Morris, *et al.* Rather the utopianism is contained in the feelings it embodies. It presents, head-on as it were, what utopia would feel like rather than how it would be organised. It thus works at the level of sensibility, by which I mean an effective code that is characteristic of, and largely specific to, a given mode of cultural production.

This code uses both representational and, importantly, non-representational signs. There is a tendency to concentrate on the former, and clearly it would be wrong to overlook them – stars are nicer than we are, characters more straightforward than people we know, situations more soluble than those we encounter. All this we recognise through representational signs. But we also recognise qualities in non-representational signs – colour, texture, movement, rhythm, melody, camerawork – although we are much less used to talking about them. The nature of non-representational signs is not however so different from that of representational. Both are, in C. S. Peirce's terminology, largely iconic; but whereas the relationship between signifier and signified in a representational icon is one of resemblance between their appearance, their look, the relationship in the case of the non-representational icon is one of resemblance at the level of basic structuration.

This concept has been developed (among other places) in the work of Suzanne K. Langer, particularly in relation to music. We feel music (arguably more than any other performance medium), yet it has the least obvious reference to 'reality' – the intensity of our response to music can only be accounted for by the way music, abstract, formal though it is, still embodies feeling. Langer puts it thus in *Feeling and Form*:

> The tonal structures we call 'music' bear a close logical similarity to the forms of human feeling – forms of growth and of attenuation, flowing and stowing, conflict and resolution, speed, arrest, terrific excitement, calm or subtle activation or dreamy lapses – not joy and sorrow perhaps, but the poignancy of both – the greatness and brevity and eternal passing of everything vitally felt. Such is the pattern, or logical form, of sentience; and the pattern of music is that same form worked out in pure measures, sound and silence. Music is a tonal analogue of emotive life.
>
> Such formal analogy, or congruence of logical structures, is the prime requisite for the relation between a symbol and whatever it is to mean. The symbol and the object symbolized must have some common logical form.

Langer realises that recognition of a common logical form between a performance sign and what it signifies is not always easy or natural: 'The congruence of two given perceptible forms is not always evident upon simple inspection. The common *logical* form they both exhibit may become apparent only when you know the principle whereby to relate them.' This implies that responding to a performance is not spontaneous – you have to learn what emotion is embodied before you can respond to it. A problem with this as Langer develops it is the implication that the emotion itself is not coded, is simply 'human feeling'. I would be inclined, however, to see almost as much coding in the emotions as in the signs for them. Thus, just as writers such as E. H. Gombrich and Umberto

Eco stress that different modes of representation (in history and culture) correspond to different modes of perception, so it is important to grasp that modes of experiential art and entertainment correspond to different culturally and historically determined sensibilities.

This becomes clear when one examines how entertainment forms come to have the emotional signification they do: that is, by acquiring their signification in relation to the complex of meanings in the social-cultural situation in which they are produced. Take the extremely complex history of tap dance – in black culture, tap dance has had an improvisatory, self-expressive function similar to that in jazz; in minstrelsy, it took on an aspect of jolly mindlessness, inane good-humour, in accord with minstrelsy's image of the Negro; in vaudeville, elements of mechanical skill, tap dance as a feat, were stressed as part of vaudeville's celebration of the machine and the brilliant performer. Clearly there are connections between these different significations, and there are residues of all of them in tap as used in films, television and contemporary theatre shows. This has little to do, however, with the intrinsic meanings of hard, short, percussive, syncopated sounds arranged in patterns and produced by the movement of feet, and everything to do with the significance such sounds acquire from their place within the network of signs in a given culture at a given point of time. Nevertheless, the signification is essentially apprehended through the coded non-representational form (although the representational elements usually present in a performance sign – a dancer is always 'a person dancing' – may help to anchor the necessarily more fluid signification of the non-representational elements; for example, a black man, a white man in blackface, a troupe, or a white woman tap-dancing may suggest different ways of reading the taps, because each relates to a slightly different moment in the evolution of the non-representational form, tap dance).

I have laboured this point at greater length than may seem warranted partly with polemic intent. Firstly, it seems to me that the reading of non-representational signs in the cinema is particularly undeveloped. On the one hand, the *mise en scène* approach (at least as classically developed in *Movie*) tends to treat the non-representational as a function of the representational, simply a way of bringing out, emphasising, aspects of plot, character, situation, without signification in their own right. On the other hand, semiotics has been concerned with the codification of the representational. Secondly, I feel that film analysis remains notoriously non-historical, except in rather lumbering, simplistic ways.

	ENERGY	ABUNDANCE	INTENSITY	TRANSPARENCY	COMMUNITY
DEFINITION	Capacity to act vigorously; human power, activity, potential	Conquest of scarcity; having enough to spare without sense of poverty of others; enjoyment of sensuous material reality	Experiencing of emotion directly, fully, unambiguously, 'authentically', without holding back	A quality of relationships – between represented characters (e.g. true love), between performer and audience ('sincerity')	Togetherness, sense of belonging, network of phatic relationships (i.e. those in which communication is for its own sake rather than for its message)
SHOW-BIZ FORMS	Dance—tap, Latin-American, American Theatre Ballet; also 'oomph', 'pow', 'bezazz' – qualities of performance	Spectacle; Ziegfeld, Busby Berkeley, MGM	'Incandescent' star performers (Garland, Bassey, Streisand); torch singing	'Sincere' stars (Crosby, Gracie Fields); love and romance	The singalong chorus numbers
SOURCES OF SHOW-BIZ FORMS	Tap—black and white folk culture; American Theatre Ballet—modern dance plus folk dance plus classical ballet	Court displays; high art influences on Ziegfeld, Cedric Gibbons (MGM)–and haute couture	Star phenomenon in wider society; the Blues	Star phenomenon in wider society; 18th-century sentimental novel	Pub entertainment *and* parlour balladry; choral traditions in folk and church
GOLD DIGGERS OF 1933	'Pettin' in the Park' (tap, roller skates; quick tempo at which events are strung together)	'Pettin' . . . ' (leisure park), 'We're in the Money' (show girls dressed in coins), 'Shadow Waltz' (lavish sets; tactile, non-functional, wasteful clothing; violins as icon of high culture—expense)	'Forgotten Man', 'I've Got to Sing a Torch Song' (Blues inflections)	'Shadow Waltz' (Keeler and Powell as couple in eye-to-eye contact)	Show girls (wise-cracking interaction, mutual support—e.g. sharing clothes)

FUNNY FACE	'Think Pink', 'Clap Yo' Hands' (tap), 'Let's Kiss and Make Up' (tap and Astaire's longevity), Cellar dance	'Think Pink' (use of materials and fabrics), 'Bonjour Paris', 'On How to be Lovely' (creation of fashion image)	'How Long Has This Been Going On?'	'Funny Face', 'He Loves and She Loves', ''S Wonderful'	(?) Cellar dance
ON THE TOWN	'New York, New York' 'On the Town' 'Prehistoric Man' 'Come up to My Place'	'New York, New York' (cf. 'Bonjour Paris') 'Miss Turnstiles' (woman as commodity-fantasy)	'A Day in New York' ballet; climactic chase	'You're Awful' (insult turned into declaration of love) 'Come up to My Place' (direct invitation)	'You Can Count on Me'
WESTERNS	Chases, fights, bar-room brawls; pounding music ('sixties onwards)	Land—boundlessness and/or fertility	Confrontation on street; suspense	Cowboy as 'man'—straight, straightforward, morally unambiguous, puts actions where his words are	Townships; cowboy camaraderie
TV NEWS	Speed of series of sharp, short items; the 'latest' news; hand-held camera	Technology of news-gathering—satellites, etc; doings of rich; spectacles of pageantry and destruction	Emphasis on violence, dramatic incident; selection of visuals with eye to climactic moments	(?) 'Man of the people' manner of some newscasters, celebrities and politicians; (?) simplification of events to allow easy comprehension	The world rendered as global village; assumptions of consensus

My adaptation of Langer seeks to emphasise not the connection between signs and historical events, personages or forces, but rather the history of signs themselves as they are produced in culture and history. Nowhere here has it been possible to reproduce the detail of any sign's history (and I admit to speculation in some instances), but most of the assertions are based on more thorough research, and even where they are not, they should be.

The categories of entertainment's utopian sensibility are sketched in the accompanying table together with examples of them. The three films used will be discussed below; the examples from westerns and television news are just to suggest how the categories may have wider application; the sources referred to are the cultural, historical situation of the code's production.

The categories are, I hope, clear enough, but a little more needs to be said about 'intensity'. It is hard to find a word that quite gets what I mean. What I have in mind is the capacity of entertainment to present either complex or unpleasant feelings (e.g. involvement in personal or political events; jealousy, loss of love, defeat) in a way that makes them seem uncomplicated, direct and vivid, not 'qualified' or 'ambiguous' as day-to-day life makes them, and without those intimations of self-deception and pretence. (Both intensity and transparency can be related to wider themes in the culture, as 'authenticity' and 'sincerity' respectively – see Lionel Trilling's 'Sincerity and Authenticity').

The obvious problem raised by this breakdown of the utopian sensibility is where these categories come from. One answer, at a very broad level, might be that they are a continuation of the utopian tradition in western thought. George Kateb, in his survey of utopian thought, *Utopia and its Enemies*, describes what he takes to be the dominant motifs in this tradition, and they do broadly overlap with those outlined above. Thus:

> . . . when a man [sic] thinks of perfection . . . he thinks of a world permanently without strife, poverty, constraint, stultifying labour, irrational authority, sensual deprivation . . . peace, abundance, leisure, equality, consonance of men and their environment. . . .

We may agree that notions in this broad conceptual area are common throughout western thought, giving it, and its history, its characteristic dynamic, its sense of moving beyond what is to what ought to be or what we want to be. However, the very broadness, and looseness, of this common ground does not get us very far –

we need to examine the specificity of entertainment's utopia.

One way of doing so is to see the categories of the sensibility as temporary answers to the inadequacies of the society which is being escaped from through entertainment. This is proposed by Hans Magnus Enzensberger in his article, 'Constituents of a Theory of the Media' (in *Sociology of Mass Communication*, edited by Dennis McQuail). Enzensberger takes issue with the traditional left-wing use of concepts of 'manipulation' and 'false needs' in relation to the mass media:

> The electronic media do not owe their irresistible power to any sleight-of-hand but to the elemental power of deep social needs which come through even the present depraved form of these media. . .
>
> Consumption as spectacle contains the promise that want will disappear. The deceptive, brutal and obscene features of this festival derive from the fact that there can be no question of a real fulfilment of its promise. But so long as scarcity holds sway, use-value remains a decisive category which can only be abolished by trickery. Yet trickery on such a scale is only conceivable if it is based on mass need. This need – it is a utopian one – is there. It is the desire for a new ecology, for a breaking-down of environmental barriers, for an aesthetic which is not limited to the sphere of the 'artistic'. These desires are not – or are not primarily – internalized rules of the games as played by the capitalist system. They have physiological roots and can no longer be suppressed. Consumption as spectacle is – in parody form – the anticipation of a utopian situation.

This does, I think, express well the complexity of the situation. However, Enzensberger's appeal to 'elemental' and 'physiological' demands, although we do not need to be too frightened by them, is lacking in both historical and anthropological perspectives. I would rather suggest, a little over-schematically, that the categories of the utopian sensibility are related to specific inadequacies in society. As follows:

social tension/inadequacy/absence	*utopian solution*
Scarcity (actual poverty in the society; poverty observable in the surrounding societies, e.g. Third World); unequal distribution of wealth	Abundance (elimination of poverty for self and others; equal distribution of wealth)

Exhaustion (work as a grind, alienated labour, pressures of urban life)	Energy (work and play synonymous), city dominated (*On the Town*) or pastoral return (*The Sound of Music*)
Dreariness (monotony, predictability, instrumentality of the daily round)	Intensity (excitement, drama, affectivity of living)
Manipulation (advertising, bourgeois democracy, sex roles)	Transparency (open, spontaneous, honest communications and relationships)
Fragmentation (job mobility, rehousing and development, high-rise flats, legislation against collective action)	Community (all together in one place, communal interests, collective activity)

The advantage of this analysis is that it does offer some explanation of why entertainment *works.* It is not just left-overs from history, it is not *just* what show business, or 'they', force on the rest of us, it is not simply the expression of eternal needs – it responds to real needs *created by society.* The weakness of the analysis (and this holds true for Enzensberger too) is in the give-away absences from the left-hand column – no mention of class, race or patriarchy. That is, while entertainment is responding to needs that are real, at the same time it is also defining and delimiting what constitute the legitimate needs of people in this society.

I am not trying to recoup here the false needs argument – we are talking about real needs created by real inadequacies, but they are not the only needs and inadequacies of the society. Yet entertainment, by so orienting itself to them, effectively denies the legitimacy of other needs and inadequacies, and especially of class, patriarchal and sexual struggles. (Though once again we have to admit the complexity and contradictions of the situation – that, for instance, entertainment is not the only agency which defines legitimate needs, and that the actual role of women, gay men and blacks in the creation of show business leaves its mark in such central oppositional icons as, respectively, the strong woman type, e.g. Ethel Merman, Judy Garland, Elsie Tanner, camp humour and sensuous taste in dress and decor, and almost all aspects of dance and music. Class, it will be noted, is still nowhere.)

Class, race and sexual caste are denied validity as problems by the dominant (bourgeois, white, male) ideology of society. We should not expect show business to be markedly different. However, there is one further turn of the screw, and that is that, with the exception perhaps of community (the most directly working class in source), the ideals of entertainment imply wants that capitalism itself promises to meet. Thus abundance becomes consumerism, energy and intensity personal freedom and individualism, and transparency freedom of speech. In other (Marcuse's) words, it is a partially 'one-dimensional' situation. The categories of the sensibility point to gaps or inadequacies in capitalism, but only those gaps or inadequacies that capitalism proposes itself to deal with. At our worse sense of it, entertainment provides alternatives *to* capitalism which will be provided *by* capitalism.

However, this one-dimensionality is seldom so hermetic, because of the deeply contradictory nature of entertainment forms. In variety, the essential contradiction is between comedy and music turns; in musicals, it is between the narrative and the numbers. Both these contradictions can be rendered as one between the heavily representational and verisimilitudinous (pointing to the way the world is, drawing on the audience's concrete experience of the world) and the heavily non-representational and 'unreal' (pointing to how things could be better). In musicals, contradiction is also to be found at two other levels – within numbers, between the representational and the non-representational, and within the non-representational, due to the differing sources of production inscribed in the signs.

To be effective, the utopian sensibility has to take off from the real experiences of the audience. Yet to do this, to draw attention to the gap between what is and what could be, is, ideologically speaking, playing with fire. What musicals have to do, then, (not through any conspiratorial intent, but because it is always easier to take the line of least resistance, i.e. to fit in with prevailing norms) is to work through these contradictions at all levels in such a way as to 'manage' them, to make them seem to disappear. They don't always succeed.

I have chosen three musicals which seem to me to illustrate the three broad tendencies of musicals – those that keep narrative and number clearly separated (most typically, the backstage musical); those that retain the division between narrative as problems and numbers as escape, but try to 'integrate' the numbers by a whole set of papering-over-the-cracks devices (e.g. the well-known 'cue for a song'); and musicals which try to dissolve the distinction between narrative and numbers, thus implying that the world of the narrative is also (already) utopian.

The clear separation of numbers and narrative in *Gold Diggers of 1933* is broadly in line with a 'realist' aesthetic: the numbers occur in life, that is, on stages and in cabarets. This 'realism' is of course reinforced by the social-realist orientation of the narrative, settings and characterisation, with their emphasis on the Depression, poverty, the quest for capital, 'gold digging' (and prostitution). However, the numbers are not wholly contained by this realist aesthetic – the way in which they are opened out, in scale and in cinematic treatment (overhead shots, etc.) represents a quite marked shift from the real to the non-real, and from the largely representational to the largely non-representational (sometimes to the point of almost complete abstraction). The thrust of the narrative is towards seeing the show as a 'solution' to the personal, Depression-induced problems of the characters; yet the non-realist presentation of the numbers makes it very hard to take this solution seriously. It is 'just' escape, 'merely' utopian.

If the numbers embody (capitalist) palliatives to the problems of the narrative – chiefly, abundance (spectacle) in place of poverty, and (non-efficacious) energy (chorines in self-enclosed patterns in place of dispiritedness) – then the actual mode of presentation undercuts this by denying it the validity of 'realism'.

However, if one then looks at the contradiction between the representational and non-representational within the numbers, this becomes less clear cut. Here much of the representational level reprises the lessons of the narrative – above all, that women's only capital is their bodies as objects. The abundant scale of the numbers is an abundance of piles of women; the sensuous materialism is the texture of female-ness; the energy of the dancing (when it occurs) is the energy of the choreographic imagination, to which the dancers are subservient. Thus, while the non-representational certainly suggests an alternative to the narrative, the representational merely reinforces the narrative (women as sexual coinage, women – and men – as expressions of the male producer).

Finally, if one then looks at the non-representational alone, contradictions once again become apparent – e.g. spectacle as materialism and metaphysics (that is, on the one hand, the sets, costumes, etc. are tactile, sensuous, physically exhilarating, but on the other hand, are associated with fairy-land, magic, the by-definition immaterial), dance as human creative energy and sub-human mindlessness.

In *Funny Face*, the central contradiction is between art and entertainment, and this is further worked through in the antagonism between the central couple, Audrey Hepburn (art) and Fred Astaire (entertainment). The numbers are escapes from the problems, and discomforts, of the contradiction – either by asserting the unanswerably more pleasurable qualities of entertainment (e.g. 'Clap Yo' Hands' following the dirge-like Juliette Greco-type song in the 'empathicalist', i.e. existentialist, *soirée*), or in the transparency of love in the Hepburn-Astaire numbers.

But it is not always that neat. In the empathicalist cellar club, Hepburn escapes Astaire in a number with some of the other beats in the club. This reverses the escape direction of the rest of the film (i.e. it is an escape from entertainment/Astaire into art). Yet within the number, the contradiction repeats itself. Before Hepburn joins the group, they are dancing in a style deriving from Modern Dance, angular, oppositional shapes redolent in musical convention of neurosis and pretentiousness (*cf.* Danny Kaye's number, 'Choreography', in *White Christmas*). As the number proceeds, however, more show biz elements are introduced – use of syncopated clapping, forming in a vaudeville line-up, and American Theatre Ballet shapes. Here an 'art' form is taken over and infused with the values of entertainment. This is a contradiction between the representational (the dreary night club) and the non-representational (the oomph of music and movement), but also within the non-representational, between different dance forms. The contradiction between art and entertainment is thus repeated at each level.

In the love numbers, too, contradictions appear, partly by the continuation in them of troubling representational elements. In *Funny Face*, photographs of Hepburn as seen by Astaire, the fashion photographer, are projected on the wall as background to his wooing her and her giving in. Again, their final dance of reconciliation to ''S Wonderful' takes place in the grounds of a chateau, beneath the trees, with doves fluttering around them. Earlier, this setting was used as the finish for their fashion photography sequence. In other words, in both cases, she is reconciled to him only by capitulating to his definition of her. In itself, there is nothing contradictory in this – it is what Ginger Rogers always had to do. But here the mode of reconciliation is transparency and yet we can see the strings of the number being pulled. Thus the representational elements, which bespeak manipulation of romance, contradict the non-representational, which bespeaks its transparency.

The two tendencies just discussed are far more common than the third, which has to suggest that utopia is implicit in the world of the narrative as well as in the world of the numbers.

The commonest procedure for doing this is removal of the whole film in time and space – to turn-of-the-century America (*Meet Me in St. Louis*, *Hello Dolly!*), Europe (*The Merry Widow*, *Gigi*, *Song of Norway*), cockney London (*My Fair Lady*, *Oliver!*, *Scrooge*), black communities (*Hallelujah!*, *Cabin in the Sky*, *Porgy and Bess*) etc. – to places, that is, where it can be believed (by white urban Americans) that song and dance are 'in the air', built into the peasant/black culture and blood, or part of a more free and easy stage in American development. In these films, the introduction of any real narrative concerns is usually considerably delayed and comes chiefly as a temporary threat to utopia – thus reversing the other two patterns, where the narrative predominates and numbers function as temporary escapes from it. Not much happens, plot-wise, in *Meet Me in St. Louis* until we have had 'Meet Me in St. Louis', 'The Boy Next Door', 'The Trolley Song' and 'Skip to My Lou' – only then does father come along with his proposal to dismantle this utopia by his job mobility.

Most of the contradictions developed in these films are overridingly bought off by the nostalgia or primitivism which provides them with the point of departure. Far from pointing forwards, they point back, to a golden age – a reversal of utopianism that is only marginally offset by the narrative motive of recovery of utopia. What makes *On the Town* interesting is that its utopia is a well-known modern city. The film starts as an escape – from the confines of navy life into the freedom of New York, and also from the weariness of work, embodied in the docker's refrain, 'I feel like I'm not out of bed yet,' into the energy of leisure, as the sailors leap into the city for their day off. This energy runs through the whole film, *including the narrative*. In most musicals, the narrative represents things as they are, to be escaped from. But most of the narrative of *On the Town* is about the transformation of New York into utopia. The sailors release the *social* frustrations of the women – a tired taxi driver just coming off shift, a hard-up dancer reduced to belly-dancing to pay for ballet lessons, a woman with a sexual appetite that is deemed improper – not so much through love and sex as through energy. This sense of the sailors as a transforming energy is heightened by the sense of pressure on the narrative movement suggested by the device of a time-check flashed on the screen intermittently.

This gives a historical dimension to a musical, that is, it shows people making utopia rather than just showing them from time to time finding themselves in it. But the people are men – it is still men making history, not men and women together. (And the Lucy Schmeeler role is unforgivably male chauvinist.) In this context, the 'Prehistoric Man' number is particularly interesting. It centres on Ann Miller, and she leads the others in the take-over of the museum. For a moment, then, a woman 'makes history'. But the whole number is riddled with contradictions, which revolve around the very problem of having an image of a woman acting historically. If we take the number and her part in it to pieces, we can see that it plays on an opposition between self-willed and mindless modes of being; and this play is between representational (R) and non-representational (NR) at all aesthetic levels.

self-willed	*mindless*
Miller as star (R)	Miller's image ('magnificent animal') (R)
Miller character – decision-maker in narrative (R)	Number set in anthropology museum – associations with primitivism (R)
Tap as self-expressive form (NR)	Tap as mindless repetitions (NR)
Improvisatory routine (R/NR)	

The idea of a historical utopianism in narrativity derives from the work of Ernst Bloch. According to Frederic Jameson in *Marxism and Form*, Bloch 'has essentially two different languages or terminological systems at his disposition to describe the formal nature of Utopian fulfilment: the movement of the world in time towards the future's ultimate moment, and the more spatial notion of that adequation of object to subject which must characterise that moment's content . . . (these) correspond to dramatic and lyrical modes of the presentation of not-yet-being.'

Musicals (and variety) represent an extraordinary mix of these two modes – the historicity of narrative and the lyricism of numbers. They have not often taken advantage of it, but the point is that they could, and that this possibility is always latent in them. They are a form we still need to look at if films are, in Brecht's words on the theatre, to 'organise the enjoyment of changing reality'.

12 · Martin Sutton: 'Patterns of Meaning in the Musical'

One aspect of the musical which has consistently received critical attention is the discrepancy in content, tone, and treatment between a film's narrative material and its musical numbers. Most critics would agree that the gap separating these two modes constitutes part of the genre's very definition (e.g. a film like Jacques Demy's *Umbrellas of Cherbourg* is not a musical because there is no spoken dialogue). Indeed, some of the most persistent critical vocabulary reserved for the musical derives from the narrative/number opposition: for example, musicals are 'integrated' or not based on the way in which they handle the transition from one mode to the other. Evaluative criticism as well often depends heavily on the narrative/number split. Some critics find musicals frivolous because the numbers appear unreal by comparison with the narrative; others find the musical self-conscious, parodic, or avant-garde for the very same reason. However we evaluate the disparity between narrative and number, the opposition between these two modes constitutes a fundamental characteristic of the musical genre; interpreting the narrative/number split thus becomes one of the critic's most fundamental concerns.

In the article which follows, Martin Sutton makes an extremely interesting attempt at structuring our thinking about the musical's two modes. The musical, he claims, projects into the narrative/number opposition two fundamental views of human value. The plot material, conventional and thus predictable, represents the text's 'superego', its allegiance to an ethic of socially defined reason, while the numbers – the film's 'id' – provide the characters as well as the spectator an opportunity to exercise imagination and personal freedom. The narrative/number opposition is thus another in culture's long line of symbolic presentations of the polity/personal, society/individual clash. I am particularly impressed and persuaded by Sutton's treatment of the 'life' of objects in the musical; by demonstrating the extent to which everyday objects achieve a new use and identity in the musical number, he shows how even the slightest details may be induced to reflect structural and thematic concerns.

In the latter half of his short but captivating essay, Sutton goes on to show how the conventional marriage which closes the musical might be seen as a resolution of the cultural opposition embodied by the narrative/number discrepancy, a notion which is further developed in the concluding essay of this collection. The value of this particular type of criticism, as I see it, lies in its simple but effective linkage of thematic and structural concerns; technique no longer seems divorced from philosophical tenets, nor the gyrations of a Gene Kelly from the values particular to American society. Like nearly all the essays in this collection, Sutton's contribution succeeds in sketching out a methodology which, by integrating structural and thematic analysis, has wide ramifications for the study of the musical as an artefact of culture as well as a self-contained work of art.

The 'classic' Hollywood musical presents us with a major contradiction: a feeling of energy, freedom and optimism is accompanied by a sense of inhibition and repression. If *Seven Brides for Seven Brothers* begins with athletically choreographed assertions of personal freedom, it also concludes with a literal shotgun wedding. These contradictory forces are located, on the one hand, in the main protagonists and the numbers (freedom) and, on the other, in the conventional, reconciliatory plot strategies (inhibition). It is this contradiction that we will enlarge upon and explore.

There are basically two kinds of musicals when it comes to the relationship between plot and number. There are those which make clear separations between the two (mainly the Busby Berkeley variety) and those which attempt to cement over the rift and present the number 'naturally' as part of the plot (mainly MGM of the 1940s and 1950s and most subsequent musicals). We are concerned here with the latter variety, which, despite number-plot integration on a general structural level, displays an interesting tension between the two stylistic modes.

The musical is essentially a genre that concerns itself with the romantic/rogue imagination and its daily battle with a restraining, 'realistic', social order. This battle grows out of a tension between realistic plot and spectacle/fantasy number. All the narrative realism inherited from the nineteenth-century novel (linear plot, chronological development, a regular graph of the emotions) is behind this tension. The number functions as a narrative interruption, a fantastical tangent that at once frustrates and releases the spectator. The plot itself, however, surrounds, regulates and keeps in check the voluptuous, non-realist excesses of the number. Plot thus takes the part of 'super-ego' to the unruly 'id' of the number.

Perhaps the most famous of all musical numbers, the title song of *Singin' in the Rain* is a classic example of this tension. In this number, Kelly's childlike dance (splashing in puddles, spinning around with an umbrella outstretched) is cut short by the appearance of a policeman who frowns on his antics. There is an immediate disparity between behaviour and setting. A city street, especially one drenched with rain, is not the place to dance. The seriousness of milieu is stressed by a large sign for 'The Mount Hollywood Art School' (which comes into frame as the policeman materializes). The policeman is heavily dressed in a black, sensible raincoat and cap, but Kelly is patently oblivious to the logical distinctions between wet and dry. The appearance of this guardian of law and order, this representative of sanity, is distinctly threatening. He gives an admonishing look and Kelly wanders off apologetically, now just another 'normal' citizen like those who pass him on the sidewalk. Kelly is here *taken over* by the verisimilitude of the plot as the forces of 'reason' (the policeman) and personal freedom (the number) clash.

In this number, the rain simply and effectively represents the adversity encountered in the day-to-day life of the average citizen. Kelly is in fact in love, but the plot connections establishing this fact are so casual that the film's *mise en scène* forces our attention onto more general psychological states. The pre-credit sequence establishes this general state of feeling as the three main protagonists march arm-in-arm towards the camera, through the rain, wearing bright yellow mackintoshes and huge smiles. In the title number, Kelly transcends adversity for a time by turning his environment into a new world.

This relationship between character and environment is something quite peculiar to the genre, and deserves closer scrutiny. The musical often uses such locations as roller-skating rinks, football fields and their environment, ship-decks, theatre stages, gymnasiums, penny arcades, farmyards, parks and, needless to say, dance-floors. These areas recur frequently, all being locations filled with an excuse for movement. These locations also have in common an element of 'play'; they are not just points for expending pent-up energy, but provide opportunities for imaginative discovery.

This aspect of play and imaginative discovery (so vital to the concept of the musical protagonist) is generally dependent upon space and props. Open space in the musical is the most expressive of media – it gives the body room to move and, through this, the mind room to expand. Neutral space is charged with vital meaning by the dancer's movement, it is encompassed by the individual or couple and becomes transformed into another world (their world). This activated space is clearly demonstrated in *Singin' in the Rain*, where Kelly and Reynolds transform a dark film studio into a new world expressive of their growing love. Space awaits an interpreter, an explorer, and the objects within it (usually very few in number and great in significance) attain a meaning beyond the utilitarian.

In *The Night They Raided Minsky's*, Norman Wisdom points out to Britt Ekland that in 'burlesque' objects have a different use from the norm: a bucket is for trapping your foot in, stairs for falling down, a jar for imprisoning your hand in, a soda siphon for firing at people. The musical, having burlesque in its family line, similarly utilizes décor and props in this way. In the scene previously mentioned from *Singin' in the Rain*, an empty film studio becomes a romantic setting by means of the magical/imaginative transformation of objects: a painted backdrop becomes a 'romantic scene', a smoke machine 'mists from the mountain', a wind machine 'soft evening breezes', an arc lamp 'moonlight', and so on. Similarly in *Three Sailors and a Girl*, the *joie de vivre* of the characters results in the open space of a garage and all its implements being turned into a totally new environment: moving trolleys provide tricky dance-floors, air hoses hiss out a rhythm, shocks off a car battery act as a catalyst to movement, and an overhead shot sees a tap dance performed on a rising car lift. Examples could be multiplied from the majority of 'integrated' Hollywood musicals: the trash-can lids hooked to the feet of the dancing trio in *It's Always Fair Weather*; the domestic objects Judy Garland turns into musical film props in *A Star is Born*; the wishing-well, pots and masks Kelly dances around in an attempt to forget his sorrows in *Anchors Aweigh*; the distorting mirrors and exotic slot machines Astaire cavorts around in *The Band Wagon*; the gym – including balls, ropes, seesaws, bikes and horses – that Durante and Sinatra investigate to escape their problems in *It Happened in Brooklyn*.

This transmutation of objects, of the quotidian, is achieved by sheer force of imagination in the protagonists. Objects and settings from the everyday world of the surrounding plot (the 'real' world) are given a new meaning by their use within the number (the idealized world). The protagonist triumphs over the plot by altering the merely logical connection between various objects. For a moment, the world turns on the thoughts of the dreamer. If the horror film reveals the darker areas of the human soul, the musical shows the brighter, more positive side prevailing. The musical protagonist is a character in conflict with his or her environment and its static nature, having much in common with the artist encompassing the world and creating it again in his or her own image.

From consideration of the typical protagonist, the number, and their relationship, we must now turn to the regulatory function of the plot. The classic trajectory of the musical narrative could, rather simply, be represented thus: a lone character or series of characters; a set of misunderstandings, confusions and personality crises; a resolution supplied by the protagonists' linking up with some established group.

The film musical has many openings that create a sense of personal isolation. Some examples: Richard Harris standing alone in the forest staring wistfully into the distance (*Camelot*); Yves Montand cracking jokes to an obediently humoured audience around his vast conference table (*Let's Make Love*); a high-angle shot of Audrey Hepburn in a darkened bookshop (*Funny Face*); three newly disbanded soldiers dancing at night in an empty New York Street (*It's Always Fair Weather*); two men lost in the mists of a Scottish moor (*Brigadoon*); the separate units of life picked up by the wandering camera (*An American in Paris*); Judy Holliday, seated in a small room at her switchboard, keeping her equally isolated clients in touch with each other (*Bells Are Ringing*); Judy Garland staring wistfully up at the clouds from the platform of her railway car (*The Harvey Girls*); Frank Sinatra kicked out of town by the police (*Pal Joey*).

In *Don Juan*, Byron points out how as a general rule 'All tragedies are finished by death, all comedies ended by a marriage.' Musical comedy is certainly no exception to the general rule, though the word 'marriage' will have to be taken in a wider sense to include the 'wedding' of culturally accepted oppositions. Musicals usually end upon a note of harmony – concluding with an actual marriage or some celebratory function (both signs of community spirit).

The Band Wagon provides a particularly useful example of these narrative patterns. Its archetypal hero (Fred Astaire) is first seen as an out-of-work dancer resolutely shuffling along a railway platform singing 'I'll Go My Way By Myself'. After several personal and professional upsets (which are, of course, related), the film draws to its end as he descends a flight of stairs from his dressing-room whistling the very same tune under his breath. Down on the stage, the entire cast of the show and the principal protagonists (including Cyd Charisse, with whom he is in love) await him in celebration of their success. They sing together a chorus of the showbiz anthem 'That's Entertainment', and the film ends. There are several points of interest here with regard to harmony. This celebration is a sign that Astaire has finally been absorbed into an established group. Although it is not actually a 'performance', it takes the form of one as they sing together *on stage* and before the décor of their show: the show is absorbed into life, and life absorbed into the show. Rather than making the ceremony appear natural and spontaneous, Minnelli uses highly stylized groupings and formal arrangements to stress the identity of characters and show, of art and life.

The actual or symbolic wedding, then, is accompanied by the bringing together of cultural oppositions. In *Seven Brides for Seven Brothers*, the final weddings unite the country (the boys) and the town (the girls), nature and culture, energy and reason. The Sleeptite Fashion Show ending *The Pajama Game*, where John Raitt and Doris Day walk down the aisle in a pretend wedding stunt (wearing one pair of pajamas between them), reconciles business and personal affairs. The number ''S Wonderful' that concludes *Funny Face*, with photographer Astaire dancing off with model Hepburn (who models a wedding gown) into a country setting, shows art and life, culture and nature reconciled. *The Harvey Girls* ends similarly as Garland and John Hodiak wed in a country setting, again uniting culture and nature. In *Annie Get Your Gun*, art and life meet as hero and heroine ride out 'partners' into a new show, an overhead shot revealing them as part of a unified pattern of horseriders. Both *Showboat* (1936 version) and *Bye Bye Birdie* conclude as people on the stage sing with characters situated in the audience. *Hello Dolly!* draws to a close with a wedding that sees the respected rural gentleman shopkeeper married to the shrewd, opportunistic city businesswoman.

The musical finally turns its wayward dreamers into conformists. The plot overtakes the numbers, and the protagonists achieve only an apparent victory. They get their partner, or even the break they have been looking for, but they are also absorbed into society and its norms via some established group. Women, for example, are forced to accept male heterosexual society's definition of themselves. Doris Day, in *The Pajama Game*, loses credibility as union leader in order to become the floor manager's girl. In *Funny Face*, the cerebral, 'beatnik' lifestyle of the heroine has to be dropped in favour of a wedding dress. *Calamity Jane* must leave behind her rogue manner of dress and behaviour in order to become more 'feminine' and attract the attention of Howard Keel. Similarly, each outsider with his or her own unique viewpoint must conform. Kelly, as the aberrant dreamer of *The Pirate*, is forced to check his imagination at the foot of a gallows. The untamed, wild heroes of *Seven Brides for Seven Brothers* are forced at gunpoint to marry and accept civilised society's mores.

The 'classic' Hollywood musical appears to want it both ways:

to create free-minded, energetic protagonists, and to create censorial narrative structures to surround them. This paradox is resolved as best it can be in the conclusions we have discussed. Dreams can be realised, but only within the framework of accepted values. In other words, one paradox is dispensed with in favour of another.

13 · Rick Altman: 'The American Film Musical: Paradigmatic Structure and Mediatory Function'

Wide Angle, 2, no. 2, January 1978, pp. 10–17

The article which follows constitutes a chapter from a forthcoming book. The opening chapter of that book attempts an analysis of the place of entertainment in American life. Forms of entertainment, it is claimed, serve as a repository for displaced consideration of actions and thoughts forbidden by society. America's Puritan heritage has permanently branded entertainment as the valueless opposite of work. When entertainment becomes a commercial affair, however, as it does in Hollywood, a contradiction is created: the very form which exists as the repository of a counter-cultural residue turns into a commodity produced by the economic system of the culture itself. This dual identity is transferred to the musical text through the identity of the protagonists, one normally representing the work ethic (or other cultural value) while the other stands for the liberating counter-cultural virtues of entertainment itself. The musical is thus always already a reflexive form, for its *dramatis personae* and narrative patterns always refer to the musical's own status as entertainment and by extension to the position of entertainment within society.

In the article which follows, I try to show how the adhesion of a specific symbolic set of values to each member of the central couple leads the musical into a realm beyond that of classical narrative, a kingdom where causality, linear progression, and psychological motivation have been divested of their civil rights. In recompense, the symbolic nature of the characters permits the film to rehearse and eventually to resolve the paradox constituted by any Hollywood musical, namely that as paid entertainment it is simultaneously a reinforcement of the reigning economic system and thus of the dominant ideology, *and* a place where that system may be threatened. Such a paradox is not easily resolved, however. Only through the agency of a mystic state, marriage, may the musical's opposites be reconciled. By convention, in Western narrative, marriage is that beyond which there is no more; it arrests discourse and projects narrative into an undifferentiated 'happily ever after'. The comic equivalent of apocalypse, marriage represents a timeless, formless state in American mythology, precisely so that it will not be open to question. Solving nothing in the world of hard facts, the musical's marriage of opposites nevertheless provides for the viewer a model of a world where his/her contradictory desires and needs no longer appear mutually exclusive. The musical's characteristically dual-focus structure thus serves as a problem-solving device.

If the essays in this volume point toward one thing, it is certainly that the musical, once considered the most escapist of genres, now must be seen in terms of its function within a cultural system. If the essay which follows has any merit, it is in its ability to reveal the kinds of structure which might permit such functioning to take place. By linking structure to function, the essay makes structure once again into the dynamic force which it has so seldom been during the recent decades of formalism, New Criticism, and structuralism.

When we look at a narrative film or read a novel, what do we tend to see? All our experience predisposes us toward a particular way of viewing. We expect certain character relationships and plot patterns just as surely as we expect a film to have a certain shape on the screen. The very vocabulary we use to describe narrative reveals a great deal about our presuppositions. We speak, for example, of the hero or protagonist of a film as if a film always had a single central character, around whom all other activity revolves. Indeed, all our notions about narrative structure seem to support this proposition. When we speak of a plot we usually mean the hero's trajectory from the beginning of the text to the end; alternately acting and acted upon, he ties the plot together by providing a psychological bridge between each action and the next. The concept of motivation is thus essential to this standard view of narrative structure. An event takes place, it motivates a second event, which in turn occasions a third, and so on until the necessary chain of causality has been extinguished and the film draws to a close.

Why belabor these seemingly obvious notions about narrative? It seems clear that most films follow the destiny of a single character, integrate other characters and happenings into his career, motivate the plot by reference to his psychology, and depend on the twin chains of chronological progression and causal sequence. Any attempt to discover these characteristics in the American film musical, however, must necessarily come to naught, for they run counter to its very essence. To be sure, the musical *looks* as if it can be properly defined by a linear, psychological model, but this impression is created by no more than a veneer, a thin layer of classical narrativity which we must learn to look beyond, discovering instead the radically different principles of organization which lie just beneath the surface.

Let us take as an extremely clear example the first two sequences of MGM's 1940 version of *New Moon*. The first few shots set the scene: the French ship *Marseilles* in 1789 en route to New Orleans, carrying a group of extremely well-dressed society ladies. The older ladies in the group soon pressure one of the younger members to share her operatic talents, a typical method of introducing Jeanette MacDonald's first song. As MacDonald holds forth on deck, demonstrating her appetizing physical features along with her well-developed voice, her song is slowly drowned out by muffled male voices. The camera immediately cuts to the source of this second song: imprisoned in the hold, a group of dishevelled young Frenchmen about to be sold into slavery sing of their plight. Their leader, played by Nelson Eddy, is introduced in the same shot sequence previously used for MacDonald's song: full shot for the first two lines, cut to medium shot at line three, then to a closeup at line seven. At the request of the ladies on deck, an emissary soon appears to order the men in the hold to cease their singing or suffer the consequences.

These first two sequences appear to correspond quite closely to the characteristics of classical narrative outlined above. An event within sequence one (the voices drowning out MacDonald's song) motivates a cut to sequence two, where we witness the logical consequences of sequence one (Eddy and friends are told to reduce the noise). What this chronological approach ignores, however, are the careful parallels set up between Jeanette MacDonald and Nelson Eddy. *She* sings on deck, *he* sings in the hold; *she* sings to entertain a bevy of society women, *he* sings to relieve the misery of a group of penniless men; *she* is free, *he* is behind bars. The first two sequences must be visualized not one after the other but one balanced against the other. Now classical narrative analysis would make the chronological relationship primary, relegating the simultaneity and parallelism of the scenes to the shadows of stylistic analysis or theme criticism. In order to understand the musical, however, we must learn to do just the opposite: we must treat the conceptual relationships as fundamental, assuming that the rather tenuous cause-and-effect connections are in this case secondary, present only to highlight the more important parallelisms which they introduce. Instead of stressing a causal progression, the first two sequences of *New Moon* present and develop the two centers of power on which the film depends: the *female* – rich, cultured, beautiful, easily offended; the *male* – poor, practical, energetic, tenacious. Yet they share one essential attribute: they both sing.

Two centers of power, two sexes, two attitudes, two classes, two protagonists. We seem to be travelling not on the *Marseilles* in 1789 but on Noah's Ark many millennia earlier. Instead of focusing all its interest on a single central character, following the trajectory of his progress, the American film musical has a dual focus, built around parallel stars of opposite sex and radically divergent values. This dual-focus structure requires the viewer to be sensitive not so much to chronology and progression – for the outcome of the male/female match is entirely conventional and thus quite predictable – but to simultaneity and comparison. We construe the first two sequences of *New Moon* not according to their syntagmatic ties but in the light of their paradigmatic relationship; that is, we subordinate their sequential connection to their parallelism. The principle which holds for the paired initial sequence also applies to the following sequence in which Eddy and MacDonald meet for the first time. In terms of traditional plot analysis we might say that this scene serves to initiate the love plot, which will eventually culminate in the couple's first embrace. If this, however, is the sole function of the scene, then it is wasted indeed. What moviegoer in 1940 needed a preliminary infatuation scene to inform him that Eddy and MacDonald would ultimately fall in love? *New Moon* was the seventh movie in five years to pair the two as lovers. In short, the matched sequences that open *New Moon* are sufficient to suggest the course which the plot will take.

What then is the purpose of the stars' first meeting in *New Moon*? In their visit to the captain, Eddy and MacDonald at first seem simply to continue the thematics of the original balanced sequences. *He* is still concerned about the fate of his singing friends; *she* still wants to be able to sing without interruption. *He* is all rebellious energy, caring little for social mores as long as the cause of freedom is served; *she* is all properness, expecting the dictates of society to be obeyed even on the high seas. It is in this context that we must interpret the simple but significant clothing motif developed in the captain's ante-chamber. When Eddy first sees MacDonald he forgets for a moment his revolutionary purpose in order to don the nearest coat; even then he apologizes for having appeared in shirt sleeves before a lady. By the end of the scene, MacDonald has reversed the process; she arrived in a shawl, but she is so captivated by Eddy she soon removes the shawl, and with it some of the propriety which has thus far defined her. If the initial paired sequences defined Eddy as energy, MacDonald as restraint, this first joint scene moves each of the prospective lovers a step towards the other, Eddy demonstrating his civility and MacDonald her desire. As this analysis suggests, the plot of *New Moon* depends not on the stars' falling in love (they do that early on) nor even on their marriage (even that takes place well before the end), but on the resolution of their differences. Each must adopt the characteristics of the other: Eddy must exercise a great deal of restraint and MacDonald must learn to reveal her desire before the love story – and the film – can end.

This simple analysis is given not as an interpretation of the film, but as an example of how the American film musical must be construed. Those aspects which form the heart of traditional narrative analysis – plot, psychology, motivation, suspense – are to such an extent conventional in the musical that they leave little room for variation: we alternate between the male focus and the female focus, working our way through a prepackaged love story whose dynamic principle remains the difference between male and female. *Each segment must be understood not in terms of the segments to which it is causally related but by comparison to the segment which it parallels. New Moon* is thus seen not as a continuous chain of well-motivated events but as a series of nearly independent fragments, each a carefully constructed duet involving the two principal personages. The presence of Jeanette MacDonald and Nelson Eddy predetermines the plot of *New Moon*, forces it to conform to certain definite criteria, even makes it stoop to the most unlikely combinations in order to set up repeated confrontations or parallels between the two stars. Whereas the traditional approach to narrative assumes that structure grows out of *plot*, the dual-focus structure of the American film musical derives from *character*.

An extended example from a well-known film should help demonstrate the importance of this new method of viewing the musical. Vincente Minnelli's *Gigi* (MGM, 1958) borrows from the French novelist Colette a story about a young girl on the verge of becoming a woman. During the course of the film, Gigi (Lesley Caron) changes from an impish girl into a dazzling beauty capable of exciting the interest of Gaston Lachaille (Louis Jourdan). Very few scenes in the film actually advance this plot, however, and those that do are singularly lacking in motivation. Gaston leaves Gigi's apartment one lovely Paris night, he stops on a bridge, looks pensive, the music swells, and presto! he suddenly realizes that his young friend has changed. To judge from the point of view of the plot, *Gigi* is a remarkably unimpressive affair; it wastes time, motivates little, seems more concerned to paint representative days in the lives of its characters than to weave the kind of tightly-knit whole which characterizes masterful narrative. But if we inspect the film from the vantage point of dual-focus structure we find that from its very first words it creates an organized and compact whole.

'Bonjour Monsieur, bonjour Madame,' says Gaston's Uncle Honoré (Maurice Chevalier) as the film opens, thus dividing the world from the very beginning into two groups, the very groups which will preside over the film's structure. The film's first song, 'Thank Heaven for Little Girls,' demonstrates the extent to which even the youngest members of society are defined by sexuality. In fact, the scenes which follow make no sense at all unless we see them as outgrowths of the basic sexual parameter introduced by Chevalier. We first see Gigi at home, where she is told by her grandmother to change her clothes, comb her hair, and hurry to the lessons in femininity which her Aunt Alicia gives her once a week. Over the music of 'Thank Heaven' we then dissolve to Gaston receiving a visit from his uncle; while Gaston buys two cars and admits having recently bought an entire railroad, his uncle reminds him that he is expected at an embassy tea. (See Figs Ia and Ib, facing p. 153.)

It is not the plot which justifies Gaston's appearance here, but the extended series of parallels linking these two scenes. We observe Gigi at home, then Gaston at home; Gigi is with an older relative, so is Gaston; Gigi has no great desire to keep her appointment, neither does Gaston; Gigi is defined by feminine preoccupations (looks, clothes, manners), Gaston by their masculine counterparts (business, politics, riches). Before they have even met on screen, Gigi and Gaston are linked in the viewer's mind by these parallel scenes, initiating the paradigm which will inform the film's structure.

The following sequences further develop this paradigm. Gaston's song 'It's a Bore,' which emphasizes his profound disgust with Parisian life, is matched by Gigi's 'I Don't Understand the Parisians.' While Gigi is trying to learn the manners of Gaston's world, Gaston is enjoying the camomile tea and cookies to which Gigi is accustomed. (See figs IIa and IIb, facing p. 153.) In fact each scene involving only one of the lovers is invariably matched by a parallel scene (song, shot, event) featuring the other lover.

From this rather simple discovery about the *structure* of *Gigi* we can deduce certain important attributes of the *interpretation process* appropriate for *Gigi* and for the American film musical in general. In any film a given scene, in order to be properly understood, must be set in its proper context. Traditional narrative analysis usually stresses other scenes involving the same character, but *in the musical the basic context is constituted by a parallel scene involving the other lover*. When Gaston wanders through the park singing 'Gigi' he sits down on a park bench. Not just any bench, however; it is the very same bench used by Gigi during her earlier song. She sang 'I Don't Understand the Parisians;' now he insists that he doesn't understand Gigi (see Figs IIIa and IIIb, facing p. 153.) Objects, places, words, tunes, positions – everything becomes colored with the other person's actions and values.

It is this aspect of *Gigi's* structure which Raymond Bellour misses in his article entitled 'Segmenting/Analysing' (translated in this volume). Building his analysis around segments which 'rhyme' – i.e., which rework the same material – Bellour limits his examples to situations where a character repeats in modified fashion an action which he performed earlier. Bellour is unable to capture the text's dialectic, paradigmatic structure because he does not recognize that one character's actions are meant to serve as the context for the other character's parallel set of actions. His presupposition about the linear, cause-and-effect, psychological nature of classical narrative have blinded him to the structural patterns particular to the musical.

When Gaston returns home from Honfleur, where he punishes his mistress's infidelity, his uncle informs him that he must not leave Paris. 'Male patriotism' requires that he give a series of parties to celebrate his triumph. The episodic sequence that follows reveals Gaston performing his masculine duty, hosting party after party. How do we interpret this short but effective sequence? From a psychological point of view it is all but useless, since it tells us nothing about Gaston which we do not already know; it motivates nothing which is not already motivated in a number of other ways. If we wait a few minutes, however, we soon find this episodic sequence matched by another, this time on Gigi's side. When Gigi returns from Trouville (the next resort down the coast from Honfleur), Aunt Alicia insists that her education must be speeded up. Gigi is no more enchanted by her aunt's lessons than Gaston is by his uncle's parties, but follow the dictates of the older generation they must, and so we are given the only other episodic sequence in the entire film, in which Gigi is forced to serve tea, to sip wine, to choose cigars, to select a dress. Throughout these parallel sequences we recall the worldly wisdom of Gigi's aunt and Gaston's uncle: if the function of men in society is to collect women, the role of women is to collect jewels. A role for men, a symmetrical role for women – such is the vision of the world which Minnelli's dual-focus editing constantly produces. Each pairing of shots reinforces the notion that men and women alike play predetermined parts in an already written scenario. Individuals have responsibilities to their sex; the older generation must remind the younger of these responsibilities. Each older character serves not so much as go-between but as symbol of the conduct expected of his younger charge.

We have seen thus far how every aspect of *Gigi* obeys a principle of duality. Instead of the traditional pattern whereby a cause calls forth an effect, we have a less linear configuration whereby each male aspect seems to call for a parallel female one, and vice-versa. This rule is by no means limited to actual events. It includes paired songs ('It's a Bore'/'I Don't Understand the Parisians'), paired montage segments (the episodic sequences), paired roles (collecting women/collecting jewels), paired trips (to Honfleur/to Trouville), paired locations (Gigi's and Alicia's apartments/Gaston's and Honoré's rooms), as well as paired activities (Gigi's lessons/Gaston's embassy tea), paired feelings (Gigi's exasperation with her aunt/Gaston's boredom), and paired scenes (Gigi at home with her grandmother/Gaston at home with his uncle). The technique even extends to paired objects: just before the couple's first 'date' we are given a single shot of Gaston in front of his mirror (choosing a jewel) from which we cut directly to Gigi in front of her mirror (dressing and primping). (See figs IVa and IVb, facing p. 153.)

What conclusions can we reach about *Gigi* based on comparison of these various pairings? The question is an essential one; on our answer rests the very variety of the American film musical. If we can say only that *Gigi*'s pairings divide the world into male and female in order ultimately to bring the two sexes together again in matrimony, then all musicals will seem identical, for nearly every musical sets up a series of male/female oppositions, eventually resolving them to harmonious unity through the device of marriage.

On careful inspection, however, we can distinguish in any musical a secondary but essential opposition alongside the primary sexual division: each sex is identified with a particular attitude, value, desire, location, age or other characteristic attribute. These secondary attributes are always seen as diametrically opposed and mutually exclusive.

If sexual differentiation represents *Gigi*'s major premise, then what will its minor premise be? What characteristics constantly inform the opposition of Gaston to Gigi? Two answers to this question are immediately apparent. First, we have learned that both sexes are collectors, men collecting women and women amassing jewels. This simple opposition remains important throughout the history of the American film musical, from the *Gold Diggers* series of the thirties (where man is seen as an endless source of gold, while woman is identified by her beauty) to the tongue-in-cheek extravaganzas of the fifties (e.g. Howard Hawks' 1953 *Gentlemen Prefer Blondes*, which turns on this simple principle: 'Don't you know that a man being rich is like a girl being pretty?'). Marriage is seen, according to this view, as the only way to join beauty and riches, to effect not a compromise but a merger between the *dulce* and the *utile*. And no wonder, for in the sexually differentiated climate of the three decades in which the musical flourished a woman could by and large become rich in only one way: by marrying for money. Similarly, a man could not fully enjoy the charms of feminine beauty without marrying. Sexual stereotyping and a strict moral code went hand in hand, leaving only one solution for young men and women alike: marriage. In this sense *Gigi*, like many other musicals, is an apology for traditional mores, an ode to marriage as the only way to combine riches and beauty.

The beauty/riches motif is a common one; however, we must search further if we are to understand the specificity of *Gigi* as a functional mechanism, one which overcomes the very contradictions on which society is founded. When we first see Gigi and then Gaston, she is preparing for her 'femininity' lessons with Aunt Alicia, while he is about to leave with his uncle for an embassy tea; she must change clothes and brush her hair, while he is buying cars and railroads. At first we characterized these activities as typically female and male: she is concerned with beauty, he with riches. On second glance, however, we note a minor premise of some importance. *She* skips and hops, plays tag and eats candy; *he* is reserved, serious, moody. *She* wears a brightly colored pinafore; *he* has formal attire and a cane. In short, *she* is a child and *he* is a man. The initial paired sequences clearly stress the stars' respective female and male qualities, yet simultaneously create a generation gap between Gigi and Gaston. This impression is reinforced at their first meeting, when Gigi speaks to Gaston as a naive child would speak to a favorite uncle; Gaston returns the compliment, treating Gigi as he would a daughter, even threatening to spank her. When they go off to the ice palace together he orders champagne for himself and the turn-of-the-century equivalent of a milkshake for her.

Now there is nothing problematic about an inter-generational relationship – unless, that is, the members of different generations suddenly develop a romantic interest in each other. And that, of course, is just what happens in *Gigi*. We even find out that Gigi's grandmother and Gaston's uncle are former lovers who might have been married were it not for his infidelity. There is something vaguely incestuous about the Gigi-Gaston relationship (since they could, indeed, be related by blood). One minute she is sitting in his lap, cheating at cards and eating caramels, the next she is being eyed, invited and embraced as a potential sexual partner. The point here, of course, is not that Gaston and Gigi violate society's prohibitions against incest but rather that society has a difficult time handling the child/adult opposition. We act as if the dichotomy were a mutually exclusive one, as if children and adults represented two diametrically opposed groups that allow no overlapping, yet every individual within the society must at some point violate the seemingly airtight partition that separates the categories. Children are not adults, yet at some indefinite point they become adults.

It is this problematic relationship between childhood and adulthood which *Gigi* mediates, with the marriage model providing the resolution: the distinction between the generations is leveled by a merging of adult and childlike qualities within the couple. As Gigi for the first time gains the right to engage in adult activities, Gaston progressively refuses to carry out the petty duties to which adulthood condemns him. Now *he* eats the caramels he brings to Gigi, dances wildly around the room with Gigi and her grandmother, plays leap-frog on the beach at Trouville. While she is becoming an adult, he is recapturing some of the excitement of youth. Instead of simply making Gigi into an adult and thus creating an adult couple, the film operates a merger of the generations through the couple's marriage. In this sense Maurice Chevalier is a perfect symbol of the film's attempt to bridge the generation gap: he is both young and old, both living in the past and constantly creating new memories, glad that he's 'Not Young Any More' and yet able to 'Thank Heaven for Little Girls.'

We have viewed *Gigi* as a series of paired segments built around a major oppositional premise, that of sexual differentiation, and two minor oppositions, beauty/riches and child/adult, both of which represent problematic dichotomies for society. Beauty and riches are treated like sex-linked chromosomes: only one is available to each sex, yet both are desirable. Society's ideal individual has both. The child/adult pairing is problematic because it treats a dynamic, diachronic process as a stable, synchronic opposition. These problematic dichotomies are eventually resolved only when the resolution of the major premise (marriage) is used as a nonrational mediatory model for the oppositions of the minor premise, bringing together categories and individuals which seemed irreconcilably opposed. The only way for the same individual to enjoy both riches and beauty is to marry. The only way to save both childlike and adult qualities is through a merger, thus blurring the barrier between the generations, thereby erasing the spectre of incest.

Though extremely simple, this method must radically change our understanding of the American film musical. No longer can we point to the musical's conventional plot, call it gauche and episodic, and walk away satisfied. Once we have understood the dual-focus approach we easily grasp the importance of the many set pieces or production numbers which so often seem to clutter the musical's program and interrupt its plot. We now see that the plot has little importance to begin with: the oppositions developed in the seemingly gratuitous song-and-dance number, however, are absolutely central to the structure and meaning of the film. Only when we identify the film's constitutive dualities can we discover the film's function.

Seen as a cultural problem-solving device, the musical takes on a new and fascinating identity. Society is defined by a fundamental paradox: both terms of the oppositions on which it is built (order/liberty, progress/stability, work/entertainment, and so forth) are seen as desirable, yet the terms are perceived as mutually exclusive. Every society possesses texts which obscure this paradox, prevent it from appearing threatening, and thus assure the society's stability. The musical is one of the most important types of text to serve this function in American life. By reconciling terms previously seen as mutually exclusive, the musical succeeds in reducing an unsatisfactory paradox to a more workable configuration, a concordance of opposites. Traditionally, this is the function which society assigns to myth. Indeed, we will not be far off the mark if we consider that the musical fashions a myth out of the American courtship ritual.

14 · Jane Feuer: 'The Hollywood Musical: An Annotated Bibliography'

This bibliography is intended as a guide to source material of a 'serious' (i.e. not merely journalistic) nature on the Hollywood musical. It does not pretend to all-inclusiveness nor to objectivity. While the 'general and theoretical' list omits nothing significant, the more specific areas – especially the section on individual directors – present only a selected list. Articles which seemed too thin, too trivial, or not relevant enough to the musical (e.g. many articles on Minnelli's *oeuvre*) are not included. Biographical material is included only when it serves to illuminate the films. Articles on individual films are included only when they have general or theoretical interest. No 'reviews' are included. As for the annotations, they include information I wish I had known when I began studying the musical. They also include my evaluations of the usefulness of the material to serious study of the genre. This bibliography was compiled in 1979.

I General and Theoretical

Action, no. 9 (May-June 1974). A series of articles and interviews devoted to American musicals. Journalistic.

Altman, Rick (Charles F.), 'The American Film Musical: Paradigmatic Structure and Mediatory Function', *Wide Angle*, 2, no. 2 (Jan. 1978), 10–17. Reprinted above.

— 'Pour une Etude sémantique/syntaxique du genre hollywoodien: Le musical folklorique', *Ça/Cinéma*, forthcoming.

— 'Toward a Theory of Genre Film', in *Film: Historical-Theoretical Speculations*, The 1977 Purdue Film Studies Annual: Part Two, Pleasantville, New York: Redgrave, 1977, 31–43.

Bellour, Raymond, 'Segmenting/Analysing', originally translated as 'To Analyse, to Segment', in *Quarterly Review of Film Studies*, 1, no. 3 (August 1976), 331–53. Reprinted above in a new translation.

Belton, John, 'The Backstage Musical', *Movie*, no. 24 (Spring 1977), 36–44. Compares *42nd Street* and *French Can-Can* as individual masterpieces.

Bizet, J. A., 'Le Musical américain', *Cinéma '74* (Feb. 1974), 34–55. Defence of *auteur* musicals.

Braudy, Leo, *The World in a Frame: What We See in Films*, New York: Anchor/Doubleday, 1976. Chapter on 'Musicals and the Energy from Within' constitutes the best general analysis of the genre currently available in book form.

Collins, Jim, 'Vers la Définition d'une matrice de la comédie musicale: la place du spectateur dans la machine textuelle', *Ça/Cinéma*, forthcoming. Expanded version printed above.

Delamater, Jerome, 'A Critical and Historical Analysis of Dance as a Code of the Hollywood Musical', Dissertation, Northwestern University, 1978.

— 'Performing Arts: the Musical', in Kaminsky, Stuart, *American Film Genres: Approaches to a Critical Theory of Popular Film*, Dayton, Ohio: Pflaum, 1974. Good brief historical overview mixed with value judgments.

Dyer, Richard, 'Entertainment and Utopia', *Movie*, no. 24 (Spring 1977), 2–13. Reprinted above.

— '*The Sound of Music*', *Movie*, no. 23 (1976), 39–49. Cultural reading of *The Sound of Music* (film). Issues raised not limited to one musical, however. Recommended.

Elsaesser, Thomas, 'The American Musical', *Brighton Film Review*, no. 15 (Dec. 1969), 15–16.

Feuer, Jane, 'The Hollywood Musical: The Aesthetics of Spectator Involvement in an Entertainment Form', Dissertation, University of Iowa, 1978. A revised version in book form is scheduled to be published by the British Film Institute and Macmillan.

— 'The Self-Reflective Musical and the Myth of Entertainment', *Quarterly Review of Film Studies*, 2, no. 3 (Aug. 1977), 313–26. Reprinted above.

— 'The Theme of Popular vs. Elite Art in the Hollywood Musical', *Journal of Popular Culture*, 12, no. 3 (Winter 1978).

Film Notebooks (Winter 1978), published at the University of California, Santa Cruz. Issue on Minnelli; includes interview, articles on *The Band Wagon*, *Cabin in the Sky*, '*Meet Me in St. Louis* and American Mythology', *Gigi*, and *On a Clear Day You Can See Forever.*

Fischer, Lucy, 'The Image of Woman as Image: the Optical Politics of *Dames*', *Film Quarterly*, no. 30 (Fall 1976), 2–11. Reprinted above.

Fordin, Hugh, *The World of Entertainment: Hollywood's Greatest Musicals*, New York: Doubleday, 1975. Meticulously researched background accounts on all Freed Unit productions. Lacks historical or critical perspective.

Freed, Arthur, 'Making Musicals', *Films and Filming*, 2 (Jan. 1956), 9–12. Don't believe for a minute that Freed wrote this history of the musical.

Giles, Dennis, 'Show-making', *Movie*, no. 24 (Spring 1977), 14–25. Reprinted above.

Hasbany, Richard, 'The Musical Goes Ironic: The Evolution of Genres', *Journal of American Culture*, 1 (Spring 1978), 120–37. Evolution of musicals in terms of Northrop Frye's modes in a developmental conception.

Hodgkinson, A. W., '*42nd Street* New Deal: Some Thoughts About Early Film Musicals', *Journal of Popular Film*, 4 (1975), 33–47. Tries to account for paucity of musicals between 1930 and 1933 as due to too many operettas rather than effects of the Depression. No original research.

Jablonski, Edward, 'Film Musicals', *Films in Review*, 6 (1955), 56–69. Chronicle with no apparent *raison d'être*.

Kidd, Michael, 'The Camera and the Dance', *Films and Filming*, 2 (Jan. 1956), 7. Should be interesting but isn't.

Kobal, John, *Gotta Sing, Gotta Dance: A Pictorial History of Film Musicals*, London: Hamlyn, 1971. Perhaps the most complete history to date. Interviews. A necessary starting point.

Kreuger, Miles, ed., *The Movie Musical from Vitaphone to 42nd Street: As Reported in a Great Fan Magazine*, New York: Dover, 1975. Practically our only record in print of the genre's formative period (1927–33). Plot summaries save one from seeing some really awful movies.

— 'Movie Musicals in the Thirties', *High Fidelity and Musical America*, 24 (April 1974), 66–72.

Lusted, David, 'Film as Industrial Product: Teaching a Reflexive Movie', *Screen Education*, 16 (Autumn 1975), 26–30. *Singin' in the Rain* as a self-reflective Hollywood text.

McVay, Douglas, 'The Art of the Actor', *Films and Filming*, 12 (Sept. 1966), 43–50. Screen musicals vs. theater musicals.

— *The Musical Film*, New York: Barnes, 1967. Year-by-year account. Tendency toward hysteria, especially regarding Judy Garland films. Most complete plot summary of *A Star is Born* on record.

Mellencamp, Patricia, 'Spectacle and Spectator: Looking Through the American Musical Comedy', *Cine-Tracts*, 1 (Summer 1977), 28–35. Analysis relying heavily on theories and jargon of Stephen Heath, also Metz, Todorov, Comolli. Analysis of musical as sub-category of 'classical Hollywood cinema'.

Movie, no. 24 (Spring 1977). Special issue on the musical. Well worth owning. Individual articles cited elsewhere.

Newton, Douglas, 'Poetry in Fast and Musical Motion', *Sight and Sound*, 22 (July-Sept. 1952), 35–7. Formalization of dance raises musicals to visual equivalent of pastoral poetry – nostalgic and utopian. Interesting analysis for its period.

Patrick, R. and W. Haislip, 'Thank Heaven for Little Girls', *Cinéaste*, 6 (1973), 22–5. American musicals as instruments of male chauvinism.

Pérez, M., 'Le musical avant Busby Berkeley', *Positif*, no. 144–45 (Nov.–Dec. 1972), 48–53. Account of a retrospective at the Museum of Modern Art covering the period 1929–31.

Roth, Mark, 'Some Warners Musicals and the Spirit of the New Deal', *The Velvet Light Trap*, no. 17 (Winter 1977), 1–7. Reprinted above.

Scher, S. N., 'The American Film Musical: Golden Age, Neglected Art', *Audience*, 7 (Apr.–May 1975).

Scheurer, Timothy, 'The Aesthetics of Form and Convention in the Movie Musical', *Journal of Popular Film*, 3 (Fall 1974), 307–25. Justification of popularity of musicals for their inherent aesthetic appeal rather than their escapist function. Highly prescriptive.

Solomon, Stanley J., *Beyond Formula: American Film Genres*, New York: Harcourt Brace Jovanovitch, 1976. Chapter on musical. Author needs to be more familiar with his material to generalize to the extent that he does.

Spiegel, Ellen, 'Fred and Ginger Meet Van Nest Polglase', *The Velvet Light Trap*, no. 10 (Fall 1973), 17–22. Art deco in set design. Good article on a much neglected area of the musical.

Springer, John, *All Talking! All Singing! All Dancing!*, New York: Citadel Press, 1966. Mostly pictures. Not as good as Kobal.

Stern, Lee Edward, *The Movie Musical*, New York: Pyramid, 1974. Rather shallow general history.

Taylor, John Russell and Arthur Jackson, *The Hollywood Musical*, New York: McGraw-Hill, 1971. Taylor's opinionated overview of musicals which forms the first half is of questionable value. Jackson's reference section with selected filmographies, indices of names, songs, titles, is indispensable.

Thomas, Lawrence B., *The MGM Years*, New York: Columbia House, 1971. Most reference material can be found elsewhere; however, 'A Chronology of MGM Musicals, 1929–71' is quite useful.

Todd, A., 'From Chaplin to Kelly', *Theater Arts*, 35 (Aug. 1951), 50–1. A history of dance in film from silents to Astaire, Berkeley, and Kelly.

Turim, Maureen, 'Gentlemen Consume Blondes', *Wide Angle*, 1 (Spring 1976), 68–76. Ideological/feminist analysis of *Gentlemen Prefer Blondes.*

Vallance, Tom, *The American Musical*, New York: Barnes, 1970. Dictionary format reference work. Not as complete or reliable as Taylor and Jackson listed above.

Vaughan, David, 'After the Ball', *Sight and Sound*, 26 (Autumn 1956), 89–91. Freed musicals as 'American lyric cinema'.

'Dance in the Cinema', *Sequence*, no. 6 (Winter 1948–49), 6–13.

Woll, Allen L., *Songs from Hollywood Musical Comedies, 1927 to the Present: A Dictionary*, New York: Garland, 1978.

Wood, Michael, *America in the Movies*, New York: Basic Books, 1975. Chapter on 'Darkness in the Dance' worth reading but a bit too simplistic in its generalizations about 1950s musicals and America in the 1950s.

Wood, Robin, 'Art and Ideology: Notes on *Silk Stockings*', *Film Comment*, 11 (May–June 1975), 28–31. Reprinted above.

II Studies on specific directors, actors, screenwriters, and films

Astaire and Rogers

Astaire, Fred, *Steps in Time*, New York: Harper, 1959. The autobiography of a very private individual.

Croce, Arlene, *The Fred Astaire and Ginger Rogers Book*, New York: Galahad Books, 1972. A witty and elegant though superficial analysis of Astaire–Rogers musicals. Very complete production information and description of films.

Freedland, Michael, *Fred Astaire*, New York: Grosset & Dunlap, 1976. Adds nothing to the biographical literature on Astaire.

Green, Stanley and Burt Goldblatt, *Starring Fred Astaire*, New York: Dodd, Mead, 1973. Indispensable reference work containing material on all Astaire's films.

Harvey, Jim, 'Fred and Ginger', *Dance Life*, 3 (Winter 1977), 1–17. Dance analysis of 'Let's Face the Music and Dance', disappointingly non-technical for a dance magazine. Borrows heavily from Arlene Croce's book.

Busby Berkeley

Benayoun, Robert, 'Berkeley le centupleur', *Positif*, no. 74 (Mar. 1966), 29–41.

Comolli, Jean-Louis, 'Kaleidoscopie de Busby Berkeley', *Cahiers du Cinéma*, no. 174 (Jan. 1965), 24–7. Translated as 'Dancing Images', *Cahiers du Cinéma in English*, no. 2 (1966), 22–6. Considers Berkeley number as foregrounding cinema itself. Interesting in light of Comolli's work on technology.

Delamater, Jerome, 'Busby Berkeley: An American Surrealist', *Wide Angle*, 1 (Spring 1976), 30–7. Examines B. B. as an 'unwitting' surrealist. Uses surrealist concepts to illuminate B. B.'s work. Recommended.

Knight, Arthur, 'Busby Berkeley', *Action*, 9 (May–June 1974), 11–16. Survey of B. B.'s musicals with emphasis on his innovative contributions to the genre.

Masson, Alain, 'Le Style de Busby Berkeley', *Positif*, no. 173 (Sept. 1975), 41–48.

Thomas, Tony and Jim Terry with Busby Berkeley, *The Busby Berkeley Book*, New York: A & W Visual Library, 1973. Includes films for which B. B. did not receive screen credit.

Comden and Green

Comden, Betty and Adolph Green, *Singin' in the Rain*, New York: Viking, 1972. The script but no shot descriptions, lyrics, or close descriptions of numbers.

Winer, S., ' "Dignity – always dignity!", Betty Comden and Adolph Green's Musicals', *The Velvet Light Trap*, no. 11 (Winter 1974), 29–32. Career chronicle written 'mostly from memory'.

Stanley Donen

Lloyd, Peter, 'Stanley Donen', *Brighton Film Review*, no. 18 (Mar. 1970), 17–19. Structural analysis of Donen's *oeuvre*. Recommended.

Mariani, John, 'Come on with the Rain', *Film Comment*, 14 (May–June 1978), 7–12. Presumably the 'true story' of the making of *Singin' in the Rain*. Facts contradicted in other interviews, however.

Gene Kelly

Griffith, Richard, *The Cinema of Gene Kelly*, New York: Museum of Modern Art, 1962.

Hirschorn, Clive, *Gene Kelly: A Biography*, Chicago: Henry Regnery Company, 1974. More than a biography, contains analysis of evolution of Kelly's filmic dance style, the Freed Unit, descriptions of films, and a fascinating portrait of Kelly as an obsessive egomaniac.

Thomas, Tony, *The Films of Gene Kelly: Song and Dance Man*, New York: Citadel Press, 1974. Pictures and plot summaries. Not as good as Hirschorn.

Vincente Minnelli

Anderson, Lindsay, 'Minnelli, Kelly and *An American in Paris*', *Sequence*, 14 (1952), 36–8.

Bathrick, Serafina, 'The Past as Future: Family and the American Home in *Meet Me in St. Louis*', *The Minnesota Review*, New Series 6 (Spring 1976), 132–9.

Britton, Andrew, '*Meet Me in St. Louis*: Smith, or the Ambiguities', *Australian Journal of Screen Theory*, no. 3 (1978), 7–25.

Casper, Joseph, 'Critical Study of the Musicals of Vincente Minnelli', Dissertation, University of Southern California, 1973. See next entry.

— *Vincente Minnelli and the Film Musical*, New York: A. S. Barnes, 1977. Based on author's dissertation (see above). Research for M.'s background based on secondary sources. Discusses M.'s musicals according to drama, enactment, spectacle, musical, and dance. Scattered insights but poorly written.

Chaumeton, Etienne, 'L'oeuvre de Vincente Minnelli', *Positif*, no. 12 (Nov.–Dec. 1954), 36–45.

Cook, Jim, '*On a Clear Day You Can See Forever*', *Movie*, no. 24 (Spring 1977), 61–2. Suggests that recent theoretical approaches would help to illuminate this neglected Minnelli masterpiece. Provocative article but too short.

De la Roche, Catherine, *Vincente Minnelli*, Paris: Premier Plan No. 40, 1966.

Durgnat, Raymond, 'Film Favorites: *Bells are Ringing*', *Film Comment*, 9 (Mar.–Apr. 1973), 46–50.

Elsaesser, Thomas, 'Vincente Minnelli', *Brighton Film Review*, no. 15 (Dec. 1969), 11–13, and no. 18 (Mar. 1970), 20–2. Very likely the best general article ever written on Minnelli. Revised version printed above.

Galling, Dennis Lee, 'Vincente Minnelli', *Films in Review*, 15 (Mar. 1964), 129–40.

Grob, Jean, 'Vincente Minnelli', *Image et son*, no. 149 (Mar. 1962), 12–13.

Harcourt-Smith, Simon, 'Vincente Minnelli', *Sight and Sound*, 21 (Jan.–Mar. 1952), 115–19.

Hogue, Peter, '*The Band Wagon*', *The Velvet Light Trap*, no. 11 (Winter 1974), 33–4. Close formal analysis of *The Band Wagon* as Pirandellian text.

Johnson, Albert, 'The Films of Vincente Minnelli', *Film Quarterly*, no. 12 (Winter 1958), 21–35, and no. 13 (Spring 1959), 32–42.

Knox, Donald, *The Magic Factory: How MGM Made An American in Paris*, New York: Praeger, 1973. Anti-auteurist oral history.

Minnelli, Vincente, *I Remember It Well*, New York: Doubleday, 1974. Not a reliable source.

Torok, Jean-Paul and Jacques Quincey, 'Vincente Minnelli ou le peintre de la vie rêvée', *Positif*, nos. 50–52 (Mar. 1963), 54–74.

Vidal, Marion, *Vincente Minnelli*, Paris: Seghers, 1973 (Cinéma Aujourd'hui no. 76). Critical study.

George Sidney

Masson, Alain, 'L'Eclat de l'artifice (sur George Sidney)', *Positif*, no. 180 (Apr. 1976), 48–54. Translation printed above.

Morris, George, 'George Sidney: A Matter of Taste', *Film Comment*, 13 (Nov.–Dec. 1977), 56–60. Sidney as example of tension between primal energy and aesthetic discipline. Not as funny as title suggests.

Charles Walters

Benayoun, Robert, 'Charles Walters, ou l'intimisme', *Positif*, no. 144–45 (Nov.–Dec. 1972), 1–8.

Henry, M., 'L'Espace vital de la comédie musicale (quatre films de Charles Walters)', *Positif*, no. 144–45 (Nov.–Dec. 1972), 9–15.

Sutton, Martin, '*The Belle of New York*', '*Lili*', *Movie*, no. 24 (Spring 1977), 54–8. Excellent but brief analyses of these films.

Miscellaneous

Green, Stanley, 'Hammerstein's Film Career', *Films in Review*, 8 (Feb. 1957), 68–77. Contains information on Hammerstein's early film musicals (1930–31) as well as the better-known ones.

Harmetz, Aljean, *The Making of the Wizard of Oz*, New York: Knopf, 1977. Lots of fascinating trivia interspersed with analysis tending toward simple Freudianism.

Knowles, Eleanor, *The Films of Jeanette MacDonald and Nelson Eddy*. New York: Barnes, 1974. Includes non-costarring films of each. Discography. Many, many facts. For those who care. Well researched.

Kreuger, Miles, *Show Boat: The Story of a Classic American Musical*, New York: Oxford, 1977. *All* versions of the Kern-Hammerstein classic are included.

Loos, Anita, *San Francisco: A Screenplay*, Carbondale, Illinois: Southern Illinois University Press, 1978.

Milne, Tom, *Mamoulian*, Bloomington: Indiana University Press, 1969. Includes filmography.

Moshier, W. Franklin, *The Alice Faye Movie Book*, New York: A & W Visual Library, 1974. One of few sources of information on Fox musicals.

Ringgold, Gene and De Witt Bodeen, *Chevalier: The Films and Career of Maurice Chevalier*, Secaucus, N. J.: The Citadel Press, 1973.

Sarris, Andrew, 'Al Jolson', *Film Comment*, 13 (Sept.–Oct. 1977), 39–41. Reviews film career of a significant but neglected film musical persona.

III Interviews

Directors always give the same basic interview, so I shall sum up each director's interview persona before listing some individual examples. I should begin by noting the obvious – the best film-makers do not necessarily give the best interviews. Minnelli, for example, tends to be incoherent. Stanley Donen gives the best interview of all; he is informative and cynical. Gene Kelly is informative and earnest; Berkeley technical and self-aggrandizing; Walters full of gossip; Sidney businesslike and politic. Comden and Green treat interviews as an opportunity to perform, yet many film historians base articles on these amusing embroideries.

Busby Berkeley

Gilson, René and Patrick Brion, 'Interview with Busby Berkeley', *Cahiers du Cinéma*, no. 174 (Jan. 1965), 27–38. Translated in *Cahiers du Cinéma in English*, no. 2 (1966), 26–38. Typical Berkeley interview: 'There was no collaboration. I did everything myself.'

Comden and Green

Hauduroy, Jean-Francois, 'Interview with Comden and Green' (translated, with filmography), *Cahiers du Cinéma in English*, no. 2 (1966), 43–50.

Stanley Donen

Harvey, S., 'Stanley Donen', *Film Comment*, 9 (July–Aug. 1973), 4–9. Claims Comden and Green's introduction to *Singin' in the Rain* is 'a lot of lies'.

Hillier, Jim, 'Interview with Stanley Donen', *Movie*, no. 24 (Spring 1977), 26–35.

Tavernier, Bertrand and Daniel Palas, 'Entretien avec Stanley Donen', *Cahiers du Cinéma*, no. 143 (May 1963).

Roger Edens

Johnson, Albert, 'Conversation with Roger Edens', *Sight and Sound*, 27 (Spring 1958), 179–82. A rare interview with the unsung hero of the MGM musical.

Bob Fosse

Gardner, Paul, 'Bob Fosse', *Action*, 9 (May-June 1974), 22–27. Profile-interview.

Gene Kelly

Bitsch, Charles and Jacques Rivette, 'Entretien avec Gene Kelly', *Cahiers du Cinéma*, no. 85 (July 1958).

Vincente Minnelli

Bitsch, Charles and Jean Domarchi, 'Entretien avec Vincente Minnelli', *Cahiers du Cinéma*, no. 74 (Aug.–Sept. 1957), 4–15.

Domarchi, Jean and Jean Douchet, 'Rencontre avec Vincente Minnelli', *Cahiers du Cinéma*, no. 128 (Feb. 1962), 3–14.

Serebrinsky, Ernesto, and Oscar Garaycochea, 'Vincente Minnelli Interviewed in Argentina', *Movie*, no. 10 (June 1963), 23–8.

Shivas, Mark, 'Minnelli's Method', *Movie*, no. 1 (June 1962), 17–24. An infamous point of controversy in the history of *auteur* criticism.

George Sidney

Higham, Charles, 'George Sidney', *Action*, 9 (May–June 1974), 17–21.

Charles Walters

Cutts, John, 'On the Bright Side', *Films and Filming*, 16 (Aug. 1970), 12–18. Walters claims to have staged all the numbers in *Meet Me in St. Louis* except 'Christmas'.

IV Recordings

Many Hollywood musicals are available on record (numbers only) in the various 'nostalgia' formats. Beware of recordings not from original soundtracks; you may not be getting the lyrics that are in the film. Two record series are worth mention:

1 'Those Glorious MGM Musicals.' MGM Records. Original soundtrack recordings but usually with numbers out of sequence and frequently shortened.
2 'Cut!', volumes 1–3. Available from Out Take Records, P.O. Box 298, Ansonia Station, New York, N.Y. 10023. Original studio archive recordings of the many numbers cut from well-known musicals prior to the original release. The only easily available record of these numbers, many of which shed light on the films that didn't have room for them.

Rick Altman · Postscript

As the essays which precede amply reveal, the past few years have witnessed many advances in the area of genre criticism in general and of criticism on the musical in particular. We are now, paradoxically, in a far better position to observe the shortcomings of our treatment of the Hollywood musical than we were even five years ago. There are, in particular, four areas which need to be more fully explored in the coming years.

1 The theory and practice of genre history

Perhaps the weakest aspect of genre criticism in general, the problem of history has hardly even been raised in respect to the musical. We go blithely along lining up one studio/personal style after another as if a simple list constituted history. Lacking a basic theory to ground and model the writing of genre history, we have simply neglected the problem all together (with certain notable exceptions, such as the Feuer dissertation listed in the bibliography). To make things worse, this global theoretical weakness is compounded by certain deep-seated prejudices regarding the relationship between Hollywood and other centers of the entertainment arts/industry. By far the majority of those involved in Hollywood musicals – actors, dancers, singers, directors, songwriters, lyricists, designers, costumers – were at one time or another also employed by Broadway shows. Yet where is the study which even breaks the surface of the sea of information implied by this interaction? To cite only one example, no attempt has been made to trace the mutual influence of Broadway and Hollywood as evidenced through the career of Rouben Mamoulian. Success with the New York plays *Porgy* (1927) and *Marco Millions* (1928) brought Mamoulian an invitation to direct the Paramount musical *Applause* (1929), but in 1930 he was already back on the stage with *R.U.R.*, *A Farewell to Arms*, a Turgenev play and a Schönberg opera, followed by a string of Hollywood successes, including *Love Me Tonight* (1932). In 1935 it was back to Broadway for the Gershwin version of *Porgy and Bess*. Between 1936 and 1942 Mamoulian directed the Kern-Hammerstein *High, Wide and Handsome* and five other films, only to return triumphantly to Broadway in 1943 with *Oklahoma!*, which was followed by a string of theatrical successes, including *Carousel*. Yet in 1947 Mamoulian was again in Hollywood, this time with MGM's version of Eugene O'Neill's *Ah! Wilderness*: *Summer Holiday*. There follows a decade of theatrical innovation and revivals, culminating in a final return to Hollywood for *Silk Stockings* (1957). If ever we are to gain a sense of the interaction between Hollywood and Broadway, it is certainly through pivotal figures like Rouben Mamoulian – yet we look in vain for the interviews, analyses, and evaluations which might lead to new understanding. Indeed, if we had the information there is no assurance that we would know what to do with it. We desperately need both a rethinking of the problem of genre history in general and a concerted attempt to collect and analyse the materials out of which such a history of the musical might be constructed.

2 The role of technology

Until recently the notion of materialist criticism and the name of Hollywood rarely even found their way into the same sentence. In spite of recent advances in this area, and in spite of the role of technology in the musical's birth, the musical has remained largely outside the realm of materialist criticism. The early history of the musical can hardly be separated from that of technology, yet accounts of the early musical centre on the Europeanness of directors, the staginess of *mise en scène*, and the operatic background of the actresses. Or to choose an entirely different realm, the musical of the 1930s depended as much on the sale of song rights (or sales of sheet music by satellite companies) as it did on actual ticket sales. When the recording industry first teamed up with the musical in the 1940s this situation changed instantly; suddenly there was still more to be made from residuals like original-cast record albums, or, conversely, from films which were sure to be attended by everyone who owned a copy of the Broadway soundtrack (surely one of the reasons why the adaptations of the late 1940s and 1950s so slavishly imitate their Broadway originals). In still another period, we need to consider the relationship between the decline in popularity of the musical and the decline of the piano as the country's fundamental source of music (both for the home and the church), not to mention the piano's replacement by a more mobile instrument, the guitar, and a more passive process of reproduction, the hi-fi. The music of the Hollywood musical in its heyday is piano music; what happens to the genre when the piano idiom is replaced by electronically (re)produced music? For a materialist history of the genre these and many others are essential questions, yet nowhere in our criticism does the musical exist anywhere but in a never-never land of idealist image analysis or vague cultural contexts. Alan Williams's article in this collection points in the right direction; it remains to be seen whether others will walk the road he has indicated.

3 The soundtrack

It seems inconceivable that a collection of the latest and best articles devoted to the musical should be all but devoid of detailed consideration of the soundtrack. To be sure, this failing is far from limited to the present collection; it is in fact one of the fundamental limitations of recent film theory and criticism alike. It is one thing, however, to ignore the soundtrack in a classical narrative film which treats its own soundtrack as secondary, and quite another to repress the soundtrack of a genre where much of the sound is actually recorded before the image is so much as conceived, where the image regularly obeys the sound (in cutting rhythm, in individual action, in group movement), where the soundtrack carries the key signifiers for the entire film. The musical provides a privileged territory for the analysis of sound, yet few have laid claim to this fertile realm. I look to the musical to lead us out of the image-oriented exile which has so plagued cinema theory in recent years. Only a genre which so regularly privileges the soundtrack can provide the material examples to support a more sound-conscious theory of cinematic practice.

4 Music and dance

It is a sad truth that students of the musical are rarely more than passable musicians, and almost never schooled beyond the basics of musical analysis. In the pecking order of musical styles, the musical's music is at the bottom. Rachmaninoff and Tchaikovsky are generally denigrated by musicologists, but the brand of music identified with the musical is treated with disdain even by Tchaikovsky fans. (Imagine. Putting words to the First Piano Concerto!) Almost by definition, those with musical training ignore (at best) the musical. We thus look in vain for careful and knowledgeable analyses of the music of Richard Rodgers or Cole Porter, let alone attempts to reveal the complex interaction between the orchestral score, the singers' rendition, and the images which accompany/mime/derive from both. The same situation holds for dance. Different performers/styles/periods practise different types of dance (Astaire and Rogers with their 'challenge' dances, Kelly and his 'Pygmalion' routines which bring inanimate objects to life, Berkeley's pattern dances and marches, Charisse's erotic siren dances, Vera-Ellen's ballet), each with its own narrative function, each with a different aesthetics, each calling for a different type of analysis. Jim Collins's typology of the song/dance numbers in the Astaire-Rogers films takes a step in the right direction, toward refining the rather undifferentiated dance analysis currently practised, but Collins's article stands nearly alone. Before we can hope to write a history of the musical we must have some idea how music and dance function not only within the genre as a whole but within single numbers, sequences, and films. Just as the materialist history of the Hollywood enterprise in general desperately needs critics schooled in the arcane sciences of legal, technological, and corporate history, so the musical history of the musical can hardly do without the attention of critics trained in the analysis of music.

These are only four major areas within an even wider realm. Serious analysis of the musical is so close to its beginnings that one would not be far wrong in suggesting that *everything* remains to be done in regard to the musical. None the less, I feel that the thirteen essays included in this collection raise myriad important questions about the genre and its function within Hollywood, American society, the film world in general, and the specific field of film criticism and theory. From now on, when people go 'back to the beginning' in their study of the Hollywood musical, they need go no farther than these essays, for they provide a new point of departure, a new beginning for study of the musical genre.

Notes on Contributors

Rick Altman splits his time between the departments of French and Comparative Literature at the University of Iowa. He is currently finishing books on the musical and narrative theory, and has recently edited an issue of *Yale French Studies* on the cinema soundtrack and an issue of *Quarterly Review of Film Studies* on the career of D. W. Griffith.

Raymond Bellour is a Professor at the Centre National de la Recherche Scientifique in Paris. He has written extensively on Hollywood cinema and his work has appeared in translation in journals such as *Screen* and *Quarterly Review of Film Studies*.

Jim Collins is finishing his dissertation in Comparative Literature at the University of Iowa. His major interest is subject placement in 'classical' narrative, both literary and cinematic.

Richard Dyer is Lecturer in Film Studies at the University of Warwick. He has edited *Gays and Film* and written *Stars*, both published by the BFI.

Thomas Elsaesser teaches film and comparative literature at the University of East Anglia and has written extensively on both American and German cinema. He was a founding editor of *Brighton Film Review* and later of *Monogram*.

Jane Feuer teaches film and mass communication at the University of Pittsburgh. Her articles on entertainment and the media have appeared in *Quarterly Review of Film Studies* and *Journal of Popular Culture*. She is currently writing a book on the backstage musical.

Lucy Fischer is Head of the Film Studies programme at the University of Pittsburgh. Her articles have appeared in *Film Quarterly*, *Cinema Journal* and elsewhere.

Dennis Giles teaches in the Communication Department at Cleveland State University. He works primarily from a psychoanalytic standpoint on genres as diverse as the musical and pornography.

Alain Masson has contributed many articles and reviews to the French film journal *Positif* and is on its editorial board.

Mark Roth, once a graduate student at the University of Wisconsin (Madison), has now, it would seem, disappeared from the film scene.

Martin Sutton did postgraduate work on the Hollywood musical at the University of Exeter and has had several articles published in *Movie.*

Alan Williams teaches film at Rutgers University. His articles have appeared in *Film Quarterly, Movietone News* and *Quarterly Review of Film Studies.* He is currently working on problems of sound and sound technology.

Robin Wood is teaching film at York University, Toronto. He is the author of many articles and books on the cinema, including *Hitchcock's Films, Howard Hawks* and, most recently, *Personal Views.*

Index

The index is organized in seven categories: studios, directors and other production personnel, actors and actresses, films, critics, journals, and subject index. Jane Feuer's bibliography has not been included in this index.

Studios

Directors and other production personnel

Actors and actresses

Films

Critics

Journals

Subject index